Return To Equilibrium:

The Proceedings of the 7th Rocky Mountain Disaster Mental Health Conference,

Laramie, WY November 6-8, 2008.

Edited by George W. Doherty, MS, LPC

Library of Congress Cataloging-in-Publication Data

Rocky Mountain Region Disaster Mental Health Conference (7th : 2008 : Laramie, Wyo.)
Return to equilibrium : the proceedings of the 7th Rocky Mountain Region Disaster Mental Health Conference / edited by George W. Doherty.
p. cm.
Includes bibliographical references and index.
ISBN-13: 978-1-932690-86-6 (trade paper : alk. paper)
ISBN-10: 1-932690-86-7 (trade paper : alk. paper)
1. Disasters--Psychological aspects--Congresses. 2. Psychiatric emergencies--Congresses. 3. Crisis intervention (Mental health services)--Congresses. I. Doherty, George W. (George William) II. Title.
RC451.4.D57R63 2008a
362.2'2--dc22

2009000388

ROCKY MOUNTAIN REGION DISASTER MENTAL HEALTH INSTITUTE
PO BOX 786
LARAMIE, WY 82073-0786

http://www.rmrinstitute.org
email: rockymountain@mail2emergency.com
Phone: 307-399-4818

The Rocky Mountain Region Disaster Mental Health Institute is a 501(c)3 Non-profit Organization.

Rocky Mountain DMH Institute Press is an Imprint of:

Loving Healing Press Inc.
5145 Pontiac Trail
Ann Arbor, MI 48105
USA

http://www.LovingHealing.com
info@LovingHealing.com
Tollfree 888-761-6268
Fax +1 734 663 6861

About the Cover

The cover montage shows a variety of disaster response scenarios. From left-to-right, and top to bottom they are credited as follows

1. Damaged boats are seen at a boatyard on the Bolivar Peninsula in Galveston, Texas, Sept. 19, 2008. Hurricane Ike struck the Texas Gulf Coast as a strong category 2 storm Sept. 13, causing wide-spread damage to the region. (U.S. Navy photo by Chief Mass Communication Specialist Chris Hoffpauir/Released)

2. The Jackson Canyon fire on Casper Mountain on August 14th, 2006 At the peak of the fire, 588 total personnel, 13 crews, 35 engines, and 7 helicopters as well as aerial tankers were assigned to the incident. A total of 55,000 gallons of red fire retardant and about 340,000 gallons of water were used to contain the blaze. By the time it was over, almost 12,000 acres burned. (Photo by George W. Doherty, RMR DMHI)

3. U.S. Air Force Maj. Christopher Collins, from the 169th Medical Group, prepares to transfer Senior Airman Daniel Dorman, a simulated killed in action from the 169th Security Forces Squadron, from a humvee to a gurney following a simulated mortar attack during a phase II operational readiness inspection at McEntire Joint National Guard Base, S.C., Dec. 14, 2008. The inspection evaluates a unit's war-fighting capabilities in a deployed combat environment. (U.S. Air Force photo by Staff Sgt. Caycee Cook/Released)

4. U.S. Air Force Airmen from the 37th and 59th Air Wing unload hospital patients at Lackland Air Force Base, Texas, Sept. 12, 2008, that were evacuated from Beaumont, Texas. These patients were transported by a combined effort from the Little Rock Air Force Base C-130 aircraft and crews and the 908th Aero medical Evacuation Squadron, Scott Air Force Base, Ill., in preparation for Hurricane Ike's landfall in southern Texas. (U.S. Air Force photo by Staff Sgt. Chris Willis/Released)

5. The logos of Homeland Security and the Federal Emergency Management Agency (FEMA) decorate a mobile disaster recovery center vehicle at the FEMA National Logistics Staging Area (Blue Team) on Fort Sam Houston in San Antonio, Texas, Sept. 12, 2008. U.S. service members and FEMA employees are preparing for Hurricane Ike emergency relief effort. (U.S. Army photo by Sgt. Teddy Wade/Released)

6. An aerial view from a U.S. Air Force helicopter is shown in Galveston, Texas, Sept. 13, 2008. The U.S. Air Force is contributing to the Hurricane Ike humanitarian assistance operations being led by the Federal Emergency Management Agency in conjunction with the Department of Defense. (U.S. Air Force photo by Staff Sgt. James L. Harper Jr./Not Released)

The Rocky Mountain Region Disaster Mental Health Institute Press
Laramie, Wyoming

Crisis Intervention Training for Disaster Workers: An Introduction (2007)

Proceedings of the 5th Rocky Mountain Region Disaster Mental Health Conference (2007)

Proceedings of the 6th Rocky Mountain Region Disaster Mental Health Conference (2008)

Return to Equilibrium: Proceedings of the 7th Rocky Mountain Region Disaster Mental Health Conference (2009)

Table of Contents

Acknowledgements

Putting together, organizing and presenting a conference involves a lot of work and includes the input and work of a number of dedicated people as well as co-sponsors. While many may go unnamed, all are vital to the success of the effort. We would like to extend thanks to the Albany County Tourism Board for providing packets for attendees that included maps, information and brochures about Laramie, the University and Albany County. They were much appreciated by the delegates. The management (Carol Jones) and staff of the Hampton Inn provided a very professional and warm welcoming environment for all of our delegates. Our partner in travel, Enterprise Rent-a-Car provided special rates for delegates attending the conference again this year. The lunches for delegates this year were catered by Home Bakery of Laramie and Grand Avenue Pizza. Many thanks to Sam's Club Foundation (Cheyenne) for their generous grant which enabled us to provide a number of things for the delegates, including the lunches and assist with some of the published materials. Their support of our first responders in the communities and of our conference is gratefully appreciated.

The exhibitors at the conference provided a little taste of local souvenirs made in Laramie for delegates. These were much appreciated. Our reception and dinner Thursday night was held at 2Bazaar, a unique quiet club setting in downtown Laramie. A fine dining setting with soft background music and a pleasant atmosphere provided delegates the opportunity to talk, network and get to know each other. A great Mexican Food Buffet dinner highlighted the evening with services and makings put together onsite. It was catered by former owners of the Café Ole in Laramie and they did an excellent job.

Dr. Dennis B. Klein's travel, other expenses and presentation was co-sponsored by the History, Sociology, Religious Studies, Psychology Departments and others at the University of Wyoming and also by St. Matthew's Cathedral in Laramie. Dr. Klein gave a Public Address at the University of Wyoming on Friday of the conference.

Thanks to all Institute members for their work throughout the year in support of the conference and other trainings and to the WYO CISM NET Coordinators and Team members around the state for their ongoing responses and their attendance and support of the mission of the Institute.

Finally, a big thank-you to each one of our delegates from around the country and to our presenters. Their willingness to present AND to compile their presentations into the articles in this volume to share with others has made it a success. Their contributions and hard work to accomplish this has been superb. Thank-you again to all involved.

George W. Doherty, President
Rocky Mountain Region
Disaster Mental Health Institute

Foreword

The 2008 Rocky Mountain Region Disaster Mental Health Conference was held November 6-8 at the Hampton Inn in Laramie, Wyoming. It was preceded by two workshops that dealt with the Colorado Crisis Education and Response Network's Field Response Training; and the Hensley Model of Biological, Psychological, and Sociological Military Wellbeing.

The conference began with an excellent introduction, direction setting presentation and discussion by Melinda Koenig, PsyD (Clinical Director, Adult Psychiatry Coordinator, Mental Health Emergency Preparedness, St. Luke's-Roosevelt Hospital, New York. Her presentation "Emphasizing Alliances: The Roles of Mental Health Professionals in All-Hazards Emergency Management" set the tone for the conference on the first day. On a very practical level, Art Storey, Voluntary Agency Liaison FEMA Region 8, discussed the Federal Emergency Service Function #6, under which Disaster mental health functions. The second half of his presentation focused on the FEMA Sequence of Delivery and Long-Term Recovery. These topics had a very lively discussion involving the focus, recruitment, training and responses of mental health professionals to disasters and critical incidents. The lack of active involvement of mental health personnel and shortages of trained and qualified mental health professionals in these areas was discussed with active suggestions that more emphasis on these areas be encouraged and promoted.

Friday's presentations and discussions focused on our returning Military Veterans and the resources available in our communities as well as how our mental health professionals and other responders can effectively work together with already existing resources and assist both communities and returning veterans re-integrate into the community, families and the workplace. LCDR Alan Hensley, USN RET presented valuable insights, backgrounds and very useful information about what many veterans are facing after their experiences in both Afghanistan and Iraq. LCDR Hensley was in both Afghanistan and Iraq and was involved in many other areas of the world during his career as a Naval Intelligence Officer. His presentations, discussions and approaches contributed greatly to the understanding of those in attendance and covered areas ranging from triage and diagnoses to causations to treatment modalities. His discussions and presentation of an assessment tool to be used 30 days prior to deployment, 90 days following return and, again, one year following return provided an innovative and, potentially very valuable, method for assessing and understanding changes in personnel as a result of exposures in war settings. His model and assessment tool will have an impact as they are currently under consideration by both the military and the Veterans Administration. He has been selected to present his model and preliminary results at the Annual Meeting of the American Counseling Association in Charlotte, North Carolina March 19-23, 2009.

The Keynote presentation on Friday was presented by Adele D'Ari, EdD. She is a Licensed Psychologist and Vice President of the Board of Give An Hour in Arlington, VA (http://www.giveanhour.org). Give an Hour is asking mental health professionals nationwide to literally give an hour of their time each week to provide free mental health services to military personnel and their families. Target population is the U.S. troops and families who are being affected by the current military conflicts in Afghanistan and Iraq. Dr. D'Ari discussed "New Wounds, New Trauma: Treating Disability and Trauma in Military Service Members and Their Families". Information about how to become involved and to volunteer is available on the Give An Hour web page. She was very impressed with the potential for this program to be made available in the rural areas of states like Wyoming in particular.

Marti Salas, LCSW and Shellie Franklin, MA, LPC from the Department of Veterans Affairs in Cheyenne provided valuable information concerning Providing Services to Returning Combat Veterans. Shellie Franklin talked about her experiences working with military personnel while stationed in Kuwait and other areas while deployed as a mental health professional with the Wyoming National Guard. Services and other information about the work VA is doing and how communities, mental health professionals and other responders can work together were discussed. Information was provided about Vet Centers and Veterans Outreach programs available in Wyoming. Marti Salas provided information about Federal Benefits for Veterans and Dependents. Finally, a panel discussion with all the day's presenters provided opportunities for attendees and presenters to discuss and share further information, respond to various concerns and questions and explore ways of working together.

The focus on Day three continued to be on Returning Veterans and our communities, as well as information about disaster planning and responses. The Keynote presentation for the day was presented by Dennis B. Klein, PhD., Director of the Jewish Studies Program and Professor of History at Kean University, Union, New Jersey. His talk was on Trauma and Forgiveness. Dr. Kean's travel, other expenses and presentation was co-sponsored by the History, Sociology, Religious Studies, Psychology Departments and others at the University of Wyoming and also by St. Matthew's Cathedral in Laramie. Dr. Klein gave a Public Address at the University of Wyoming on Friday. His presentation provided additional, relevant and important insights into the conference topics and emphases.

Curt Drennen, PsyD, RN (Colorado Behavioral Health Disaster Response Coordinator and Planner) presented information about Behavioral Health Considerations on Triage, Treatment and Tracking for a Mass Casualty Event. He also discussed the Colorado Crisis Education and Response Network (CoCern). This, particularly, generated much discussion about how such approaches could be integrated and adapted for Wyoming. An additional presentation by Dr.Drennen focused on mental health Planning for Pandemic-Quarantine, Isolation and Social Distancing: Behavioral Health Concerns. Attendees were provided with copies of a Toolbox for Public Health and Public Behavioral Health Professionals developed by the Colorado Department of Human Services, Division of Mental Health. It is a laminated handbook sponsored by the Colorado Division of Mental Health, The Colorado Department of Public Health and Environment, and The Center for Disease Control. It was discussed that this would be a great asset to Wyoming Mental Health Professionals in planning for pandemic and related events. It is in the public domain, and can be adapted to Wyoming with little tweaking.

Additional Military Veteran related information was presented with current updates and training and handout materials by Debbie Russell, Specialist, Coordinator and FAC Supervisor and Daniella Hamilton, Family Assistance Specialist, both with the Wyoming

National Guard Family Assistance Program. Their program has been very busy over the past year and is becoming more so. Each attendee was provided with relevant materials and resource information. One of the valuable resources provided is the ISFAC (Inter Service Family Assistance Committee) Directory which contains descriptions and contact information for Community Agencies. Wyoming Army National Guard Family Program Planners were made available and their importance discussed. If interested in registering as a counselor, the following was suggested: http://www.militaryonesource.com Discussion also centered on available Program Services for Reunion and Reintegration with the Family after Deployment, DOD Family Assistance Centers, Family Pre-deployment Preparation Academy, Reunion Briefs, Tips for Returning Service Members, Marriage Enrichment (PREP), Family Enrichment/Veterans Coalition, and other programs.

An experiential workshop was provided for attendees by Jamie Egolf, MSW, LCSW (Jungian Psychotherapist) and Chivawn Kelley, MA (Writer) on "In the Moment Relief and Training for Responders Utilizing Dramatic Re-enactment and Authentic Witnessing' for the Treatment of Trauma in Returning Soldiers, Accident Victims and Others Traumatized by Disastrous Events".This workshop provided attendees with a hands-on personal experience.

The Thursday evening reception was held at 2Bazaar, a unique quiet club setting in downtown Laramie. A fine dinner setting with soft background music and a pleasant atmosphere provided a great opportunity for attendees to talk, network and get to know each other. Dinner included a fine Mexican Food Buffet with services and makings put together onsite. The food was made and catered by former owners of the Café Ole in Laramie. Lunches were provided at the conference by Home Bakery (sandwiches and salad) on Thursday and Grand Avenue Pizza on Friday (best pizza west of the Mississippi – gourmet) and Saturday (gourmet sandwiches).

The current volume documents contents of the conference. Presenters have placed their presentations into articles included here in order for others to be able to update their knowledge and information about these topics. The theme of this conference was "RETURN TO EQUILIBRIUM". Two major topic areas were addressed within this theme: *Disaster Mental Health* and *Returning Military and Families*. A panel discussion and other discussions generated much interest in both topics. It is hoped that this volume will allow further dissemination of these presentations to others in the first responder, disaster mental health, academic and research communities and provide a useful addition to these very important and critical fields. Further goals of the conference included learning from research, field experiences and networking as well as providing a safe, fun, relaxing time to enjoy away from regular responder activities.

This volume is dedicated to our Veterans of the wars in Iraq and Afghanistan, their families, and those who support them before, during and following deployments. It is also dedicated to our first responders without whom our communities would be less resilient following disasters, critical incidents and other emergencies.

George W. Doherty, President
Rocky Mountain Region
Disaster Mental Health Institute

Returning To Equilibrium: Community Mental Health Response to Disasters, Critical Incidents and Returning Military

George W. Doherty, MS, LPC

Abstract

This paper begins by discussing the importance of the mental health profession in the responses to disasters, emergencies and other critical incidents, including war. It presents a model for Emergency Preparedness and the roles of mental health professionals. An overview of both the National Incident Management System (NIMS) and Incident Command is presented with a view toward emphasizing both their importance and their efficiency of response as well as why and how mental health is involved. Mental health awareness and responses in disasters is reviewed and discussed in the first part. This is followed by an overview of mental health concerns about our returning military and their families. Finally, an in-depth discussion is presented on how the concept of "Return to Equilibrium" is a more appropriate approach to dealing with disasters, trauma, war, etc. than is the attempt to return to normal – a term that is difficult to define because "normal" has changed.

Introduction

National traumas in recent years (e.g., 9/11/2001; other terrorist acts and threats; military actions in Afghanistan and Iraq; natural disasters such as Katrina and Rita; etc.) have heightened interest in the mental health needs of emergency responders, military personnel, law enforcement professionals, and disaster relief workers. Attending to the mental health needs of persons responding to emergencies, providing disaster relief, defending national interests, participating in peacekeeping missions, and maintaining a civil society is a critical part of strengthening and maintaining our national infrastructure.

Adjustment disorders can cause a variety of problems for individuals affected, including psychological pain and suffering, increased health care utilization, decreased family, social and occupational functioning, and premature mortality. These problems can extend to spouses and children in the form of child and family adjustment disorders. Due to their occupational roles in society, certain groups (e.g., first responders, military) are at heightened risk for trauma exposure and associated health and functional sequelae. Similar to the general population of trauma survivors, risk and adverse adjustment are not equally distributed among emergency responders and other high-risk occupational groups.

Current research is focusing on a variety of approaches to help improve our ability to deal with the results of traumatic exposure. Many of these include early interventions to reduce the likelihood of chronic posttraumatic stress. Other research is trying to identify biomarkers of vulnerability and disorder to help inform preemptive intervention approaches to avoid or prevent long-term posttraumatic stress disorder and related disorders. This has led some researchers to study preventive strategies that are based on concepts of protective factors, including psychological hardiness and resilience. Their focus is on risk and resilience factors (biological, cognitive-emotional, behavioral, social) that are considered important in the development and maintenance of post-trauma adjustment disorders in order to develop and test preventive interventions.

Conditions such as acute anxiety, depression, and PTSD can occur as a result of interacting individual and environmental circumstances. The nature, intensity and duration of exposure to trauma are clearly related to risk for adjustment disorders. Additionally, a host of other factors such as low Socio-Economic Status, lack of education, previous trauma, adverse childhood and developmental factors, lack of social support, life stress, psychiatric history, family psychiatric history, peritraumatic psychiatric history and peritraumatic emotion contribute to such risks. Sex and age are also specific risk factors involved in susceptibility.

Potential targets for selective prevention strategies include environmental interventions to limit or manage exposures, exposure-based interventions to increase familiarity with high-probability events and cultivate accurate expectations about their impact, educational interventions to increase the controllability of acute stress reactions, shaping coping behaviors, and/or fostering help-seeking, social interventions to build team/unit cohesion and bolster social support networks, and interventions to prepare family members for stressors introduced by their relative's deployment. A variety of intervention techniques or tactics for increasing high-risk employees' resilience during short-term, intermediate, and long-term adjustment periods are needed.

An Emergency Preparedness Model

In order to meet the needs of people affected by a disaster, it is necessary to have an emergency plan that is well structured and ready to be implemented at any time. Disasters and tragedies cannot be foreseen. However, they happen and it is important to react effectively. Any emergency plan must be operational.

An emergency plan consists of a master plan which determines the steps to be taken to optimize the mental health response in the event of a disaster. It explores the different possibilities for intervention with the community.

This master plan should provide first of all, for the designation of a mental health services coordinator in the context of emergency services. It is suggested in the specialized literature that this person not participate directly at the time of the intervention (Titchner, 1982), in order that he/she maintain a certain objectivity and control over the activities.

The many urgent tasks that must be carried out simultaneously at the time of a disaster and afterwards require a basic team to be involved right from the planning stage. There are many advantages in doing this planning as a group, including that of beginning to develop a team spirit that will last over the course of the intervention. Following are some elements that should be included in an emergency mental health intervention plan:

- an on-call system that will permit any responder to reach the mental health team at any time;
- an internal organizational chart showing the responsibilities of each person in the event of a disaster;
- a call list system (telephone tree and/or email contact system);
- internal directives on the use of communications equipment;
- an inventory of public and private resources that can be used by the mental health team and memorandums of understanding established among them;
- a formal structure for the reception and coordination of offers of mental health assistance by organizations that wish to provide assistance;
- a method of very quickly identifying clients who are likely, because of their physical or psychological state, to be more vulnerable in the event of a disaster;
- the organization of a telephone listening service to provide information and psychological support for the disaster victims;
- instructions for establishing contact with the disaster victims;
- a standard outline for an information session provided by the mental health team for the community;
- program elements for a verbalization session on the event for the disaster victims and responders;
- the elements of a specific short-term follow-up program for individuals or groups;
- an activity for the re-evaluation of the needs of the disaster victims in order to establish if there is a need to offer a program for returning to normal life;
- directives with regard to relations with the media.

The emergency plan will be a useful instrument in the event of a disaster, and may, of course, be adapted to the specific circumstances of the event. It is important to plan for and address the needs of both the victims and responders (including disaster relief workers).

ORGANIZATION OF EMERGENCY PREPAREDNESS: How to Help Foster Equilibrium

In the area of emergency preparedness, local authorities, concerned for the security of their citizens and in keeping with their responsibilities, should, by a local resolution, create an emergency preparedness committee. This committee could be made up of mental health professionals, representatives of citizens and businesses, as well as persons from outside, especially from the fields of health and social services. The primary mandate of such a committee should be to prepare and recommend to the authorities an emergency preparedness plan. This plan should include all the measures and activities of the municipality or governmental entity whose purpose is to avoid the occurrence of a disaster or a dangerous situation. Its aim should be to ensure the protection of individuals, the preservation of property and the return to normal life. Moreover, in order to ensure the execution of the plan, these same authorities should provide for an appropriate organizational structure.

Each department and/or organization participating in the organization of emergency preparedness measures should develop and set up an emergency structure and allocate to it the human and material resources required. Such an emergency measures plan which identifies hazards should be flexible and permit the rapid mobilization of personnel, both locally and at state and national levels.

Once developed, the department's emergency measures plans should form a larger plan in which resources, roles and interventions are clearly articulated. The suggested model favors interdepartmental action which precisely takes into account the importance of coordination.

The following is proposed as a model. The goal of coordination will be to establish the contribution of each partner in accordance with the needs created by the event and to integrate all of these activities into a coherent whole. The structure of the organization of local emergency preparedness suggested includes four roles: decision making, coordination, direction and execution.

Goals

The goals of the emergency plan should be:

- to provide for the coordination and dispensing of physical health services, mental health services, social services, and services related to public health before, during and after a disaster.
- to ensure that all communities are covered by an emergency measures plan for health, mental health and social services. The aim of these measures is:
    - to preserve, as far as possible, the life and health of the population endangered by the actual or apprehended action of destructive elements;
    - to provide the care required to persons;
    - to minimize the psychological and social impacts through appropriate services.

Responsibilities

The following tasks can be the responsibility of the committee:

- to develop and keep up-to-date a local emergency health, mental health and social services plan;
- to provide support in the development and updating of regional plans, and to ensure that they are carried out;
- to apply the government policy on communications in emergency situations;
- to coordinate the physical health, public health, mental health and communications response when a disaster affects more than one region;
- to ensure that the communication role is filled at the appropriate level; to support or replace according to the needs identified;
- to coordinate participation in local, state and national activities;
- to ensure the updating of knowledge and expertise by maintaining relations with the main bodies concerned on both the international and national levels;

- to develop local support and expert resources in order to permit communities, in particular:
    - to identify health problems and mental health problems and hazards to the health of the community;
    - to provide the authorities with appropriate recommendations in the areas of public health and mental health;
- to determine the training needs and develop programs, tools, and teaching materials;
- to ensure the training of local and state instructors;
- to develop a 24-hour-a-day response system for the areas covered;
- to participate in the local community emergency planning committee and its task forces;
- to determine, in cooperation with appropriate emergency planning groups, the financial framework for the planning of emergency measures;
- to evaluate the effectiveness of operations.

Responsibilities of Emergency preparedness Committee

- to develop and update the plans for emergency health, mental health and social services, determining which institutions, organizations and resources should be involved;
- to maintain links among the different institutions and organizations involved in emergency health, mental health and social services working in their respective areas;
- to assist the institutions, organizations and other resources in the planning of their emergency measures in the event of a disaster;
- to coordinate the physical health, public health, mental health, social services, and communication services response when a disaster occurs;
- to take responsibility for the communications role assigned in line with the policies on communications in emergency situations;
- to develop and coordinate regional and state resources;
- to coordinate participation in local and state activities;
- to participate in the emergency services committees and their task forces;
- to determine training needs in cooperation with its partners of the network;
- to develop a statewide instructors' network;
- to coordinate and organize statewide training;
- to develop a statewide warning system;
- to evaluate the effectiveness of emergency plans.

Each state emergency committee should, in cooperation with the institutions of the network, determine, for each of the communities in the state, which is the best resource to provide emergency services in physical health, public health, mental health, and social services.

Decision Making

This involves the ultimate decision-making power on any important question concerning the governmental entity in the area of disasters and emergency measures. The Emergency Operations Center should be in direct contact with each organization/department and should keep them informed during the application of emergency preparedness measures. The specified mental health coordinator should also participate in the decision making by advising on the cooperation required in the circumstances.

It is also at this stage that relations with the media and with governmental authorities are established. This role is the responsibility of the elected municipal officials, that is, the mayor and members of the local city council or other local governmental body.

Coordination

Coordination should be the responsibility of various department coordinators. Its make-up may vary according to the emergency situation. The mental health coordinator should advise and inform the emergency coordinator or governmental entity about the measures to be taken and the resources to be mobilized in the event of an emergency.

Coordination is very important since it involves seeing to the application of the emergency measures plan, evaluating the overall disaster situation, obtaining the additional resources required for the emergency measures, and communicating decisions to the political authorities.

Direction

Each department or organization must carry out the functions stipulated in their plan and that are agreed upon by the emergency planning committee.

The overall management of the activities of the various services is part of this role. There should be a direct and constant link between the persons responsible for coordination and execution, in order to ensure the effectiveness of the intervention. For activities being carried out on the disaster site, these roles should be the responsibility of the operations director. For all activities outside the disaster site, they should be the responsibility of the service managers.

Execution

Any action decided upon and ratified by the emergency planning committee should be carried out on the site of the emergency by the mental health teams assigned. The mental health team coordinator should inform the emergency services coordinator of the progress of events, the problems encountered and the resources required to manage the intervention.

On the disaster site or outside it, each responder should be responsible for the execution of the operations in his/her specific area. Emergency services are provided for disaster victims and assistance given to the other emergency responders as part of this role. It is the coordinator of mental health services who should report on the situation to the director of operations. There should also be cooperation between the local manager and the coordinator at a disaster site with respect to any question involving expertise in their specific sector.

Summary

In summary, the organization of emergency preparedness measures should be the instrument provided by the emergency services committee to ensure that there is coherent and effective intervention in the event of an emergency.

What is the National Incident Management System (NIMS) and Incident Command (IC) and What is the Role of Mental Health Professionals?

Two areas that mental health professionals need to be familiar with when responding to critical incidents, emergencies and disasters are the Incident Command (IC) System and the National Incident Management System (NIMS).

The National Incident Management System (NIMS) provides a systematic, proactive approach to help guide departments and agencies at all levels of government, nongovernmental organizations, and the private sector to work seamlessly to prevent, protect against, respond to, recover from, and mitigate the effects of incidents, regardless of cause, size, location, or complexity, in order to reduce the loss of life and property and harm to the environment.

NIMS works hand in hand with the *National Response Framework* (NRF) [see http://www.fema.gov/pdf/emergency/nrf/nrf-core.pdf]. NIMS provides the template for the management of incidents, while the NRF provides the structure and mechanisms for national-level policy for incident management.

Incident Command is responsible for overall management of the incident. Overall management includes Command Staff assignments required to support the command function. The Command and General Staffs are typically located at the Incident Command Post (ICP). This includes an active mental health presence.

A basic premise of both NIMS and the NRF is that incidents typically be managed at the local level first. In the vast majority of incidents, local resources and local mutual aid agreements and assistance agreements will provide the first line of emergency management and incident response. If additional or specialized resources or capabilities are needed, Governors may request Federal assistance. However, NIMS is based on the concept that local jurisdictions retain command, control, and authority over response activities for their jurisdictional areas. Adhering to NIMS allows local agencies to better utilize incoming resources. The NRF provides the structure and mechanisms for national-level policy and operational direction for incident management to ensure timely and effective Federal support to State, tribal, and local related activities. The NRF is applicable to all Federal departments and agencies that participate in operations requiring a coordinated Federal response. NIMS and the NRF are designed to improve the Nation's incident management capabilities and overall efficiency. During incidents requiring coordinated Federal support, the NRF provides the guidelines and procedures to integrate capabilities and resources into a cohesive, coordinated, and seamless national framework for incident management.

Preparedness requires a unified approach to emergency management and incident response activities. To achieve this, components of NIMS should be integrated within a jurisdiction's or organization's emergency management and incident response structure. The unified approach concept is at the core of the Command and Management component, as it is based on chain of command, unity of command, unity of effort, and when implemented, Unified Command. These characteristics allow organizations with different jurisdictional, geographical, or functional responsibilities, authorities, and resources to coordinate, plan, and interact effectively in support of a commonly recognized objective.

Effective emergency management and incident response activities begin with a host of preparedness activities conducted on an ongoing basis, in advance of any potential incident. Within NIMS, preparedness focuses on the following elements: planning; procedures and protocols; training and exercises; personnel qualifications, licensure, and certification; and equipment certification. Effective adoption, implementation, and training of all NIMS components in advance of an incident or planned event will facilitate collaborative emergency management and incident response activities. Preparedness is a foundational step in emergency management and incident response. The concepts and principles that form the basis for preparedness are an integration of the concepts and principles of all NIMS components.

Flexibility to manage incidents of any size requires coordination and standardization among emergency management/response personnel and their affiliated organizations. NIMS provides a set of standardized organizational structures that improve integration and connectivity among jurisdictions and disciplines, starting with a common foundation of preparedness and planning. Personnel and organizations that have adopted the common NIMS framework are able to work together and foster cohesion among the various organizations involved in all aspects of an incident. NIMS also provides and promotes common terminology, which fosters more effective communication among agencies and organizations responding together to an incident.

The components of NIMS are adaptable to any situation, from routine, local incidents to incidents requiring the activation of interstate mutual aid to those requiring a coordinated Federal response, whether planned (e.g., major sporting or community events), notice (e.g., hurricane) or no-notice (e.g., earthquake). This flexibility is essential for NIMS to be applicable across the full spectrum of potential incidents, including those that require multiagency, multijurisdictional (such as incidents that occur along international borders), and/or multidisciplinary coordination. Flexibility in the NIMS framework facilitates scalability of emergency management and incident response activities. NIMS also provides the flexibility for unique implementation in specified areas around the Nation. The National Integration Center (NIC), as appropriate, will review and support implementation plans, which reflect these individual requirements

NIMS is based on the premise that utilization of a common incident management framework will give emergency management/response personnel a flexible but standardized system for emergency management and incident response activities. NIMS is flexible because the system components can be utilized to develop plans, processes, procedures, agreements, and roles for all types of incidents. It is applicable to any incident regardless of cause, size, location, or complexity. Additionally, NIMS provides an organized set of standardized operational structures, which is critical in allowing disparate organizations and agencies to work together in a predictable, coordinated manner.

OVERVIEW OF NIMS

What NIMS Is:	What NIMS Is NOT:
• A comprehensive, nationwide, systematic approach to incident management, including the Incident Command System, Multiagency Coordination Systems, and Public Information • A set of preparedness concepts and principles for all hazards • Essential principles for a common operating picture and interoperability of communications and information management • Standardized resource management procedures that enable coordination among different jurisdictions or organizations • Scalable, so it may be used for all incidents (from day-to-day to large-scale) • A dynamic system that promotes ongoing management and maintenance	• A response plan • Only used during large-scale incidents • A communications plan • Only applicable to certain emergency management/incident response personnel • Only the Incident Command System or an organization chart • A static system

Incident Command System (ICS)

ICS was developed in the 1970s following a series of catastrophic fires in California's urban interface. Property damage ran into the millions, and many people died or were injured. The personnel assigned to determine the causes of these outcomes studied the case histories and discovered that response problems could rarely be attributed to lack of resources or failure of tactics. Surprisingly, studies found that response problems were far more likely to result from inadequate management than from any other single reason.

Anytime a large group of people gather to perform some activity, an organizational structure is needed. Someone needs to be in charge, others need to follow. In most response activities, a group of volunteers is mixed together with other volunteer groups and employees from one or more County, State or Federal agencies. Out of this mix of individuals, an organizational structure capable of performing all of the necessary response activities needs to be quickly and efficiently formed. The Incident Command System allows this to happen.

The ICS is a management system designed to enable effective and efficient domestic incident management by integrating a combination of facilities, equipment, personnel, procedures, and communications operating within a common organizational structure, designed to enable effective and efficient domestic incident management. A basic premise of ICS is that it is widely applicable. It is used to organize both near-term and long-term field-level operations for a broad spectrum of emergencies, from small to complex incidents, both natural and manmade. ICS is used by all levels of government—Federal, State, local, and tribal—as well as by many private-sector and nongovernmental organizations. ICS is also applicable across disciplines. It is normally structured to facilitate activities in five major functional areas: command, operations, planning, logistics, and finance and administration. Incident Command:

- Provides an organizational framework that defines all necessary management/work positions needed to conduct operations in single or multi-agency or jurisdictional settings.
- Provides an associated set of forms to help individuals collect and disseminate the information needed in the operation.
- Provides a time-table of activities that need to be completed on a recurring basis to keep the operation moving and information flowing.
- Provides common terminology across the entire structure—ensuring that everyone is talking about the same things
- Is a standardized management tool for meeting the demands of small or large emergency or nonemergency situations.
- Represents "best practices" and has become the standard for emergency management across the country.
- May be used for planned events, natural disasters, and acts of terrorism.
- Is a key feature of the National Incident Management System (NIMS).

Mental Health professionals who wish to respond to disasters, emergencies and other critical incidents need to complete the Incident Command System (ICS) 100 and NIMS 700 courses for those seeking the Disaster Response Crisis Counselor credentials. The Incident Command System or ICS 100 level course provides an overview of the standardized, on-scene, all-hazard incident management concept. It is designed to introduce mental health responders to basic ICS concepts and terminology.

The National Incident Management System (NIMS) 700 course explains the purpose, principles, key components and benefits of NIMS.

Additionally, ICS 200 is designed to enable personnel to operate efficiently during an incident or event within the Incident Command System (ICS). ICS-200 provides training on and resources for personnel who are likely to assume a supervisory position during a disaster or crisis response. ICS-100 is a pre-requisite to the ICS-200 course. For further information about these courses, go to: http://www.fema.gov/pdf/emergency/nims/ics_700_fs.pdf

Additional information about the roles of mental health professionals, CISM Teams and Incident Command are available online through links provided at the end of this article.

Background and Identification of Critical Areas: What do Mental Health Professionals need to address?

Crisis intervention is commonly thought of as acute psychological first aid applied within close temporal proximity to the precipitating event. While all disaster workers should have familiarity with the common patterns of reaction to unusual emotional stress and strain, relatively few are versed in the principles of care for the psychological or emotional casualty. What is Psychological First Aid? How, where and when should it be used? Who can provide it? How does it apply in different situations, with different groups or organizations? Is it applicable to military personnel, first responders, etc.? How effective is it?

How do victims, first responders, and the public in general deal with the fears generated by natural and man-made disasters, terrorism threats and acts, and war-related events? What can mental health professionals do to deal with these? Are there resources available to mitigate these?

What is strategic planning and how do we use it to adequately address problems and issues identified as possible risks in the future? How do we identify threats and target groups? How are resources developed and allocated? How are CISM Team protocols and disaster responder approaches developed? What should plans include in terms of response and what is the importance of follow-up? What criteria are needed for proper referrals for more intensive assistance? How are these referral resources developed and what training should they have? How do we develop efficient ways to identify factors that buffer against acute and long-term stress reactions; the potential costs and benefits of various intervention strategies; and gauge whether current training and preparation activities have a beneficial impact on post-trauma adjustment? How can we clarify high probability targets for intervention? What interventions preempt disorder mechanisms and promote functioning in various contexts and populations? How effective are prevention approaches for members of high risk occupations? How can we measure risk/resilience, response benchmarks, clinical and functional endpoints that are relevant to employers and individuals?

When states, cities and towns are affected by increased development and growth in industries and population, how are the effects dealt with in these communities and states? When they boom due to these events, how are social and physical and other infrastructures affected? How do responders such as law enforcement, firefighters, nurses and other healthcare professionals, hospitals, schools, social service and mental health agencies approach and deal with changing situations and populations? How do these groups strategically plan for the future? What do long-time residents do to adjust and how do newcomers fit in? What effects do various forms of energy development (e.g., wind, solar, oil, nuclear, gas, coal, etc.) have on communities, agriculture, vacation sites, national parks, forests and others and how do we adjust?

What cultural factors need to be considered when responding to critical incidents, disasters, local emergencies and other events? If responding to events in a culture not one's own, what do CISM Teams and mental health professionals need to be aware of and prepare for? How do we do strategic planning for such events whether locally, nationally or internationally?

These are just a few of the questions and concerns that mental health professionals who respond to disasters, emergencies and other critical incidents need to address. It is beyond the current purview of this article to discuss them in detail. They will be addressed and discussed in detail in an upcoming book on these topics. However, one will be addressed more directly here: Psychological First Aid.

Psychological First Aid

Nearly every survivor of mass violence, critical incidents or disasters experiences stress-related reactions in the immediate aftermath. Most recover. The emotional and psychological impact of disasters is not easily absorbed, and survivors may benefit from some immediate psychological support even under the best of conditions. However, it is no simple task to determine who should deliver what kind of support to whom and at what time. Disasters and wars are so dangerous and disruptive that it would be absurd to address people's psychological needs when their very lives are threatened. Moreover, even after the imminent threats have subsided, there continue to be imperative survival needs that must be given the utmost priority. Therefore, if immediate psychosocial support is to be supplied at all, it will most likely require an informal method of delivery that fits seamlessly with the provision of the most essential services (e.g., medical, nutritional, and sanitation) and must neither conflict with the priorities of the humanitarian operations or the cultural values of the beneficiaries.

Psychological First Aid (PFA) consists of a systematic set of helping actions aimed at reducing initial posttrauma distress and supporting short- and long-term adaptive functioning. Designed as an initial component of a comprehensive disaster/trauma response, PFA is constructed around eight core actions: contact and engagement, safety and comfort, stabilization, information gathering, practical assistance, connection with social supports, information on coping support, and linkage with collaborative services. PFA for children and adolescents focuses on these same core actions, with modifications to make them developmentally appropriate.

PFA is akin to the concept of physical first aid. First aid refers to preliminary physical care provided by members of the general population, not by medical professionals. In minor cases of physical injury, first aid may suffice to provide the care an individual needs for recovery. There is often no need for follow-up with a medical professional. Similarly, PFA is basic "grassroots" psychological support provided for family, friends, neighbors, and colleagues by members of the general population, not by mental health professionals. Just as physical first aid can be used for injuries ranging from minor scratches to serious wounds, PFA can be used to provide psychological support for experiences ranging from minor stressors in daily life to traumatic events. Just as physical first aid teaches participants how to know when an injury requires professional medical attention, PFA teaches providers when and how to make referrals for professional mental health care. The principles of psychological first aid are an evidence-informed approach to providing early intervention after disaster. Early intervention after disaster is both a social and health necessity.

The need for mental health intervention is substantial and increases as time passes post-disaster. Much of today's psychological trauma can be identified as resulting from sudden and seemingly random events, and particularly from events that involve the loss of human life. Due to the often overwhelming and ongoing nature of disasters and the recovery efforts they necessitate, building competency in a variety of intervention techniques and prioritizing assessment and education is essential for effective response. Experts agree that most people will recover from the effects of a disaster with little or no formal psychological intervention. Providing well planned and targeted psychological first aid may help many access coping skills and resources more quickly and may also allow disaster mental health providers to identify populations or individuals at greater risk for developing distressing psychosocial issues. In doing so, these individuals may be linked with the resources they need to ensure better outcomes. Different populations benefit from a variety of approaches applied at different stages of disaster response and recovery.

The role of mental health clinicians in the aftermath of disaster and terrorism is growing in importance. Assessment and treatment of acute responses to traumatic stress has received much attention since September 11, 2001. Those events underscore the value of having a trained and ready mental health workforce. Training in psychological first aid, crisis intervention, and early interventions may well become a part of graduate and postgraduate training in clinical programs in psychology, psychiatry, and social work. The scope and the depth of the psychological impact coming from such events warrants such an investment of time and resources. Coordinated efforts that cross geographic, political, and social lines would be welcome additions to societal efforts to understand the impact of mass violence and to provide the best possible interventions directed at recovery. It is clear that most survivors of traumatic events are resilient and do recover. However, a significant minority of survivors may endure prolonged periods of distress. It is for these people that interventions should be developed with the hope of minimizing the impact of trauma exposure, limiting disability and dysfunction, and maximizing optimal emotional recovery. Go to this site (Psychological First Aid in a Crisis) for further information about Psychological First Aid. http://www.samhsa.gov/SAMHSA_News/VolumeXV_3/article10.htm

The following is a combination video/PowerPoint presentation on Psychological First Aid (about 20 minutes). It is a good introduction and can be used as a discussion starter at team meetings http://mentalhealth.samhsa.gov/samhsadr/presentation3.htm

RETURNING MILITARY AND FAMILIES

Our military personnel (Regular, Reserve and National Guard) have been deployed for tours of duty in Afghanistan and Iraq that have varied in length and number of times deployed. Our Reservists and National Guard personnel in particular have left jobs, family and college for extended periods to serve our country. In some cases, they have been deployed two or even three or four times. While deployed, they have been in harm's way constantly 24/7. Some have been severely wounded physically while many others have been wounded emotionally and behaviorally. Their families (spouses and children) are all affected by their deployments.

Returning military members receive assistance from the military in their re-entry into the community upon return. Family members are supported through military and Guard Family Services groups while the Service member is deployed and continues upon their return. Veterans organizations have members who also provide various types of support.

In the news we hear of reports of increasing numbers of Service members returning with Post-Traumatic Stress Disorders and related symptoms of post-traumatic stress such as anxiety, depression and somatic problems. Problems associated with Traumatic Brain Injury (TBI) are also present. Another particularly disturbing statistic is the number of suicides occurring among military personnel. Each of these directly affect family relations among spouses and children of varying ages. They also affect many friends, relatives and fellow employees in our communities. Most affected, of course, is the individual returning military member. Adjusting to their changed lives and re-adjusting to families and the community is not always smooth. How can our communities better understand these adjustments, support our returning veterans and become constructively and positively involved in re-integrating our returning military back into our communities? What resources are available? What is the role of our mental health professionals. Who do they network with and interact with? Do they have a role with other healthcare providers, public health, hospitals, veterans organizations, veterans administration, military support groups and others? How can all these groups, other community organizations, first responders, and others strategically plan how to address and respond to these needs in a combined effort? What issues need to be addressed?

Invisible Wounds

Since October 2001, approximately 1.64 million U.S. troops have been deployed for Operations Enduring Freedom and Iraqi Freedom (OEF/OIF) in Afghanistan and Iraq. Early evidence suggests that the psychological toll of these deployments—many involving prolonged exposure to combat-related stress over multiple rotations—may be disproportionately high compared with the physical injuries of combat. In the face of mounting public concern over post-deployment health care issues confronting OEF/OIF veterans, several task forces, independent review groups, and a Presidential Commission have been convened to examine the care of the war wounded and make recommendations. Concerns have been most recently centered on two combat-related injuries in particular: post-traumatic stress disorder and traumatic brain injury. With the increasing incidence of suicide and suicide attempts among returning veterans, concern about depression is also on the rise.

The study discussed in a RAND (2008) monograph focuses on post-traumatic stress disorder, major depression, and traumatic brain injury, not only because of current high-level policy interest but also because, unlike the physical wounds of war, these conditions are often invisible to the eye, remaining invisible to other service members, family members, and society in general. All three conditions affect mood, thoughts, and behavior; yet these wounds often go unrecognized and unacknowledged. The effect of traumatic brain injury is still poorly understood, leaving a large gap in knowledge related to how extensive the problem is or how to address it.

Some Key Findings:

- Approximately 18.5 percent of U.S. service members who have returned from Afghanistan and Iraq currently have post-traumatic stress disorder or depression; and 19.5 percent report experiencing a traumatic brain injury during deployment.
- Roughly half of those who need treatment for these conditions, slightly more than half who receive treatment, get minimally adequate care.
- Improving access to *high-quality care* (i.e., treatment supported by scientific evidence) can be cost-effective and improve recovery rates.

DEPLOYMENT SUPPORT RESOURCES

A special collection of resources focusing on this topic. Several of these resources focus specifically on deployment and how it affects military families. Other resources are targeted more toward helping children deal with war, terrorism, and a parent being away from home due to a deployment. Additional ones focus on suicidal behaviors.

Center for Military Health Policy: A joint endeavor of Rand Health and the Rand National Security Research Division: "Invisible Wounds: Mental Health and Cognitive Care Needs of America's Returning Veterans"

http://www.rand.org/pubs/research_briefs/RB9336/index1.html
http://www.cfs.purdue.edu/mfri/pages/military/deployment_support.html
http://www.cfs.purdue.edu/mfri/pages/military/index.html
http://www.cfs.purdue.edu/mfri/pages/research/reports.html
http://www.rand.org/pubs/research_briefs/RB9336/index1.html

Suicide as a Risk Among Military Personnel

How can mental health professionals know which of the many variables in an individual's clinical presentation are most salient to that person's suicide risk? Such certainty requires an empirically validated prediction model that is specific to the population served. Data obtained through the U.S. Air Force (USAF) Office of Special Investigations and the USAF Institute for Environment, Safety, and Occupational Health Risk Analysis were analyzed using multivariate strategies of prediction based on an empirically validated model of suicide prediction (Brown, Beck, Steer & Grisham, 2000) and suicide completion versus non-completion status. The usefulness of the model to the USAF sample were discussed, and several factors unique to a military population were highlighted.

Implications

There are several practical implications of their findings for clinicians (Brown, Beck, Steer & Grisham, 2000). Given the increased stress and suicide risk factors in our society and the fact that suicide is considered to be one of the most common clinical emergencies faced by psychologists and other mental health practitioners, knowing what risk factors contribute most to a client's self-injurious behavior is essential to good risk management and client care. This information helps guide decision-making concerning hospitalization, referral, consultation, and the frequency of outpatient follow-up monitoring or intervention.

There are also potential implications for mental health professionals operating within industrial settings. For example, suicide risk assessments (and more general assessments of emotional stability) impact personnel selection, particularly for high-stress environments such as military, law enforcement, national security, etc. Unique to military settings, both individual risk factors as well as those that are systemic in nature are used to shape and support a healthier armed force. In keeping with this perspective, the USAF Surgeon General asserted that "we have to stop thinking of suicide prevention as something only mental health professionals do" (Redovian, 1999, p. 1). This emphasis resulted in the continued development of surveillance tools (such as the SESS) and prevention efforts (such as the USAF community awareness program). Through such identification and refinement of population-specific suicide risk factors, researchers and practitioners can create more focused prevention and intervention strategies. In most cases these strategies include a thorough biopsychosocial evaluation. Taking into consideration the variables outlined above can provide most practitioners with an excellent overview of potential risk factors in a client's risk profile. The ultimate goal of research on the subject of suicide is to one day be able to predict risk and avert clients from it. In the absence of such capability, we must continue to strive to reduce risk in the environment, identify those at risk through systemic prevention tools, and intervene in a way that minimizes the impact of the risk factors present.

Rozanov, Mokhovikov and Stiliha (2002) discuss the problem of suicidal behavior in the Ukraine military environment and give an example of the successful prevention approach they implemented. Their model of prevention is based on (1) education of the responsible officers, (2) training of the representatives of the most vulnerable risk groups, and (3) follow-up procedures based on distribution of pocket books for soldiers, educational booklets, and sets of helpful materials for officers. One of their main conclusions was that the prevention activity must be organized as a continuum of actions, seminars, consultations, and materials distribution.

Veterans and Military Suicide Prevention

Male veterans are twice as likely to die by suicide as male non-veterans, and the suicide rate in the Army is at a 26 year high. The Joshua Omvig Veterans Suicide Prevention Act (PL 110-110) and the successful Air Force Suicide Prevention Program are important steps in addressing suicide in the veteran and military communities. http://www.spanusa.org/index.cfm?&page_ID=7ECD7BB1-C613-FA47-9E53D64729C8A88C

Military personnel live with extraordinary stress these days, as they return from overseas or face the prospect of deployment. A recent study by the Department of Psychiatry at the Walter Reed Army Institute of Research demonstrated that a significant percentage of soldiers who have experienced combat suffer from major depression, generalized anxiety or post-traumatic stress disorder. But less than half of those exhibiting symptoms of such disorders sought mental healthcare, fearing they would be stigmatized by superiors and peers.

Families of military personnel experience considerable mental stress of their own. They fear for the safety of loved ones. At the same time, they often face the challenge of feeling like a single parent and experiencing the sense of loss that occurs when someone is missing from the family unit. Many find themselves living far from friends and relatives, causing feelings of isolation. What can be more distressing are soldiers who return home with untreated mental issues that cause emotional disturbances within the family. Family members with persistent anxieties may want help from a mental health professional. That's where our community mental health professionals come in.

Counseling needs for military families vary, and may include marriage and family counseling, individual psychotherapy and addiction counseling. Nearly every military installation has a family service center, where family members can access information, a referral, counseling and crisis intervention services. In addition, all military families—including those of National Guard and Reserve members who are active for more than 30 days—are eligible for at least limited free mental healthcare benefits at either a military treatment center or a civilian facility.

Insurance coverage for counseling services at a civilian facility may be provided—in whole or in part—by TRICARE, the healthcare program offered by the Department of Defense to active duty and retired uniformed services members and their families.

If military families come to you for help, learn all you can about this unique group and get the information you need on counseling services covered by TRICARE at www.tricare/osd.mil/Factsheets/viewfactsheet.cfm?id=127

http://www.state.sd.us/applications/mv91mvainternetrewrite/download/ResourceCenterContactListing4-1-08.htm?navid=23

Additional knowledge can only benefit your practice.

http://www.navytimes.com/benefits/health/online_hbml08_tricareother_mentalhealth/

http://www.govtrack.us/congress/bill.xpd?bill=h110-2739

- The NEW GI Bill also expands educational benefits for veteran: www.gibill.va.gov/
- Suicide Prevention Hotline: Veterans will be connected immediately to VA suicide prevention and mental health service professionals by calling 1-800-273-TALK (8255) and pressing 1.
- VA Housing Assistance: http://www1.va.gov/opa/pressrel/pressrelease.cfm?id=1514

Mental Health Services: Women in Military

Katz et al (2007) studied eighteen women who served in Operation Iraqi Freedom/Operation Enduring Freedom (OIF/OEF) and sought mental health services at a Veterans' Affairs (VA) medical center. Ten of the 18 women (56%) reported military sexual trauma (MST) while serving in OIF/OEF. All 10 with MST reported sexual harassment, 6 of the 10 (33% of the sample) reported unwanted physical advances, and 3 (17%) reported completed assault or rape. Fifteen women also completed a questionnaire about their experiences and the Iraq Readjustment Inventory (IRI) developed for this study. High reliability and high correlations with clinician ratings make the IRI a promising measure for future research. A comparison between those with and without MST revealed that those with MST had higher clinician ratings and IRI scores, suggesting greater difficulty with readjustment. And, while MST was significantly correlated with clinician ratings and readjustment scores, the variables "being injured" and "witnessing others injured or killed" were not. These preliminary data suggest that MST OIF/OEF women seeking mental health services is a critical factor for predicting symptoms and difficulty with readjustment to civilian life.

RETURN TO EQUILIBRIUM

There comes a time when the military member (Regular, Reserve, or National Guard) returns from deployment; there comes a time when the first responder and the disaster worker returns from deployment; and there comes a time when the disaster or the war victim seek to re-establish their lives. All attempt to return to what many refer to as normality. However, it is very difficult to define what normality is or involves. That is because, as the result of their experiences, normality as previously understood, no longer exists. However, a return to an equilibrium that incorporates their recent experiences is a more viable concept.

Balance

A mechanical system is at equilibrium if the forces acting on it are in balance. For example, when a body floats, the force of gravity is balanced by the buoyant force due to displacement of the liquid. The "balance of nature" (Pimm 1991) is an extension of this idea to the natural world. The concept usually refers to steady flows of energy and materials, rather than to a system whose components do not change.

What Is Equilibrium?

In 1884, a French industrial chemist, Henri-Louis Le Chatelier (1850-1936), when commenting on chemical systems in equilibrium observed that :

> "When a stress is applied to a system in equilibrium, the system will change so as to undo or offset the effect of the stress" (le Chatelier, 1884).

He used this principle to describe the changes that occurred in chemical reactions at equilibrium when external changes were made to the concentration of the components of the reaction or to temperature or pressure. This principle has a much wider relevance and can be applied to a wide range of everyday situations, including any system in stable equilibrium. This also includes environmental systems in the political, cultural, scientific, technical, economic and physiological areas. It can also provide a very useful analytical and predictive tool.

By applying Le Chatelier's Principle to systems in equilibrium, a system is said to be in **stable** equilibrium if, after a small perturbation is applied to it, it returns on its own to its original equilibrium state. An example of a system in stable equilibrium would be a ball at the bottom of a curved bowl. When the ball is deflected from the bottom of the bowl, other things being equal, gravity will always bring it back to the bottom center of the bowl.

Not all systems in equilibrium are stable. An example of a system in **unstable** equilibrium would be a pencil balanced on its point. Any small deflection will cause the pencil to fall over. The fallen pencil will be in a very different equilibrium state from when it was balanced on its point and therefore, the original equilibrium was unstable.

Le Chatelier's Principle did not require the system to return to its original equilibrium nor is that required here. Application of Le Chatelier to situations outside of the chemical equilibria, to which it was originally applied, is only likely to prove to be valid where relatively small stresses and perturbations are being applied to the system in question.

A system in equilibrium is comprised of a number of inputs and outputs that have achieved a "balanced" state. In many everyday situations, the systems will be very complex and the inputs and outputs may be numerous. Because of this, a system under stress will not necessarily return to its original equilibrium state but may well return to a different one. What Le Chatelier says is that the system will respond by resisting the changes and try to retain its original equilibrium state or at best achieve a slightly changed equilibrium state.

Most everyday situations that we encounter are systems in some form of equilibrium. If they were not, we would not view them as a system at all since they would be changing continuously. We can use Le Chatelier to try to analyze and predict the outcome of other situations that affect us all. One such situation is actually occurring right now, where the equilibrium is already under significant stress. This involves the earth's atmosphere and global warming. This stress is being produced by our releasing into the atmosphere ever increasing amounts of carbon dioxide and other waste gases. These end up as a layer in the upper atmosphere and lead to the well-known "greenhouse effect", resulting in the average temperature of the earth's surface rising slowly. The impact of this if continued unabated would be catastrophic to the earth. Among the other bad things that could happen is that the ice caps would melt and large areas of the earth would become flooded. We would also get major changes in climate, etc.

A Corollary to Le Chatelier

A corollary to Le Chatelier's Principle, called "The Goodwill Overshoot Principle", states that:

> In the absence of sufficient damping force, when a system in equilibrium is put under stress, the offsetting changes that occur, following Le Chatelier's Principle, will likely overcompensate before equilibrium becomes re-established, i.e. the system will "overshoot".

The equilibria we find in everyday systems are formed from fairly complex sets of inputs and outputs. Le Chatelier's Principle applies just as well to these situations as it did to the chemical equilibria for which it was originally prescribed. It should always be considered when evaluating the possible impact on the equilibrium of a system from stresses applied through changes to one or more of the input variables. Doomsday Scenarios are nearly always wrong because they do not take Le Chatelier into account.

As a direct consequence of Le Chatelier's Principle, it can be argued that it is usually safer to assume that a system that exhibits stable equilibrium is more likely to self-correct when small stresses are applied to it than it is to become unstable or to bring about fundamental changes to the system. Le Chatelier gave us this important piece of scientific observation and understanding, although in the limited area of chemical reactions.

The usefulness of Le Chatelier can be extended through the addition of the corollary of "The Goodwill Overshoot Principle" which states that in adapting to a stress, a system in equilibrium usually overcompensates in an attempt to sustain that equilibrium. As such, this can help in using Le Chatelier as a predictive tool when examining systems in equilibrium and under stress. This approach can be applied and used when analyzing and dealing with those who have been exposed to a traumatic event or critical incident that has disrupted their equilibrium.

Resilience and stability

We are interested in characterizing natural systems that are resilient, i.e., that tend to maintain their integrity when subject to disturbance (Holling 1973). This is related to the idea of stability. The informal concept of stability refers to the tendency of a system to return to a position of equilibrium when disturbed. If a weight is added suddenly to a raft floating on water, the usual response is for the weighted raft to oscillate, but the oscillations gradually decrease in amplitude as the energy of the oscillations is dissipated in waves and, eventually, in heat. The weighted raft will come to rest in a different position than the unweighted raft, but we think of the new configuration as essentially the same as the old one. The system is stable.

If we gradually increase the weight on the raft, eventually the configuration will change. If the weight is hung below the raft, the raft will sink deeper and deeper into the water as more and more displacement is required to balance the higher gravitational force. Eventually, the buoyant force cannot balance the gravitational force and the whole configuration sinks: the system is no longer stable. On the other hand, if the weight is placed on top of the raft, the raft may flip over suddenly and lose the weight and its other contents long before the point at which the system, as a whole, would sink. This sudden loss of stability may be more dangerous than the gradual sinking, because there may be little warning or opportunity to prepare for it. We may think of the raft system as losing its resilience as more weight is placed on it.

Suppose that we accept the ``balance of nature'' and the steady flows of resources that it implies. As we demand more and more of the products of natural systems, and we load them with more and more of our waste products, are we likely to experience a gradual loss of stability or a sudden one? In order to clarify such questions, we must refine our terminology. To decide whether a system is stable or not, we must first specify what we mean by a change in configuration or loss of integrity. If we don't care whether the raft flips over when weighted, then there is no problem of sudden loss of stability for the floating raft. We must also specify the types and quantities of disturbances that may affect the system. Suppose that a fixed weight is placed on top of an occupied raft. If the occupants of the raft move about, the raft may float at a slightly different angle, but if they move too far or all at once, the raft may tip. The range of possible movements of the occupants that do not lead to tipping is called the domain of stability, or domain of attraction, of the upright state. If the amount of the fixed weight is gradually increased, the balance becomes more precarious and, hence, the domain of attraction will shrink. Eventually, the weight becomes large enough so that there is no domain of attraction at all, and the raft will flip over no matter what its occupants do.

The preceding example makes a distinction between the weight loading the raft and the positions of the occupants. If the amount of the weight changes very slowly or not at all, we may think of the "system" as consisting of the raft and weight. The occupants change position relatively quickly, and these changes may be thought of as disturbances of the system. On the other hand, we may adopt a more comprehensive point of view, seeing the raft, the weight, and the occupants as a single system. If the occupants organize themselves to anticipate and correct for external disturbances, then the system may be able to maintain its integrity long enough for them to achieve their objectives. Another possible response to disturbance might be to restructure the raft itself. If it were constructed of several loosely coupled subunits, then excessive weighting or a strong disturbance might flip one part of the system, but leave the rest intact. Such a structure might not require as much vigilance to maintain as the single raft, and it might be able to withstand a greater variety of external disturbances. On the other hand, if the bindings that link the subunits become stiff, then the structure may become brittle and, hence, more prone to failure. This simple example illustrates how the notion of resilience of a system depends upon our objectives, the time scale of interest, the character and magnitude of disturbances, the underlying structure of the system, and the sort of control measures that are feasible.

In order to understand complicated systems, it is often convenient to consider a simpler system that exhibits the type of behavior of interest. A full theory of the floating raft would require a combination of the theories of hydrodynamics and of rigid body dynamics, but the essential features can be captured in a one-dimensional model. We are mainly concerned with the notion of stability and the fact that the domain of attraction of a stable equilibrium may depend upon slowly varying parameters. These features are present in a one-dimensional system.

Individuals exist in a normal state of "equilibrium" or balance. That emotional balance involves everyday stress, both positive and negative- like being late to work, getting a promotion, having a flat tire, getting ready for a date, or putting the children to bed. Occasionally, stress will be severe enough to move an individual out of his or her normal state of equilibrium, and into a state of depression or anxiety, as examples. But most people most of the time stay in a familiar range of equilibrium

Well Being and Equilibrium

While psychologists have developed some models of behavior modification and mental reinforcement to help people achieve an elevated state of well being (Seligman 2002) and economists have used theories of consumer behavior to give insights into the importance of relative income in explaining variations in well being (for example Duesenberry (1949), Friedman (1957), Veblen (1899) and Scitovsky (1976), there have been fewer attempts to develop a more general theory of well being that incorporates both economic and psychological factors.

Individuals achieve a higher state of well being and happiness when they are in a homeostatic equilibrium. This equilibrium state has physical, emotional, psychological and environmental dimensions. Characteristics of this equilibrium include feelings of safety, trust, connectedness with friends, family and community, and a predictable and welcoming social and work environment. Individuals make decisions that help them move toward and achieve this state of equilibrium.

When individuals are displaced from this equilibrium as a result of abrupt and strong changes (shocks, trauma) in the overall environment, well being and happiness are affected. If the shock is positive (marriage, birth of a child, promotion, windfall inheritance), the individual experiences an increase in well being. If the shock is negative or traumatic (death of a child, parent or spouse, falling seriously ill, demotion or getting fired), well being is adversely affected.

Behavior adjusts to restore the individual to homeostatic equilibrium through a combination of physical, emotional, behavioral and psychological adjustments. This behavioral readjustment is known as allostasis. This process of adjustment to external shocks/traumas creates physical, emotional and psychological stress.

The concept of homeostasis as it relates to human, ecological and physical systems pays particular attention to the impact of external shocks/traumas (such as unemployment, deteriorating health, divorce, emotional challenges) on agents and how agents react to these shocks or traumas. Behavioral adjustments by these agents are then related to the concept of homeostasis and allostasis, and to research findings on the determinants of happiness and well being.

An aspect of the relationship between risks and the homeostatic equilibrium relates to behavior that has been referred to as risk homeostasis. This behavior implies that there is an optimum or equilibrium level of risk that people are generally comfortable with. If this is true, then efforts to decrease risk may be met by riskier behavior. Consider the case of farm tractors and road design. When tractors were designed for greater stability, farmers used them on steeper slopes and the accident rate remained constant. When highways were designed to be safer, drivers increased their speed and took more risks and the accident rate remained at previous levels (Slovic 1984). Ample evidence also illustrates that when individuals are placed in dangerous situations where there is risk of injury or death, they experience a higher level of stress (Seligman 2004; Spitzer et al 1995) which implies that they have the urge and motivation to take action to return to their equilibrium level of stress which is consistent with their desired comfort zone.

The nature of an individual's disposition also affects the rate of return to the equilibrium set point. For example, research suggests that optimistic patients live longer than pessimistic patients (Palmore 1969a, 1969b). Happy people recover faster and some diseases can be cured or treated more effectively when the patient has a happy and upbeat attitude (Diener and Seligman 2004). As a corollary to this, a pleasant mood seems to lower blood pressure and that a high level of stress reduces the ability of the immune system to fight off disease. Furthermore, depression and anxiety, two major forms of mental illness, lead to significant declines in well-being (Spitzer et al 1995; Packer, Husted, Cohen and Tomlinson 1997). On the other hand, there is evidence that happy people show low signs of mental illness (Diener and Seligman 2002). In addition, duration of unemployment and well being are negatively related, and absenteeism and turnover rates are lower when workers are happier (Clegg 1983, Clark 2001; Akerlof et al 1988).

There is also ample evidence that agents who experience negative shocks or traumas that reduce well being make persistent attempts to return to the homeostatic equilibrium and to increase their levels of well being and happiness. Those who are unemployed look for work. Those who are sick go to the doctor. Those who are divorced begin to date and often remarry. Those who move to a new city or neighborhood make efforts to make new friends.

While the desire to return to a set point or homeostatic equilibrium may not always be synonymous with an increase in happiness and wellbeing, the various behaviors described above do suggest that the motivation to return to such an equilibrium set point is strong and highly desirable in a wide variety of circumstances, including disasters and other critical incidents. This behavioral pattern generally reflects a desire to return to or move toward the familiar, predictable and comfortable, and away from undue stress and aggravation. To the extent that these states of equipoise and relaxation are preferred, we can infer that they are also positively associated with higher levels of well being and happiness. When life circumstances such as stress, trauma, critical incidents, war, death of relatives/close friends and other negative social developments disrupt this equilibrium, well being is also compromised.

Some researchers have pinpointed the importance of such a homeostatic set point in determining the level of wellbeing. For example, Cummins and Nistico (2000) suggest that life satisfaction responses from questionnaires, on average, are not free to vary over the full range of possible outcome (say from being very unhappy to very happy). Instead, the distribution of responses is confined to a narrow range in the happy to very happy area. Commins and Nistico (2000) argue that this is because of the operation of such a homeostatic mechanism. They suggest that high self esteem control, optimism about life's circumstances and the understanding that we are in control of our own destiny help to constrain responses to a narrow range. This optimistic approach to life in general serves as a psychological buffer against misfortune, if and when it arises. Furthermore, this narrow range of variation in average subjective well being is reinforced by observations that people's feeling of well being responds quickly following misfortune. Even those who have suffered serious accidents involving paralysis return to a fairly optimistic view of life after some time. Such a view of behavior stresses the powerful psychological forces that lead to a return to a set point or homeostatic equilibrium. Psychologists refer to this belief pattern as positive cognition bias. This bias leads to a variety of observed behaviors that buffer the psyche. These include people's need to preserve their self esteem by downplaying the ability of others; to control essentially random outcomes (like roll of dice) by mental concentration or to predict many more positive than negative outcomes when asked to think about the future.

In summary, according to Pimm (1991) and others, long return times may be indicative of a loss of resilience. Pimm is concerned with behavior near a stable equilibrium. In that case, a long return time for a given displacement from the equilibrium indicates a small coefficient or, equivalently, a small derivative. Others are concerned with behavior of a system with two or three equilibria, one of which is stable. Resilience describes the tendency of the system to return to its stable equilibrium. A long return time is due to disturbances that bring the system near an unstable equilibrium, or possibly to a weak repulsion from an unstable equilibrium.

One should not interpret the strong desire to return to a set point as a reason to forsake explanations for variations in observed well being. Despite the relatively small variation in responses (vis a vis the full range of possibilities), models which try to describe the causes of well being are only successful in accounting for a small proportion of the variation. In large cross-sections such the world value surveys or US General Social Surveys, less than 10 percent of the variation in individual response is explained. Where panel data are available, analysis suggests that happiness over time varies directly and significantly with several dimensions of people's lives including family life, health, work and social environment (Easterlin 2004).

Life *disruptions* have a strong negative and very strong impact on happiness and well being. Social mobility as reflected by the number of moves also has a significant impact on well being. Making more moves tends to reduce trust, while fewer moves tend to increase trust and social cohesion in neighborhoods. Twenge (2002) and Magdol (2002) conclude that frequent moves have a detrimental impact on families, particularly in wives. Long distance mobility discourages individuals in forming long-lasting community ties and has a negative impact on well being. Illness, mental anguish and death in families also have a very strong negative impact on well being (Di Tella et al 2003, Layard 2005; Diener and Seligman 2004). Disruption in the form of vulnerabilities to floods, hurricanes, earthquakes, tornadoes and other natural disasters, also results in lower levels of well being (Veenhoven 1994)

Poor health and illness diminishes well being quite dramatically as shown in several studies (World Values Study Group, 1994; Packer, Husted, Cohen and Tomlinson, 1997; Diener and Seligman 2004; Gerlach and Stephan 1996). Depression and other psychiatric illness together make up about 30 percent of the various causes of disability. This is a much higher rate than disability from alcohol and drug addiction (together10%), respiratory illness, cancer and heart trouble (together 15%) (Layard 2005, Chapter 11). There is also evidence that happy people show fewer signs of mental illness (Diener and Seligman 2004).

Rewarding social interactions are key components of wellbeing (Baumeister and Leary, 1995). This entails frequent and pleasant interactions with a few people within the context of a stable, trusting and mutual caring environment. Ongoing relationships, within a framework of mutual concern, provide a stronger and more substantive bond and feeling of belonging than one based on self interest alone (Clark 1984; Clark and Mills 1979). Superficial social contacts cannot substitute for deeper and more intimate relationships (Weiss 1973; Baumeister and Leary 1995). Positive social bonds are associated with positive emotions and higher levels of well being (see Sternberg 1986 and McAdams 1985). Conversely, the loss of friends leads to loneliness and depression (Leary 1990) as well as anxiety (Baumeister and Tice 1990). Other research shows that intimate relationships and close social and family ties are highly valued by respondents and, in the case of sexual intimacy, results in a significantly high increase in well being. (Kahneman, Krueger, Schkade, Schwartz and Stone 2004, Diener and Seligman 2002; Blanchflower and Oswald 2003)

Two specific events that have a strong impact on a person's need to belong are divorce and death. Even though marriages that end up in divorce court may not have been joyful, divorce nevertheless results in negative feelings and reduced well being (Weiss 1979, Price and Mc Kenry 1988). The death of a spouse, child or close friend rank high on the list of stressful and difficult events and can result in a period of depression (Holmes anRahe 1967 and Weiss 1979).

People are adversely affected by negative disruptions such as illness, unemployment and divorce yet they recover more rapidly than they expect from these disruptions. People value their freedom and are adversely affected by rigid constraints and governmental controls. People value friends, family and social relationships more than work and yet they spend more time involved in activities they don't like including work and commuting. Extra income increases happiness less and less as people get richer. Motivation for maintaining the status quo (being comfortable) is consistent with homeostasis and is reinforced by social nature and the search for trust.

When trauma occurs, people are thrown so far out of the range of equilibrium that it is difficult for them to restore a sense of balance in life. Trauma may be precipitated by stress: "acute" or "chronic." Acute stress is usually caused by a sudden, arbitrary, often random event. Chronic stress is one that occurs over and over again—each time pushing the individual toward the edge of his or her state of equilibrium, or beyond. Most trauma comes from acute, unexpected stressors such as violent crime, natural disasters, accidents or acts of war. Some trauma is caused by quite predictable (but hated) stressors .such as the chronic abuse of a child, spouse, or elder abuse. "Developmental crises" come from transitions in life, such as adolescence, marriage, parenthood and retirement.

Before a disaster occurs the majority of people are usually in a state of relative equilibrium. When a stressful incident occurs, people experience a state of disequilibrium and there is a perceived need to return to an equilibrium. Faced with this dynamic situation, the role of mental health professionals and related responders is to support, and at the same time, accelerate the re-equilibrium process. Thus the worker may have to deal with disaster victims who are in various states of recovery. On the one hand there are those who, because of the presence of compensation factors, situational support and appropriate adaptation mechanisms, have a realistic perception of the incident. This usually leads to resolution as one's equilibrium is regained without crisis. On the other hand, there are others who, because of the absence of compensation factors, of situational support, and of adaptive mechanisms, may have a distorted perception of the incident. Problems then remain unresolved resulting in disequilibrium and crisis. A crisis intervention referral is needed. (Aguilera and Messick, 1976).

When a disaster or other critical incident occurs, people are traumatized at different levels, mostly dependent upon how directly affected they are. Much effort and much discussion revolves around returning to normal. However, "normal" has changed. It is a concept with many different meanings. It tends to be a term that is very difficult to define and, consequently implement. What was "normal" before can never be the same again. What can happen and what is constructive, and more easily defined is a "Return to Equilibrium". This involves integrating the event, its effects and its meanings into one's life and recognizing it as now part of one's life. Taking that and building a new balance in life can bring one into a new and enriched life. To use a concrete example, it is quite akin to taking an old-fashioned balance and adding or subtracting to one side or another in order to gain a balanced scale. Experience in life changes each of us whether the experience is good or bad. Integrating that experience into our life creates that new balance. It is a changed normality that results from the new balance and a return to equilibrium.

Returning to Equilibrium following a major hurricane or other natural event is different from Returning to Equilibrium following a man-made traumatic event, critical incident, terrorism event or war. However, in all cases, re-establishing a balance in life that integrates the event as part of one's life and moving forward into the future in a constructive manner is what develops our new "normality". Such a "Return to Equilibrium" is a goal of recovery.

A stress response that fails to return to a state of equilibrium becomes unresolved psychological/emotional trauma . Emotional or psychological trauma is the extreme end of the stress disorder continuum. It is stress run amuck—a deregulation of the nervous system that remains fixed and contributes to lifelong mental, emotional and physical disorders including anxiety and depression. Emotional or psychological trauma can result from such common occurrences as an auto accident, the breakup of a significant relationship, a humiliating or deeply disappointing experience, the discovery of a life-threatening illness or disabling condition, or other similar situations. Traumatizing events can take a serious emotional toll on those involved, *even if the event did not cause physical damage.*

Summary

Following a disaster it is common for individuals to feel pressure to reduce distressing emotions brought on by the event and return to adaptive, independent everyday functioning. For first responders, returning to everyday functioning involves managing residual effects from the disaster, being able to handle the day-to-day stressors of work, and being prepared to respond to any future crisis. First responders may want to avoid talking about the disaster. Avoidance can also take on other forms, such as missing work or even working too much. Although avoidant strategies may be initially highly adaptive, allowing the first responder to continue working, continuous use or overuse of avoidance can impede long-term positive readjustment. An active problem-solving approach that actively addresses difficulties posed by the stressor can help with both chronic and acute stressors. For example, finding meaning in some outcome of the disaster may minimize feelings of helplessness, instill a sense of control and mastery, and is typically associated with better physical and psychological outcomes than avoidant coping.

Following an intensely stressful event, first responders may believe that by talking about the event they will burden family and friends or that other people "just don't understand." However, talking about, or even writing about, the experience can be healthy and therapeutic. Discussing the event does not need to take place immediately following the stressful experience. Judgment should guide the decision about to whom and when to open up. If a trusted confidante extends an offer to listen and discuss the experience and reactions to the disaster, and the first responder desires to talk about his or her experiences, this might be beneficial. If, on the other hand, first responders are not yet ready to discuss their experiences, their decision should be respected. It is important that all relationships be built upon communications, including the right to not communicate. It is helpful, however, for first responders to remember to keep their options open and to let those who have offered their support at least know that their offer has been heard and appreciated. This is especially true with family members.

Every time a *stressful event* happens, there are certain recognized compensating factors which can help promote a *return to equilibrium*. These include:

- perception of the event by the individual
- the situational reports which are available
- mechanisms of adaptation

The presence or absence of such factors will make all the difference in one's return to a state of equilibrium. The strength or weakness of one or more of these factors may be directly related to the initiation or resolution of a crisis.

When stress originates externally, *internal changes* occur. This is why certain events can cause a strong emotional reaction in one person and leave another indifferent.

References

Adler PS & Kwon S. 2000. Social Capital: The Good, the Bad, and the Ugly. Knowledge and Social Capital: Foundations and Applications. Boston: Butterworth-Heinemann, 89-115.

Akerlof, George A & Yellen J. 1990. "The Fair Wage-Effort Hypothesis and Unemployment." Quarterly Journal of Economics.

Akerlof, George A, Rose, A.K. & Yellen J. 1988 "Job Switching and Job Switching in the U.S. Labor Market," Brookings Papers on Economic Activity. 2 495-582.

Alesina, Alberto F, Di Tella R & MacCulloch R. 2001. "Inequality and Happiness: Are Europeans and Americans Different?" Harvard University, Department of Economics.

Argyle, M. 1999. "Causes and correlates of happiness," in D. Kahneman, E.Deiner and N. Schwarts eds, Well Being: The Foundations of Hedonic Psychology New York: Russel Sage Foundation pp. 353-73

Arrindell WA, Hatzichristou C, Wensink J & Rosenberg E. 1997. "Dimensions of national culture as predictors of cross-national differences in subjective well-being." Personality and Individual Differences 23: 37-53.

Arrow, K., B. Bolin, R. Costanza, P. Dasgupta, C. Folke, C. S. Holling, B.-O. Janssen, S. Levin, K.-. Mäler, C. Perrings, and D. Pimentel. 1995. Economic growth, carrying capacity, and the environment. Science 268: 520-521.

Austin JH. 1998. Zen and the Brain: Toward an Understanding of Meditation and Consciousness. Cambridge, MA: MIT Press.

Barber, Brad M. and Terrance Odean. 1999. "The Courage of Misguided Convictions." Financial Analysts Journal November/December.

Baumeister, R.F. and Leary, M.R.1995. "The Need to Belong: Desire for Interpersonal Attachments as a Fundamental Human Motivation," Psychological Bulletin 117(3): 497-529.

Baumeister, R.F. and Tice, D.M. 1990. "Anxiety and social exclusion." Journal of Social and Clinical Psychology 9, 165-195.

Bernknopf, Richard L,, David S. Brookshire, and Mark A. Thayer. 1990. "Earthquake and Volcano Hazard Notices: An Economic Evaluation of Changes in Risk Perceptions." Journal of Environmental Economics and Management, Vol 18, No 1, pp. 35-49.

Biderman, Albert D. 1960. "Social-Psychological Needs and Involuntary Behavior as Illustrated by Compliance in Interrogation." Sociometry vol. 23, 120-47.

Bolton, Gary E & Zwick R. 1995. "Anonymity versus punishment in ultimatum bargaining." Games and Economic Behavior 48,287-292.

Brookshire, David S., Mark A. Thayer, John Tschirhart, and William D. Schulze, [1985] "A Test of the Expected Utility Model: Evidence From Earthquake Risks," Journal of Political Economy.

Brown, John P. 1972. The Economic Effects of Floods, (Springer-Verlag: New York).

Butler, James R. and Daniel P. Doessel. 1981. "Efficiency and Equity in Natural Disaster Relief," Public Finance, Vol 36, No 2, pp. 193-213. California," Westview Press: Boulder, Colorado.

Carpenter, S. R., and J. F. Kitchell. 1993. The trophic cascade in lakes. Cambridge University Press, Cambridge, UK.

Carpenter, S. R., and P. R. Leavitt. 1991. Temporal variation in the paleolimnological record arising from a trophic cascade. Ecology 72(1): 277-285.

Carpenter, S. R., B. O. Jannson, D. Ludwig, J. Pastor, G. Peterson, and B. Walker. 1996. A comparative analysis of total system resilience. Notes from the Beijer Institute Resilience Network Planning Workshop April 10-16.

Cochrane, Harold. 1974. "Predicting the Economic Impact of Earthquakes," in Harold C. Cochrane, J. Eugene Haas, Martin J. Bowden, and Robert W. Kates (eds), Social Science

Congressional Budget Office. 1992. "A Descriptive Analysis of Federal Relief, Insurance, and Loss Reduction Programs for Natural Hazards." Report to the Subcommittee on Policy Research and Insurance of the Committee of Banking, Finance, and Urban Affairs.

Consequences of a Catastrophic Earthquake, National Academy of Sciences Press: Washington, D.C., pp. 112-118.

Cordes, Joseph J. and Anthony M.J. Yezer. 1998. "In Harm's Way: Does Federal Spending on Beach Enhancement and Protection Induce Excessive Development in Coastal Areas?" Land Economics, Vol. 74, No. 1, pp. 128-145.

Cummins, J. David, and Helyette Geman, 1995, "Pricing Catastrophe Insurance Futures and Call Spreads: An Arbitrage Approach, Journal of Fixed Income, 46-57.

Dacey, Douglas C. and Howard Kunreuther [1969], The Economics of Natural Disasters:

D'Antonio, C. M., and P. M. Vitousek. 1992. Biological invasions by exotic grasses, the grass-fire cycle, and global change. Annual Review of Ecology and Systematics 23: 63-87.

De Alessi, Louis [1975], "Toward an Analysis of Postdisaster Cooperation," American

Disasters, Working Paper #61, Institute of Behavioral Science, University of Colorado.

Discretionary Reinsurance Markets for Natural Disasters," Journal of Risk and Insurance, 567-597.

Done, T. J. 1992. Phase shifts in coral reef communities and their ecological significance. Hydrobiologia 247: 121-132.

Dublin, H. T., A. R. E. Sinclair, and J. McGlade. 1990. Elephants and fire as causes of multiple stable states in the Serengeti-Mara woodlands. Journal of Animal Ecology 59: 1147-1164.

Economic Review, (March) 127-138.

Edelstein-Keshet, L. 1988. Mathematical models in biology. Random House, New York, New York, USA.

Ellison, Richard W., Jerome W. Milliman, and R. Blaine Roberts, "Measuring the Regional Economic Effects of Earthquakes and Earthquake Predictions," Journal of Regional Science, Vol 24, No. 4, (1984) pp. 559-579.

Estes, J. A., and D. Duggins. 1995. Sea otters and kelp forests in Alaska: generality and variation in a community ecological paradigm. Ecological Monographs 65(1): 75-100.

Frame, David E., "Housing, Natural Hazards, and Insurance," Journal of Urban Economics, Vol 44, (1998), pp. 93-109.

Guckenheimer, J., and P. Holmes. 1983. Nonlinear oscillations, dynamical systems, and bifurcations of vector fields. Springer-Verlag, New York, New York, USA.

Harper, D. 1992. Eutrophication of freshwaters. Chapman and Hall, London, UK.

Harvard Business School-Business, Government and the International Economy Unit and Princeton University-Center for Health and Wellbeing.

Henri-Louis le Chatelier, Comptes rendus., 99: 786-789 (1884). Journal of the French Academy of Sciences.

Hirschleifer, Jack. 1987. Economic Behavior in Adversity, (University of Chicago Press: Chicago). Jaffee, Dwight and Thomas Russel, "Catastrophic Insurance, Capital Markets, and Uninsurable Risks," Journal of Risk and Insurance, (June 1997), pp 205-230.

Holling, C. S. 1973. Resilience and stability of ecological systems. Annual Review of Ecology and Systematics 4: 1-23.

Hughes, T. P. 1994. Catastrophes, phase shifts, and large-scale degradation of a Caribbean coral reef. Science 265: 1547-1551.

Implications for Federal Policy, (New York: Free Press)

Jansson, B.-O., and H. Velner. 1995. The Baltic: the sea of surprises. Pages 292-372 in L. H. Gunderson, C. S. Holling, and S. S. Light, editors. Barriers and bridges to the renewal of ecosystems and institutions. Columbia University Press, New York, New York, USA.

Jones, R. I. 1992. The influence of humic substances on lacustrine planktonic food chains. Hydrobiologia 229: 73-91.

Katz, Lori S.; Bloor, Lindsey E.; Cojucar, Geta; Draper, Taylor. Nov 2007 Women who served in Iraq seeking mental health services: Relationships between military sexual trauma, symptoms, and readjustment. Psychological Services, Vol 4(4), 239-249.

Kunreuther, Howard, and Anne E. Kleffner. 1992. "Should Earthquake Mitigation Measures Be Voluntary or Required?" Journal of Regulatory Economics, 321-333.

Kunreuther, Howard, and Richard Roth, Sr (editors). 1998. Paying The Price: The Status and Role of Insurance Against Natural Disasters in the United States, (Joseph Henry Press: Washington, D.C.), 1998.

Kunreuther, Howard. 1978. Disaster Insurance Protection: Public Policy Lessons. (John Wiley and Sons: New York).

Kunreuther, Howard. 1996. "Mitigating Disaster Losses through Insurance," Journal of Risk and Uncertainty, 171-187.

Lewis, Christopher, and Kevin C. Murdock. 1996. "The Role of Government Contracts in

Lewis, Tracy, and David Nickerson. 1989. "Self-Insurance Against Natural Disasters," Journal of Environmental Economics and Management, Vol 16, (1989) pp. 209-233.

Ludwig, D., D. Jones, and C. S. Holling. 1978. Qualitative analysis of insect outbreak systems: the spruce budworm and the forest. Journal of Animal Ecology 47: 315-332.

Mangelsdorf, A.D. (1985). Lessons learned and forgotten: The need for prevention and mental health interventions in disaster preparedness. Journal of Community Psychology, 13: 239-257.

McClanahan, T. R., A. T. Kamukuru, N. A. Muthiga, M. Gilagabher Yebio, and D. Obura. 1996. Effect of sea urchin reductions on algae, coral, and fish populations. Conservation Biology 10(1): 136-154.

National Research Council. 1992. Restoration of aquatic ecosystems. National Academy Press, Washington, D.C., USA.

Nemetz, Peter N. and Kelvin Dushnisky. 1994. "Estimating Potential Capital Losses from Large Earthquakes," Urban Studies, 99-121.

Odum, E. P. 1993. Ecology and our endangered life support systems. Second edition. Sinauer, Sunderland, Massachusetts, USA.

Palm, Risa, M. Hodgson, R. Blanchard, and D. Lyons. 1990. "Earthquake Insurance in

Palm, Risa. 1995. Earthquake Insurance: A Longitudinal Study of California Homeowners. (Westview Press: Boulder, Colorado).

Perspectives on the Coming San Francisco Earthquake, Natural Hazards Research Paper No.25, Boulder: University of Colorado.

Pimm, S. L. 1991. The balance of nature? University of Chicago Press, Chicago, Illinois, USA.

Redistribution, and Urban Property Values," Journal of Urban Economics.

Rose, Adam, and Tim Allison. 1989. "On the Plausibility of the Supply-Driven Input-Output Model: Empirical Evidence on Joint Stability," Journal of Regional Science, 451-458.

Rose, Adam, Juan Benavides, Stephanie E. Chang, Philip Szczesniak, and Dongsoon Lim, "The Regional Economic Impact of an Earthquake: Direct and Indirect Effects of Electricity Lifeline Disruptions, Journal of Regional Science, Vol. 37, No 3, (1997), pp. 437-458.

Rozanov, Vsevolod A.; Mokhovikov, Alexander N.; Stiliha, Richard. (2002). Successful model of suicide prevention in the Ukraine military environment.

Rubin, Claire. 1982. "Managing Recovery from a Natural Disaster." Management Information Service Representative. Vol 14, No. 2, 1-15.

Scawthorn, Charles, Hirokazu Iemura, and Yoshikazu Yamada [1982], "The Influence of Natural Hazards on Urban Housing Location," Journal of Urban Economics, (March) 242-251.

Scheffer, M., S. H. Hosper, M.-L. Meijer, B. Moss, and E. Jeppesen. 1993. Alternative equilibria in shallow lakes. TREE 8(8): 275-279.

Schindler, D. W. 1990. Experimental perturbations of whole lakes as tests of hypotheses concerning ecosystem structure and function. Oikos 57: 25-41.

Shilling, James D., C.F. Sirmans, and John D. Benjamin. 1989, "Flood Insurance, Wealth

The Journal of Crisis Intervention and Suicide Prevention. Vol 23(4), 2002, 171-177.

Tanielian, T. and Jaycox, L.H. (Eds). 2008. Invisible Wounds of War: Psychological and Cognitive Injuries, Their Consequences, and Services to Assist Recovery A Joint Endeavor Of RAND Health and The RAND National Security Research Division Center for Military Health Policy Research

Titchner, James (22-24 Oct 1982). Psychological response to disaster and trauma. Expose presente au 3e colloque national sur les facteurs psychosociaux en medecine d'urgence.

Vollenwieder, R. A. 1976. Advances in defining critical loading levels for phosphorus in lake eutrophication. Memorie dell'Istituto Italiano di Idrobiologia 33: 53-83.

Walker, B. H., D. Ludwig, C. S. Holling, and R. M. Peterman. 1981. Stability of semiarid savanna grazing systems. Journal of Ecology 69:473-498.

West, Carol T. and David G. Lenze. 1994. "Modeling the Regional Impact of Natural Disaster and Recovery: A General Framework and Application to Hurricane Andrew," International Regional Science Review, Vol 17, No 2, pp. 121-150.

Yezer, Anthony M.J. 1992. "Differential Impact Of Earthquake Events" in The Economic

Yezer, Anthony M.J., and Claire B. Rubin. 1987. "The Local Economic Effects of Natural

Zimov, S. A., V. I. Chuprynin, A. P. Oreshko, F. S. Chapin, III, J. F. Reynolds, and M. C. Chapin.1995. Steppe-tundra transition: a herbivore-driven biome shift at the end of the Pleistocene. American Naturalist 146(5): 765-794.

Online References and Resources

National Incident Management System
http://www.fema.gov/pdf/emergency/nims/NIMS_core.pdf

Incident Command System / National Incident Management System Training Series for Disaster Mental Health Responders
http://www.disastermentalhealthnj.com/NIMS_ICS_genl_announce.pdf

Incident Command System Primer for Public Health and Medical Professionals
http://www.hhs.gov/disasters/discussion/planners/mscc/appendix/b.html

Organizational Preparation and Response to Mass Violence and Terrorism and the Mental Health Role
http://mentalhealth.samhsa.gov/publications/allpubs/sma-3959/chapter4.asp

Incident Command System (ICS)
http://www.nydis.org/nydis/downloads/manual/Manual_NYCRL_SectionIII-Chapter16.pdf

Crisis Management Information "Incident Command System"
http://www.ebasedprevention.org/toolbox/school-safety-planning/incident-command

Groups Discussing Incident Command System
http://groups.yahoo.com/phrase/incident-command-system

Disaster Recovery Plan
http://www.cityofripon.org/DisasterManagement/Appendices/Appendix_S.pdf

Understanding the Incident Command System (ICS) Manuel M. Fontes, MA Research Specialist Yvette M. Corral, BS Instructional Specialist Coordinator
http://azcphp.publichealth.arizona.edu/Resources/Documents/CHRMasterPowerPoint.ppt

Scenarios
http://www.oregon.gov/DPSST/AT/docs/ScenarioOpenings.pdf
Medsys Health Network: Center For Bioterrorism Preparedness And Planning
http://www.nyc.gov/html/doh//downloads/pdf/bhpp/bhpp-focus-mh-emaccess.pdf
Final Report: American Psychological Association Task Force on the Mental Health Response to the Oklahoma City Bombing
http://books.google.com/books?vid=9780788148309
Syllabus Hospital Incident Command System Sftx-2300
http://www.wncc.net/programs/coursepdf/SFTX-2300.pdf
Incident Command Structure
http://www.garretthealth.org/preparedness/pdfs/Appendix%20K%20Cover%20&%20Contents.pdf
Primary Incident Command
http://www.hhs.gov/disasters/discussion/planners/mscc/chapter5/5.4.html
Incident Command for Public Health: A Compilation of Education Resources from theCenters for Public Health Preparedness
http://preparedness.asph.org/documents/incident_command.pdf
Annual Colorado Volunteers Active in Disaster (VOAD/COAD) Conference November 18, 2008
http://dola.colorado.gov/dem/weekly_report/oct/info10-20-08.htm
Public Health, Mental Health, and Emergency Medicine
http://www.colorado.edu/hazards/resources/web/med.html
INCIDENT COMMANDER – Job Action Sheet
http://www.bioprepare.org/Resources/HICS-JAS/Command.doc
Developing a Crisis Management Plan in the Wake of the Virginia Tech Tragedy
http://www.suny.edu/University_Life/files/Developing%20a%20Crisis%20Management%20Plan.txt
Incident Command System (ICS)
http://www.norcalbt.com/Region3/ics.htm
Incident Command Staff: Mission Chaplain – Civil Air Patrol Model
http://level2.cap.gov/documents/Command_Staff_and_the_Mission_Chaplain_Role.pdf
Incorporating Community Mental Health into Local Bioterrorism Response Planning: Experiences from the DeKalb County Board of Health
http://www.springerlink.com/content/p05711t53h3533gx/
Texas A&M University at Galveston Pandemic Response Plan
http://www.tamug.edu/emergency/Pandemic.htm
All Disaster Mental Health Planning Steering Committee Group Memory1 of Meeting January 20, 2004
http://www.disastermh.nebraska.edu/files/2004.01.20.pdf
PA DOH SNS Incident Command System: Dispensing Site Organization
http://www.dsf.health.state.pa.us/health/lib/health/sns/DispensingSiteOrganizationChart.pdf
Disaster Response and Recovery
http://books.google.com/books?vid=9780788131264
Medical Incident Command
http://www.authorstream.com/Presentation/aSGuest1081-95711-medical-incident-

command-emergency-cycle-medicalincidentcomand-science-technology-ppt-powerpoint/

US Coast Guard - Commandant Instruction 1754.3 Subj: Critical Incident Stress Management http://www.uscg.mil/directives/ci/1000-1999/CI_1754_3.pdf

Coordinating a Multiple Casualty Critical Incident Stress Management (CISM) Response Within a Medical/Surgical Hospital Setting http://www.icisf.org/articles/Acrobat%20Documents/TerrorismIncident/MassCasHosp.pdf

CISM Critical Incident Stress Management http://www.pimahealth.org/bioTerr/conference/3-CISM_TRAINING_publichealth.ppt

Minnesota Department of Corrections – Critical Incident Stress Management http://www.doc.state.mn.us/DocPolicy2/Document/103.090.htm

Team Management http://cism.wikispaces.com/TeamManagement?f=print

Ground Team Leader Course http://www.mncap.org/es/docs/ground_courses/gtl_ics_cism.ppt

US Coast Guard - C.I.S.M. HELPING THE HEROES By Petty Officer 2nd Class Christopher Evanson, Fifth District Public Affairs http://www.piersystem.com/go/doc/651/179859/

Managing A CISM Team and Program http://www.kingcounty.gov/healthServices/health/ems/community/~/media/healthServices/publichealth/documents/ems/managing_cism_team.ashx.

Grant County CISM Team http://www.co.grant.wa.us/EM/HTM/CISM.htm

Orange County Sheriff's Office – Critical Incident Stress Management Team http://www.ocso.com/LinkClick.aspx?link=Policies%2F17.1.1.pdf

Colorado Crisis Support Network Guidelines for Crisis Support Services in Extraordinary Events http://www.healthoneems.com/pdf/Guidelines_for_Extraordinary_Events.pdf

Critical Incident Stress Management – Command and Staff Officer Course http://www.nmcap.org/labs/DO02_-_CISM_Command_and_Staff_Officer_2007.ppt.

Incident Command Systems http://www.sortteam.org/ICS_Present_SMAT2.pdf

Invisible Wounds of War - Psychological and Cognitive Injuries, Their Consequences, and Services to Assist Recovery http://rand.org/pubs/monographs/MG720/

Part I:
Disaster Mental Health

Placing Emphasis on Alliances in All-Hazards Emergency Management

Melinda Koenig, PsyD

Abstract

The literature on prior collective trauma indicates that a vital aspect in maintaining the ability to respond to emergency situations and to prevent post traumatic stress is the cohesiveness and empathic support of the participants of the response team. Forming and maintaining strong relationships among the diverse professionals on the emergency management team are key components necessary for successful response and recovery. Doing so prior to an event ensures that these alliances strengthen the response team by creating emotional cohesiveness and promoting resilience to anticipated traumatic stress. During the event, solid relationships form the support system required to sustain the responders during the operation. After the event, these emotional bonds weave together a common experience, enabling recovery through support, empathy, and ongoing connection as the responders debrief. Mental health professionals are an important component of the response team, but are often overlooked during the all-hazards approach to emergency management.

As part of the response effort, mental health professionals become real: the stigma of speaking to those in this field disappears. These professionals are trusted confidants, whose ongoing connections can identify pathological stress reactions or other psychological dysfunction within the response team both during and after the event. During recovery, mental health professionals maintain their connections to prevent the development of psychological illness and to refer appropriately for treatment. This presentation addresses the importance of creating working alliances between mental health professionals and other key members of the emergency management community. It takes the points of view of the emergency manager and the mental health professional to demonstrate the need for such work. Using practical examples from actual exercises and events, it answers questions such as: What resources and assets do mental health professionals bring to the emergency management table? What are their roles in the National Incident Management System (NIMS)? With whom do they network, partner and ally with to increase collaboration? How can they increase involvement in all-hazards emergency management activities? Further, attendees will be taken through each point of view individually, and then guided through the development of mutual goals. Finally, it gives recommendations as to the formation and maintenance of these key alliances.

Placing Emphasis on Alliances in All-Hazards Emergency Management

All too often emergency management services—and the responders who work with them—work singly, performing difficult work in their own areas of expertise. Although they may train together, they are primarily focused outward, on meeting the needs of those affected by various catastrophic events. Out of necessity they may form loosely knit collaborations or they may reach out informally to others during their work. These collaborations create essential support systems for emergency personnel, permitting the emotionally draining and complex work of disaster management to proceed effectively. However, it is unusual for emergency management organizations to look at the alliances formed to see not only how they nurture those involved in them, but also to learn how to create solid alliances prior to an event.

Typical emergency management organizations have widely diverse groups that must learn to work together: doctors of all specialties, nurses, administrators, business personnel, EMS, Fire Department, police, and construction workers are just a few—all with disparate mind-sets, training, and mission. They are tied together in the emergency management mission, yet work essentially "alone." Would our services be improved if, taking a cue from the business literature, we actively focused on building and maintaining alliances?

Why should we look at our connections with others? As infants our first experiences are attachments: how we bond with our mothers and fathers forms the basis for our sense of self, for our ability to individuate from our family system, and for the formation of relationships with others. As adults, working with others is unavoidable. We know that working well with others gets things done in a way that working individually does not. People in stressful situations bond naturally, as group cohesiveness appears to be emotionally protective, but few organizations focus on the skills needed to build strong alliances.

Research focusing on the curative nature of group psychotherapy has found clear benefits from the affiliative experience, as well. In order for its members to experience an emotionally corrective experience group therapy seeks to form connections with group members as they form a microcosm of the original family. Groups impart a feeling of universal bonding: "we're all in this together." Members recognize that life is difficult, often unfair, and may discuss real issues of life and death, terrifying to contemplate alone, but bearable with support from others. Alongside others the group member is able to experience and/or express powerful emotions that he or she may have previously defended against or suppressed. Through this social support a group may encourage altruism, a stepping out of one's own cares to share helpful information. This altruism, in turn, forms the basis for yet greater, emotionally healthy bonding with others.

Other research has noted that the bonding of group members has been beneficial, as well, in medical situations. Van Andel (2003) looked at treatment outcomes of cardiac patients, finding that the attachment of group members and the group's working alliance contributed "significantly and independently to the reduction of risk factors and an increased quality of life." Michael Wiensner, looking at the effectiveness of EMT services found that group cohesion was the most important factor contributing to more rapid response time, fewer missed or cancelled shifts, and smooth functioning of larger programs.

Donald Meichenbaum, Ph.D. (1985, 1993), has developed a cognitive-behavioral program of "Stress Inoculation" that has at its core various elements that foster the development of a cohesive team. This program has been used successfully to anticipate and prepare for the emotional effects of profound and prolonged stress or catastrophic trauma. By creating small worlds in themselves, strong groups reinforce our ability to see the world as benign and meaningful, to experience the self as worthy; to view others as trustworthy; to see our environment as secure. All this is necessary for accurate perception without the cognitive distortion that leads to unhealthy emotional reactions. Traumatic events disrupt these basic beliefs that we need to live emotionally healthy lives. This program of "inoculation," implemented pre-stress, has been demonstrated to decrease vicarious traumatization typically seen in military personnel or first responders. The debilitating effects of "secondary PTSD" or "compassion fatigue" are viewed as extreme, yet typical, disruption in our world view as a reaction to the stressful and traumatizing work with victims. The development of affiliative behaviors encourages us to think of the world as benign in spite of catastrophe; people we know reinforce our belief that others are trustworthy; during a time when beliefs are shaken, we develop security in our connections with others.

Data from the World Trade Center Medical Working Group of New York City's 2008 Annual Report on 9/11 Health point toward resilience encouraged by culturally affiliated groups. Post Traumatic Stress symptoms and full-blown disorders were lower among police, volunteers with organizations, and firefighters. They were higher in unaffiliated volunteers. This may suggest that to some degree group cohesiveness is an important factor in resilience.

As "disaster mental health professionals" we work with other responders from various areas. We have important roles in the National Incident Management System (NIMS), we are members of the Health Management System (HICS), and research tells us that we are likely to be called upon frequently during any catastrophic event. But—we rarely focus on the groups as a whole that we work with; and the operations we work with are, of necessity, focused on training for the events to come. All of us are self-starters; all of us are experts. Although we know that strong group cohesiveness is key to a strong response effort, and although we know that the more strongly we are bonded with our responder colleagues the healthier we all will be, few of us know how, or are in a position to implement a formal program designed to promote alliances among ourselves. Too often this is seen as unimportant, or as something that will occur naturally or informally. In fact, alliance building is a skill requiring specific tasks and a specific type of leader.

We often organize ourselves in ways that resist the development of strong alliances. Experts—as we are—think they should know how to do this intuitively and do it well! So, we put a lot of experts on our teams. Surprisingly, counterintuitively, Gratton and Erickson (2007), writing in the *Harvard Business Review*, have found that "the greater the proportion of experts a team has, the more likely it is to disintegrate into nonproductive conflict or stalemate." This means we may not be as effective as we think we are: we have to work at it. Our teams, as well as the nature of the work, make it difficult to get things done: we convene quickly in response to an unexpected event. Our teams are large, with a high proportion of strangers. We are diverse—encouraging innovation but creating problems, as well. Group theory emphasizes the need to find common ground, which may be difficult within diverse collections of responders. We collaborate "virtually"—online, over long distances. We are, therefore, less likely, without other influences, to share knowledge freely, to learn from one another, to help one another complete jobs, to share resources, to shift workloads flexibly to break up unexpected bottlenecks—in other words, we are less likely to "collaborate" effectively.

The organization that takes steps to establish a collaborative culture has an advantage over the one that does not. Certain principles, when established early and continued over time, encourage improved response and a level of functioning that supports the organization's members.

As we've learned in afteraction reports from the most recent catastrophic events, emergency management operations must develop pre-disaster emergency operations plans. They must measure performance. They must conduct collaborative planning, training, exercising, and response. They must learn various regulations and work in accordance with FEMA, HHS, regional, state, and local stakeholders. It is easy to become caught up in establishing systems and structures to the detriment of the types of management steps that build alliances. Simple shifts, however, can move the organization toward cohesive strength. As a value for collaboration is established, these structures are created, and they enable increased collaborative behavior through frequent communication simply about communication itself. Structures must be put into place that provide formal space for frequent contact among members. While developing a clear chain of command, leaders must develop the right working relationship—how will the team work together? While creating "ends metrics" (numbers focusing on the final product), create "means metrics", as well: how many meetings? How many ideas were proposed? How many problems have been addressed? Emergency management organizations must support alliances: hold regular meetings, emphasize affiliation, and prioritize togetherness. Rather than attempting to eliminate differences, talk about how to embrace those differences—find an operational place for talking about the diversity of the group and the varying points of view that diversity brings to the group. While it is clear that the emergency response team must focus outward on its "external relationships," (victims, government agencies, etc.), a shift toward inclusion of principles of managing "internal stakeholders" can make a difference in morale and performance. Pay attention to the relationships among those working together.

With so many other, often overwhelming things to do, how, specifically, can we pay attention to the "us factor?" Here are some suggestions:

- Create a high-level department specifically assigned to strategic alliances. This legitimizes alliances, recognizing their importance. It identifies a point person, centralizes organizational functions. Problem solving in four key areas improves: knowledge management, external visibility, internal coordination, and accountability.
- Create a collaborative structure. Opportunities for interaction, open rooms, and face to face meetings must be frequent and clear.
- Work on a specific project together.
- Choose senior leaders who value collaboration and demonstrate it. Perceived behavior of leaders plays a significant role in how cooperative teams will be ("role modeling").
- Choose leaders with specific skill sets. Flexible, with task AND relationship oriented, leaning more heavily on task orientation at the outset, shifting toward relationship orientation once the work is in full swing.

- Define roles: members of the team must have sharply defined roles so as not to waste time focusing on turf rather than task.
- Allow "task ambiguity:" the team must have latitude on how to achieve the task—collaboration increased if they have a shared path to the goal.
- Create a "gift culture" —generosity of spirit. Leaders mentor and coach, especially informally; help others build networks; appreciate others openly; engage in purposeful conversations; manage programs; creatively resolve conflicts.
- Teach specific collaborative skills (e.g., how to build relationships, communicate well, resolve conflicts) that are modeled, as well.
- Create balanced teams: people who know each other and who don't. All strangers are reluctant to share knowledge; all friends increase probable conflict among subgroups.
- Support a strong sense of community via: a group identity; "external symbols—shirts? Emblems? Hold regular meetings as a group. Groups with a strong sense of community are more generous in reaching out to others, more supportive of each other.

Although it appears to be common sense that individuals who work together develop a group identity and a sense of bonding, in truth some organizations work better than others. Some emergency response teams seem to develop less emotional trauma than others. Investigation into the commonalities of these healthy, high-functioning teams has produced a specific set of guidelines, supported by research and recent data, resting on a foundation of psychological development theory, principles of attachment, and group therapy. Emergency management is a difficult field, with multiple demands. Paying attention to the elements of building a strongly bonded team provides resiliency to each member so that the vital response work in our communities will continue unabated.

Selected References:

Gratton, L. and Erickson, T. J. Ways to Build Collaborative Teams. Harvard Business Review. November 2007, 101-109

Hughes, J. and Weiss, J. Simple Rules for Making Alliances Work. Harvard Business Review. November 2007, 122-131.

Kanter, R.M. Collaborative Advantage: The Art of Alliances. *Harvard business review,* July-August, 1994, 96-108/

Maddi, S. R. (2002) The story of hardiness: Twenty years of theorizing, research and practice. *Consulting Psychology Journal, Vol, 54,* pp. 173-185.

Meichenbaum, D. (2005). Trauma and suicide: A constructive narrative perspective. In T. E. Ellis (Ed.), *Cognition and suicide: Theory, research and practice.* Washington, DC: American Psychological Association.

Meichenbaum, D., & Deffenbacher, J. L. (1988). Stress inoculation training. *Counseling Psychologist,* 16, 69~90.

Meichenbaum, D., & Fitzpatrick, D. (1993). A narrative constructivist perspective of stress and coping: Stress inoculation applications. In L. Goldberger & S. Breznitz (Eds.), *Handbook of stress* (2nd Ed.). New York: Free Press.

Meichenbaum, D., & Fong, G. (1993). How individuals control their own minds: A constructive narrative perspective. In D. M. Wegner & J. W. Pennebaker (Eds.), *Handbook of mental control*. New York: Prentice Hall.

Meichenbaum, D., & Jaremko, M. E. (Eds.). (1993). Stress reduction and prevention. New York: Plenum Press.

Meichenbaum, D., & Novaco, R. (1978). Stress inoculation: A preventative approach. In C. Spielberger & I. Sarason (Eds.), Stress and anxiety (Vol. 5). Washington, DC: Hemisphere.

Meichenbaum, D. (1985). *Stress inoculation training*. New York: Pergamon Press.

Meichenbaum, D. (1993). *Stress inoculation training: A twenty year update*. In R. L. Meichenbaum, Donald. Stress Reduction

Okie, S. Dr. Pou and the Hurricane—Implications for Patient Care during Disasters. *New england journal of medicine*, 358:1. January 3, 2008, 1-5

Van Andel P. Group Cohesion and Working Alliance: Prediction of Treatment Outcome in Cardiac Patients Receiving Cognitive Behavioral Group Psychotherapy *Psychotherapy and Psychosomatics 2003, Vol. 72, No. 3* http://content.karger.com/ProdukteDB/produkte.asp?Doi=69733

World Trade Center Medical Working Group of New York City. 2008 Annual Report on 9/11 Health. New York: New York City Department of Health and Mental Hygiene. 2008.

Yalom, I.D. *The theory and practice of group psychotherapy*, Second Edition. New York:: Basic Books, Inc. 1975.

ABOUT THE AUTHOR

Melinda Koenig, Psy.D. is a clinical psychologist and the Director of Outpatient Adult Psychiatry Services at St. Luke's -Roosevelt Hospital Center in New York and maintains a private practice. She is an Assistant Clinical Professor of Psychiatry at Columbia College of Physicians and Surgeons. She has been an active participant in the St. Luke.s-Roosevelt Emergency Management Committee, sits on the Continuum Health Partners Emergency Management Committee, and most recently has been the Continuum Health Partners Coordinator for Emergency Mental Health Services.

Disaster Mass Care: Emergency Support Function #6

Art Storey, Department of Homeland Security

Abstract

What is the .new Mass Care for federal government under ESF # 6? How it has and does work on recent regional and national disasters. Who is responsible for what? What about special needs population? What about pets? What about temporary housing or long evacuations out of an impacted area? What happens in host states that receive evacuees?

• • •

One thing that is consistent in life is change and Emergency Management is no exception and lessons learned and not applied means we are destined to make the same mistakes.

The Federal Emergency Management Agency (FEMA) was the overall Emergency Support Function #6 (ESF 6) coordinator and the American Red Cross was the primary agency for Mass Care. FEMA was the primary agency responsible for Housing and Human Services. Those traditional assignments and responsibilities are now part of an expanded ESF 6 in the new National Response Framework (NRF).

The Post Katrina Emergency Management Reform Act of 2006 and the Pets Evacuation Act of 2006, both passed by congress, have created substantial changes in the Robert T. Stafford Disaster Relief and Emergency Management Act. ESF 6 now includes four primary functions: Mass Care, Emergency Assistance, Housing and Human Services. FEMA now has been designated to be the lead agency for the delivery of all of these services to ensure that the needs of disaster impacted populations are addressed by coordination federal and private agency assistance to impacted areas.

1. **Mass Care:** now includes general population sheltering, mass feeding, emergency 1st Aid, bulk distribution of emergency items and disaster welfare information.
2. **Emergency Assistance:** goes beyond the "traditional mass care" to include support to non-conventional shelters, as well as support for special needs shelters, mass evacuations, registration and reunification, animal evacuation and care, coordination of Undesignated In-Kind Goods and unaffiliated Volunteers, coordination of Voluntary Agency assistance and the National Shelter System.
3. **Housing:** Involves the provision of assistance of short and long-term housing needs of victims. This includes temporary housing which is financial assistance for lodging expenses and/or rental. It could also involve direct housing such as travel

trailers or mobile homes. Financial assistance is also given to help the home owner with minimal repairs to the primary residence. Financial assistance can also be given to the homeowner to assist with the replacement of their destroyed primary home. Finally, permanent and semi-permanent construction can be provided if none of the above is possible.

4. **Human Services**: This includes Individual and Household Programs, to include Other Needs Assistance. This might be Small Business Administration low interest loans, emergency food stamps, crisis counseling and training program, disaster unemployment assistance, disaster legal services and other federal agency programs.

In summary, the ESF #6 mission has greatly expanded. There have been revisions regarding the lead agency responsibilities in both response and recovery activities. ESF #6 has to work within the Incident Command System (ICS) and ESF #6 execution involves an extended federal, state, county and Non-Government Organization family. Where do or can you and/or organization fit in this new way of assisting people at a critical and emotional need in their lives? Contact your local or state emergency management agency in your area or state or your state Voluntary Organizations Active in Disaster (VOAD) group in your state. To get a point of contact for VOAD in your state, visit www.NVOAD.org

ABOUT THE AUTHOR

Art Storey is the Voluntary Agency Liaison for FEMA Region 8 which includes the states of Wyoming, Montana, Colorado, Utah, North Dakota and South Dakota. He has been in this position for the past 7 years. In this position he has responded to 21 declared and 11 non-declared disasters in 18 states including the 9-11 attack in New York and Katrina in Louisiana. He served with The Salvation Army for 20 years in many assignments throughout the Western United States including the Territorial Disaster Coordinator for the Western Territory extending from Alaska to Guam and from Texas to the Canadian border. Also was a Deputy Sheriff for Los Angeles County including corrections, patrol and a SWAT team member.

Federal Emergency Management Agency's Sequence of Delivery,

Art Storey, Department of Homeland Security

Abstract

This article focuses on explaining how a Federally Declared Disaster occurs. It also explains how voluntary organizations pick up the pieces for recovery after a disaster. It includes recent examples of disaster recovery from local disasters.

• • •

All disasters are local events. All disasters start and end locally. What will you do in the event of an emergency or disaster strikes you? Are you prepared individually at work and home in case of such an event? What is the plan for your business? What is your personal and family disaster plan? You can visit www.ready.gov for information on how to be prepared for emergencies and disasters.

When a disaster strikes, local emergency responders are first on the scene. Police, fire, EMT's and local emergency management personnel, along with local volunteer organizations, community and faith based groups are there to try to meet the urgent and emergency needs. This normally includes life and property saving activities, shelter, food, clothing and other emergency needs.

If it goes beyond their resources, they call upon their county for additional assistance. If it gets too big for county assets, the county will call upon their state for additional help. With the governor of a state making an Emergency Declaration, state help will be sent. If it goes beyond the states resources, they can request Federal Government assistance.

When the governor of a state requests federal government assistance, preliminary damage assessments (PDA) teams are sent to verify the amount of damage done and assistance needed. There is an exception for this process on a "catastrophic" event. When the federal PDA team verifies the losses, with the help of state and local emergency management, the governor can formally request the federal assistance from the President of the United States. The President (and only the President) can make a Federal Disaster Declaration which makes federal government assistance available under the law passed by congress (Robert T. Stafford Act).

After the President makes a Federal Disaster Declaration, the Federal Emergency Management Agency (FEMA) is called upon to coordinate disaster assistance. Under an Individual Assistance Declaration, individuals are directed to resister as a victim with FEMA to begin the federal assistance process. The first "line of defense" is personal insurance. The law does not allow for "duplication of benefits", so personal insurance is considered first.

After that, FEMA housing can be made available to assist individuals who are displaced from their primary residence. This can be temporary rental assistance for up to 18 months, if needed, repair assistance is made available along with replacement and/or permanent or semi-permanent construction. (It should be noted that the total Stafford Act Grant for uninsured losses for 2009 is $30,300).

Other federal assistance may then be available such as emergency food stamps, emergency unemployment assistance, crisis counseling grant and other federal government programs.

After registration with FEMA, victims will probably receive a loan application from the Small Business Administration (SBA). If this is received, this application MUST be filled out and returned to receive further federal financial assistance. SBA can make a low interest loan for up to $200,000 for a residence and up to $40,000 for uninsured personal property losses (renters and others may qualify for personal property losses).

After a determination by SBA is done, a victim can accept the total loan offer, accept a partial loan, defer making a decision on the loan or reject the loan, like any other loan offer.

If a victim does not qualify for the loan, additional assistance may be available through the Other Needs Assistance (ONA) program. This could include personal property losses, transportation, moving and storage and group flood insurance. (Again remember, under the Robert T. Stafford Act, the total FEMA grant cannot exceed in 2009 over $30,300)

After all the available assistance is provided by personal insurance, FEMA, SBA and others and there are still unmet needs, voluntary agency Long Term Recovery Committees are formed to assist an applicant with those needs. This process can be found on www.NVOAD.org under documents describing Long Term Recovery Committees.

Where would you and/or your organization fit into this process of assisting individuals at their critical time of need? Contact your local or state emergency management agency or your state VOAD. A list of all state VOADs and their points of contact can be found at www.NVOAD.org

About The Author

Art Storey is the Voluntary Agency Liaison for FEMA Region 8 which includes the states of Wyoming, Montana, Colorado, Utah, North Dakota and South Dakota. He has been in this position for the past 7 years. In this position he has responded to 21 declared and 11 non-declared disasters in 18 states including the 9-11 attack in New York and Katrina in Louisiana. He served with The Salvation Army for 20 years in many assignments throughout the Western United States including the Territorial Disaster Coordinator for the Western Territory extending from Alaska to Guam and from Texas to the Canadian border. Also was a Deputy Sheriff for Los Angeles County including corrections, patrol and a SWAT team member.

Community in Times of Disaster

Bruce L. Andrews, MS, CCMHC, LPC, LMFT, NCC

Abstract

This paper presents a personal account and reactions about an assignment with the Red Cross in response to Hurricane Ike in Texas in 2008. It is an After Action report by the author.

Introduction

From September 18 to October 8, 2008 I was deployed as an American Red Cross Disaster Mental Health Provider in response to Hurricane Ike. I served in an area of operations around Galveston Bay. During my deployment, I was repeatedly reminded of three of the six basic principles espoused by Unitarian Universalists (Unitarian Universalist Association, 1993).

1. The inherent worth and dignity of every person
2. Justice, equity and compassion in human relations
3. The respect for the interdependent web of all existence of which we are a part

In regard to communities, a person could probably list hundreds of characteristics of communities, but, don't worry, I won't. Martin Luther King wrote of "beloved community" (Smith and Zepp, 1998). Beloved communities and the multiple communities I witnessed are quite similar. Here some of the characteristics they share.

1. They are welcoming, inclusive, & hospitable.
2. They build and maintain community.
3. Community is a means to spiritual growth.
4. Gratefulness and warmth are abundant.
5. A sense of belonging exists.
6. There is a replacement of oppression with inclusion.
7. People are more genuinely integrated.
8. Agape is apparent, i.e., an understanding, redeeming good will for all.
9. Sanctuary is provided.
10. Reverence is expressed for all.
11. Equity and compassion are pervasive.

These are very positive characteristics upon which I will focus. However, to paraphrase, during disasters, there exist "the best of behaviors and the worst of behaviors". Thus, there are looters and those who would shoot them right alongside heroes trying to save lives. Reality is what it is and cannot be denied.

Understanding the structure of the American Red Cross and the Phases of Disasters will help to give you context for the multiple communities I experienced and, simultaneously, to give you context for the examples of their interactions over time and space. For descriptions of the structure and phases, I am drawing heavily on *Disaster Mental Health Services: An Overview* – The ARC Participant's Manual, 2005 Edition that is used for training Disaster Mental Health Providers.

The Red Cross is made up of various departments serving various purposes during disaster response. These departments, as in any large organization, all have their acronyms. The main department upon which I will focus is Disaster Mental Health Services (DMHS). DMHS was initially established in 1992 as an entity separate from Disaster Health Services (DHS). I was in the inaugural group of Disaster Mental Health Providers (DMHP) who trained in 1992 and responded to Hurricane Andrew in that same year.

The two main goals of DMHS are to meet the emotional needs of the people affected by the disaster (clients) and to help assure the emotional well being of Red Cross Disaster workers (staff and volunteers). Two key ways DMHS workers achieve these goals are by serving as a part of immediate disaster response teams and by providing specialized assistance for people who need mental health care beyond everyday emotional support. DMHS workers supplement and assist, but do not supplant, local community mental health care delivery systems and personnel. DMHS work is crisis intervention rather than therapy. It may feel therapeutic, but it is not therapy. Crisis intervention helps people to emotionally stabilize and to begin again to use their own emotional resources to cope. The intervention is time-limited until, if needed, local mental health providers take over.

All Red Cross workers are trained in the phases of disasters. These include:

1. The **Heroic Phase** that occurs before, during and immediately after the disaster. During this phase many emotions or behaviors may occur. For example, risk-taking to save lives or property, confusion, shock, denial, grief, anxiety, and fear.
2. The **Honeymoon Phase** occurs during early relief efforts when there are feelings of relief, hope and high expectations of assistance.
3. The **Disillusionment Phase** evolves as the relief effort continues during which frustration and increased stress possibly lead to behaviors such as abuse of children, spouses, and elders or increased alcohol use, drug use, and looting.
4. The **Reconstruction Phase** occurs after the relief effort ends and when the acceptance of personal responsibility for recovery or resignation may begin.

This is a generic description of the phases. Individuals and communities may experience these phases at different speeds, in different sequences and in different ways.

The "multiple communities" I mentioned earlier varied significantly. For me, these ranged in size from two to 200 or more. They were my partners and I, the DMHS team in a specific area of operations, client and staff shelter members, Red Cross Headquarters staff, North Carolina Men's Convention kitchen operators and client communities. I shouldn't exclude the million or so people in the Houston metropolitan area. There was also a Vietnamese fishing community on Galveston Bay, as well as a small bayou community isolated from others. Even now I almost neglected to mention nature's "communities" including horses, cows, dogs, cats, armadillos, water moccasins, alligators, fish, trees, bushes, grass, water, etc.

I found that community is not defined by time, or space, or culture, or disasters, or other demographic data or environmental events alone. I now believe that community is defined more by the relationships that occur within these human and environmental parameters. These relationships include a primary, if not the primary, community, which is with one's self. If one cannot commune with one's self, community with others is far more difficult. Clearer connections with one's self allow clearer connections with all else. Like John Muir, the great naturalist, said, "If you try to pick something up by itself, you'll find it is connected to everything else in the universe." I have learned and known that through different experiences for some time. Life just seems to keep reminding me. I think Life is patiently providing me repetitions of life experiences until I really see and understand the connections.

Now for the part of this paper to which I have been looking forward—telling stories that reflect Unitarian Universalist Principles and Beloved Community. More formally, these are examples to make the point, but thinking of them as stories is a lot more fun.

That reminds me. One of the primary skill sets for DMH workers is to remain flexible and to keep and express a sense of humor. If one doesn't, one cannot provide support and solace without greater risk of experiencing compassion fatigue. Compassion fatigue is when one absorbs so much of others' pain that one cannot function as effectively as needed in one's helping role. When a person's cage has been rattled, that person needs a helper whose cage is firm. If there are two emotionally wobbly cages, it is akin to "the blind leading the blind" emotionally.

Now for the stories. I find it difficult not to tell all of the stories. However, space requires that I tell only one or two associated with each of the three UU Principles I mentioned.

The Inherent Dignity and Worth of Every Person

My partner and I were assigned to check out a report of a man who lived alone in an isolated place and who may not have had food or contact for several days. We made a wrong turn and came upon another man whose home at the water's edge was torn in half. He had built it himself and was already determined to build again. In fact, he wanted us to take pictures of the damaged home and to walk with him as he described how he would rebuild his dream home. The resilience in these people is amazing. Having shared his dreams, he directed us to the home of the man whom we were seeking. He said that the man wasn't "quite right in the head, but a good man". He went on to say that we needed to be aware of that "redneck next door who was unpredictable, but mostly made noise". The "redneck" did not show or make a sound.

We found the man for whom we were looking at his home where he was mowing the lawn. We were immediately aware that the man, whom I'll call Bo, was mentally challenged. He was cordial and invited us into his home. It was clear he kept his home clean. Bo's brother had died right after the storm and he needed to show us his brother's funeral program. It was clear he had water, but we weren't sure about food and other necessities although he assured us he was OK.

As we were leaving, a couple of men drove up and dropped off a case of Meals-Ready-To-Eat (MREs) and told him to come to their house two doors down to learn how to use them safely. One of the men had been Bo's employer for many years although Bo was now retired.

The other was a neighbor who also kept an eye on him. They also added that Bo's sister-in-law lived right behind Bo.

Bo was safe and well. He, literally, had a community watching out for him. Not only does it take a community to raise a child, but it also takes a community to recognize the inherent worth and dignity of every person in order to take care of each other. Where would we be if that were not so?

Justice, Equity and Compassion in Human Relations

One day we were assigned to follow an Emergency Response Vehicle (ERV) crew as they fed people in the community. One of their stops on previous days had been at a huge garbage dump where debris was taken. There they provided meals and water for the truck drivers at the dump. On this day some headquarters (HQ) people had business there so the ERV crew led them to the dump. After arriving, the HQ people told the ERV crew they couldn't feed the garbage men because the garbage men supposedly should have had access to food and water through their employers. They didn't have access, but the ERV crew followed orders and went on to serve in other places on the west side of Galveston Bay. The mental health team helped with the serving. While I was serving, one of the women on the crew standing next to me broke into tears because she was so worried about the garbage men with no food or water in the heat. Believe me. These ARC volunteers are not in this work for the money. They are in it for the 18-hour days, exhaustion, and lack of sleep.

Another day while I was serving meals from another ERV, a man came for a meal. I asked him how things were going. He replied that he had cleaned out his home because all the contents were lost. Yet he said he was working. When asked for whom he was working, he said that he didn't have a job. He was just helping others clean out their houses because they needed help. "Just helping"? He had lost everything, was thinking of others, and asking, "What else is a guy to do?"

I'll be mentioning a couple of surprises later, but this one fits here better. While working in an extremely poor neighborhood, we came upon a group of somewhat unkempt-looking white people each of whom had a beer in hand. Remember that I mentioned clearer connections with one's self? I am ashamed to admit that at that moment I had a reactive stereotypic response to these people as possibly being bigoted or racist. They proved me wrong in about five seconds. They had introduced me to another Vietnam vet who, like myself, had been in an airborne unit. Jose and I chatted. Then I was told the story of their awareness of Jose's war injury that made walking very difficult for him. When water was rising rapidly during the storm, they knew Jose would need help. They went to his home at their own peril in waist deep water to bring him to safety. Justice, equity, and compassion? You bet! I also learned something about looking into the mirror rather than looking out the window and pointing one's finger with preconceived notions!

Respect for the Interdependent Web of All Existence

While working the very rural east side of Galveston Bay, I saw all sorts of wildlife as well as cattle, horses and other domestic animals. People were gathered to help round up stock to return them to safety as miles of fencing had been destroyed. Sadly, there were dead cattle, armadillos, snakes and others of the animal kingdom.

In most disaster operations volunteers of different local organizations help to locate and, if possible, return pets to their owners. Of course, pet owners also desperately search for beloved pets. One day we were serving in a town called Seabrook. We saw a man with a cat in his arms and took a meal to him. Just before we took him a meal his cat had come to him out of the pile of lumber that had been the man's home. The cat had been there for almost two weeks while the man searched for it every day. At that moment, the man didn't give a darn about his house. Instead, he wanted us to take pictures of his cat in his arms with the "pile of splintered lumber" house right behind them. We took a picture with his cell phone so he could send it to his friends.

In addition, talk was already beginning regarding restoration of the land. Although reclamation of the bottom of Galveston Bay had to be addressed later, I knew the bottom of Galveston Bay must have been a junkyard if the debris on land was any indication of the extent of debris spread across the bottom of the bay.

Surprises, Learning, and Relearning

There are many surprises and much learning in these conditions. One of many instances of learning for me was that community is not limited by time or space. One day I was covering the Mental Health "desk" next to the port-a-potties near the kitchen area when I saw a nurse striding purposefully toward me. She was clearly and intently looking at me. I immediately thought that we had a mental health crisis situation with which to deal. However, as I stood up, she asked, "Do you remember me?" As I frequently am, I was embarrassed to say, "No." She then said that we had served together 16 years before at Hurricane Andrew. I then recognized her and we had a wonderful "mini-reunion." We had had no contact since Hurricane Andrew. She had recognized my boonie hat that I had worn at Hurricane Andrew and tracked me down.

That boonie hat led to another humbling experience of self-awareness and learning or reminding. A person must be aware of one's self while also being open to the perspective of others. That may not sound especially profound or difficult, but living it in the moment is another matter.

While visiting a small Vietnamese fishing village on Galveston Bay, we met with a Vietnamese woman whose seafood business had been devastated. I greeted her in Vietnamese. She thanked us profusely for checking on her village. Then she noticed my boonie hat and asked if I had been in Vietnam. I said, "Yes." She hugged me and said, "Thank you for coming." I had received many hugs and thanks for coming to Texas at that point and it took me a moment to realize that she meant to thank me for coming to Vietnam 40 years before that day. Forty years ago I was so lost in my hate for that war or any war that I couldn't or wouldn't see that it was a life saving event for some. In forty years a Vietnamese person had never thanked me for my service. This lady's home and business had been destroyed. She was grieving her loss. Yet she took the opportunity in that moment to thank me for my service so long ago. How humbling.

It seems that when one is at the "tip of the spear in combat" or, in this case, in the path of the devastation of the "eye of the storm", something basic in human relationships happens. Their focus narrows to what is really primary and important and, simultaneously, beloved community expands to include all that is really primary and important. That which is secondary or tertiary falls away at least for a moment in time. Words like cooperation, commitment, connection, compassion, community, humanity, and, yes, love come to the fore. They are more completely and consistently alive and well in relationships. I believe that each of us can help to expand that moment in time. I really do. I invite you to join me in trying every moment of every day to do so.

In conclusion, I want to share a reading sent to me by one of my mental health team friends from Hurricane Ike. It is entitled *A Part of You—A Part of Me*. As you listen, please allow "You" to be singular and plural and permit "Me" to be "Us" as well. I ask this because I believe it applies to you with yourself, with another person, or you with an entire community whatever form that community takes.

A Part of You – A Part of Me

Every moment that we are together I am learning something and that knowledge becomes a permanent part of me. Though my feelings will be different a year from now, or ten years from now, part of that difference is you.

Because of you, I am a different person and the person I will grow to become, with or without you by my side, will have [grown to become that person] partly because of you. If you were not in my life right now, I could not be who I am right now, nor would I be growing in the same way.

Much of what I grow toward and change within myself, has to do with what I respond to in you, what I learn from you, what I understand about myself through you and what I learn about my feelings in the dynamics of our relationship. I do not worry about our "future together" since we have already touched each other and affected each other's lives on so many levels that we can never be totally removed from each other's [experience].

A part of me will always be you, and a part of you will always be me. That much is certain, no matter what else happens.

References

American Red Cross. (2005). *Disaster mental health services: An overview - participant's workbook,*

Smith, K.L. & Zepp, I.G. Jr., (1988) *Search for the beloved community: The thinking of martin luther king, jr.,* Judson Press, Valley Forge , PA, 1998 [See the chapter on "Vision of the Beloved Community]

Unitarian Universalist Association. (1993). *singing the living tradition*, Unitarian Universalist Association.

ABOUT THE AUTHOR

Bruce L. Andrews, MS, CCMHC, LPC, LMFT, NCC , Counseling Psychology Bruce graduated from Laramie High School in 1962 and obtained a BA with a major in Psychology from the University of Wyoming in 1967. He served in the U.S. Army stateside from January 1968 to December 1968 and in Vietnam with 82nd Airborne medics from January 1969 to December 1969. He earned his MS in Counseling Psychology at Southern Illinois University in September 1972.

Bruce worked for two years in medium and maximum security prisons of the Ohio Youth Commission. From July of 1974 to November 2002, he was a Child and Family Therapist at Northern Wyoming Mental Health Center. He served as a member of Sheridan County Child Protection Team for 14 years from 1979 to 1993.

Since February 3, 2003, he has been in private practice providing general practice mental health services as a member of the Cottonwood Clinic Family Medical Practice staff. He is also pursuing the development of a private consulting practice focused on organizational development and personal and executive coaching.

South Sheridan Medical Center (SSMC) Counseling Services
1842 Sugarland Drive, Suite 103
Sheridan, WY 82801
Phone: (307)673-5586
Email: brucelandrewsmslps@vcn.com

The Colorado Crisis Education and Response Network (CoCERN): A Model for Multi-Agency Coordination of Disaster Mental Health Services Utilizing the Incident Command System.

By Curt Drennen PsyD. RN

Abstract

In December of 2006 the Colorado Department of Human Services gathered a group of community stakeholders to develop a standardized structure for mental health/behavioral health disaster response. The result of this first gathering and two years of work is the Colorado Crisis Education and Response Network (CoCERN), which is a statewide asset based in community partnerships formed to deliver effective, efficient and professional disaster behavioral health services.

An inclusive, organized, collaborative and cooperative network for disaster behavioral health response, CoCERN is activated if local disaster behavioral health response resources are depleted or overwhelmed. When requested, the member organizations will provide support and services to the lead local responding behavioral health agency, survivors, responders, responder families and the public following any large-scale event. Based on strong partnership values including trust, collaboration, cooperation, coordination, communication and inclusion, CoCERN addresses the core issues of a disaster behavioral health response: Command (identifies specific roles and responsibilities of behavioral health command personnel, tying the behavioral health response to the Incident Command System), Resource Management (identifies key structures of responding teams and core response activities), Communications (identifies and addresses issues of technology and process) and Credentialing (sets standards for training and capacity expectations).

Introduction

The usual suspects in any disaster response include a wide variety of professionals from fire and police, emergency management, emergency medical and a host of "VOADs" or Voluntary Organizations Active in Disaster. The strength in the system is that each of these professional groups has a strong organizational or agency structure that maintains the focus of the mission (life saving, fire fighting, peace keeping, food and shelter, rebuilding, etc). In contrast is the typical "mental health" aspect of a disaster response. A mental health response to a disaster situation or community crisis can be multi-faceted, and includes anything from Critical Incident Stress Management, to a chat over a donut, to providing direct support to the larger response effort. Historically, what has been lacking is any semblance of organization paired with varying degrees of professionalism, and a void of mission focus other then the ambiguous "to help people."

On December 19, 2006 the Colorado Department of Human Services Division of Behavioral Health called together a group of 59 individuals representing 44 different agencies that either had direct response capacity or held a close interest in disaster behavioral health response. At this initial four hour meeting the vision of developing a partnership structure for behavioral health disaster response was laid out with the following five goals: 1. Identify who was missing and bring them to the table; 2. Adoption and modification of the Incident Command System for behavioral health disaster response, 3. The development of true cross agency and cross organizational partnerships, with the possibility of Memorandums of Understanding and Mutual Aid Agreements, 4. The development of communication systems that are inclusive and redundant, and 5. Standardization of Training and Credentialing.

With this framework, the group developed four subcommittees each with primary goals. The Command subcommittee was tasked with developing a structure for developing a process for implementing a unified command structure that would cross agencies and organizations. The Resource Management subcommittee was tasked with developing guidance for field response teams, management of personnel resources, building team structures and their core activities. The Communications subcommittee was tasked with identifying core lines of communication within the group and connection to the larger incident command structure. The Credentialing subcommittee was tasked with identifying core training requirements and the process for credentialing all involved in a behavioral health disaster response.

While initial estimates for completion of this project were 9 to 12 months, the actual development time was two years. The first year was spent with a heavy focus on subcommittee work developing the necessary structures for the partnership which was known as the Disaster Behavioral Health Planning Council. The second year was spent writing the guidance and protocol document and creating an identity for this blooming partnership named CoCERN (the Colorado Crisis Education and Response Network).

While yet untried, CoCERN has been developed with several key foundational elements in mind. First, CoCERN is not an entity in and of itself. It is a partnership and an agreement to work collaboratively and cooperatively in planning and response and it does not exist without that partnership. CoCERN does not recruit for paid or volunteer responders. That is the duty of the individual partner agencies. CoCERN is only the umbrella structure for all behavioral health disaster response. Second, CoCERN is designed for the immediate response period, not the long term recovery of the community from the event. Finally, CoCERN is not a "state asset", it is a community asset. While the Colorado Department of Human Services Division of Behavioral Health provided the leadership and supported the development process, CoCERN is "owned" by all of the partners and each partner has a responsibility for maintaining its sustainability through continued work at building the partnerships, sharing training, exercising as a larger group and assuring that disaster response efforts follow the CoCERN guidance.

The CoCERN Protocol and Guidance document has become the central element of this partnership and primary output of the CoCERN Council, the body of people that created this project. The document addresses all core issues identified at the first gathering in December of 2006. The following is a brief overview of this core guidance.

Contextual Framework

This section of the document lays out the foundational elements of CoCERN including the vision, mission and values statements. It illustrates the variety of partner agencies that have been assembled for a strong behavioral health disaster response. It outlines several organizations and their identified "authorities" during a disaster response. Finally, this section lays out several situational and response assumptions.

Command

The Command section of the Protocols and Guidance document is a core element of the partnership and the document. This section describes how agencies can activate the partnership, bringing in other resources from CoCERN to support the behavioral health aspects of the disaster response. It outlines how to select a behavioral health "commander" from those individuals available and it specifies duties for that position. The document also outlines core "command staff" including a deputy commander, a safety officer, a communications officer and a liaison officer and their specific duties. Other topics covered include how CoCERN operates within the larger ICS structure, how it interacts with the MACC (Multi-agency Coordination Center), and how to address issues around demobilization and after action reports.

Resource Management and Deployment

The Resource Management and Deployment section of the Protocol and Guidance document covers the primary issues of what happens in the field. It lays out a structure for teams in the field including a team leader, communications, logistics, and safety officers and how teams should interact in the field with each other and with other parts of the response effort. This section outlines the processes for deployment and response activities in the field including triage, basic support and psychological first aid. In closing, this section provides guidance on what types of activities should be focused on depending on the number of personnel available for the response.

Communications

The Communications section covers the basic processes of initiating a CoCERN response as well as several aspects of internal and external communications. This section also covers how to work behavioral health response issues into the public information and joint information center processes as well as issues regarding technologies available for communications.

Credentialing

The Credentialing section of the CoCERN Protocol and Guidance document is a critical part of the interagency partnership. It sets the basic floor training values for individuals who wish to be a behavioral health disaster responder. The CoCERN Council agreed upon two basic levels of credentialing, the Behavioral Health Disaster Responder and the Behavioral Health Disaster Specialist. The Responder is typically a behavioral health para-professional and is required to have some basic disaster behavioral health training as well as introductory training in the Incident Command System. The Specialist is typically a behavioral health professional, holding a license to practice in a behavioral health field and someone who has a higher level of disaster behavioral health training and experience. The document outlines the specifics for these levels of credentialing as well as expectations for further training and maintance of the credential.

Conclusion

We are looking forward to finalizing and putting the Colorado Crisis Education and Response Network to the test. Our current time line includes the following: December of 2008 all CoCERN partner agencies will sign the Protocol and Guidance Document as a Memorandum of Understanding. During the Spring and Summer of 2009, the Division of Behavioral Health will be working to educate State and County Emergency Managers regarding CoCERN and how it is to be used. Finally, during FY 2010 CoCERN will be exercised as part of other statewide disaster response exercises.

References

Drennen, C.H. (2009, In Press). The Colorado Crisis Education and Response Network Protocols and Guidance. Colorado Department of Human Services Division of Behavioral Health; Denver, CO

About the Author:

Curt H Drennen, PsyD, RN is a licensed psychologist with the Colorado Department of Human Services Division of Behavioral Health. He has worked in disaster response since 2002 and is the Colorado Behavioral Health Disaster Response Coordinator and Program Manager for the Disaster Behavioral Health Planning and Response Section. He has 17 years of experience in the field with an emphasis in Public Psychology and Administration, Emotional Intelligence, Servant Leadership, Systems and Systems Conflict Management as well as Crisis Intervention and Behavioral Health Disaster Management.

Mass Casualty Behavior Triage (MCBT): A Model for Efficient, Rapid, Mass Casualty Disaster Behavior Health Triage

P.J. Havice-Cover, LPC, CACIII, CEM and Curt Drennen, PsyD, RN

Abstract

When dealing with a mass casualty event that is taxing resources, triage is a necessary tool for assuring that those resources are used appropriately. undreds or thousands of people seeking medical services can quickly overwhelm a system of care. The Mass Casualty Behavioral Health Triage is designed to functionally support the disaster response system at medical facilities and in the field at disaster sites. Based on the Simple Triage System that considers severity, viability and rationing resources for the greatest good, this system quickly identifies behavioral health (BH) related crises and directs appropriate resources to meet the need. When people become agitated, angry, anxious and/or frightened, they are more likely to cause disruption, discord or even panic, resulting in a diverting of necessary medical resources and professional focus. Rapid identification and intervention with individuals who are unable to or are struggling with following directions, are a threat to themselves or others, or are causing disruption to the larger response effort results in a greater level of safety and order during the event.

Introduction

While true mass casualty incidents (MCI's) are rare, and few chances to practice and train for them exist [1], the inclusion of psychological casualties in the calculations of expected victims ensures better preparedness. How are psychological casualties defined? How can a reasonable estimate of psychological casualties be made if there is no standard tool to identify those casualties? In disaster mental health, a list of indicators and risk factors are used for consideration such as: dose exposure, types of losses, complicated grief, failed coping mechanisms, guilt, helplessness, hopelessness, traumatic amnesia, dissociation, depersonalization, derealization, mental status, and traumatic history- to name a few. These issues are important to consider. However, during the immediate response to an incident that threatens to overwhelm the available resources, it is unrealistic to attempt to gather this information. When casualties are great, altered standards of care must be implemented to promote the greatest good for the greatest number of people.

It has been estimated that for each medical/physical casualty, the number of mental health casualties ranges from 4 to 500.[2] Terrorist incidents generally produce high levels of extreme stress, but depending on circumstances, natural disasters can result in significant dysfunction and psychological sequelae as well. In 1987, 250 people were exposed to a radiological gas release in Brazil; 125,000 sought screening. During the 1991 Gulf War, of the 773 people taken to hospital in Israel following scud missile attacks, 43% were considered "mental health casualties".[3] Following the 1995 Sarin gas attacks within the Tokyo subway, hospitals saw 5,510 patients: 17 were deemed critical, 37 severe, and 984 moderately ill with vision problems. Many of those reporting to hospitals were the "worried well," who had to be distinguished from those that were ill.[4]

In 2005 Hurricane Katrina hit the Gulf Coast resulting in the largest population evacuation in the history of the United States. Over 300,000 people self evacuated or were forced to evacuate as part of the disaster response effort. The Astrodome in Houston, Texas sheltered tens of thousands of people. Disaster responders worked to meet basic needs, including medical, public health and mental health needs. The number of available trained disaster behavioral health professionals was low or non-existent in the early response phase. Symptoms of extreme stress and exhaustion were common, resulting in problems with functioning (individual and group), as well as community/group cohesion. These dynamics negatively impact response efforts, significantly slow community recovery and threaten lives. Often when trained disaster behavioral health professionals are available the need is so great, it is difficult if not impossible to identify the highest priorities and appropriately channel available resources. The availability of an effective and efficient form of rapid, behavioral health triage in a MCI would result in significantly higher levels of positive outcomes for the individuals and communities impacted by such an event.

Medical triage is a system to quickly assess the levels of medical care needed and prioritize resources to meet those needs. In a disaster or mass casualty event, triage is a quick and effective way to communicate the most pressing needs to resource limited medical response units. It typically uses a color-coding system for easy identification of those needing immediate transport based on injuries; those with the greatest chance for survival and those that delayed treatment will not negatively impact outcomes. Simple Triage and Rapid Treatment (S.T.A.R.T.)[5] is a commonly used medical triage system. S.T.A.R.T. was designed in 1983 and updated in 1994. It can be used by rescuers with basic first aid skills. This system is based on urgency of medical need—not "first come- first served" and uses four colors that communicate the level of need. Another type of medical triage system used by the the military and many governmental agencies originated in military medicine, when limited resources faced many wounded soldiers. It is used in civilian settings during disasters or epidemics and in emergency rooms. This system has perforated color sections that allow the triaging professional to leave the tag intact if the person has minor injuries (green) or to tear off a color block, leaving the the current level of care displayed on the bottom. The colored sections are defined as follows:

- Black- Deceased or not breathing and repositioning the airway is not successful
- Red- Immediate transportation of those who can be helped by advanced medical care or within one hour
- Yellow- Delayed; injuries not life threatening
- Green-Minor; not treated until all red and yellows have been sent for treatment—may need basic first aid (wound cleaning, antiseptic and bandages).

According to a report published by the CDC *"Predicting Casualty Severity and Hospital Capacity"* [6] it may be expected that 1/3rd of victims of terrorrist bombings will be critical casualties, tagged as either black or red, and 2/3 will be designated as non-critical (either yellow or green).

A Review of Existing Models of Behavioral Health Triage (BHT)

A comprehensive search of the literature was completed utilizing Pub Med and PsychINFO databases over the past ten years (August 1997 to August 2007), and searching the following keywords: disaster mental health triage, trauma triage, psychiatric emergency services and disaster, and early assessment of trauma.

Several authors have argued that strong behavioral health or mental health triage is needed during times of disaster. As Murdoch and Cynmet [7] state "Triage of the initial waves is important to prevent the system from becoming overwhelmed and to begin looking for those who will suffer long-term psychological sequelae." Providing a balance, Everly [8] points out that triage must help to identify those that most need support or referral, but not be so aggressive that it interferes with the natural resilience of individuals and communities. Either extreme can result in loss of functionality. We must also be able to identify extreme responses without interfering with the normal and functional processing of extreme stress. In a 1999 editorial, Everly [11] argued that a form of triage was needed for disaster behavioral health and suggested that no models existed. He offered some basic guidelines, which have at their core the following assumptions:

1. "Psychological homeostasis has been disrupted;
2. One's usual coping mechanisms have failed in their efforts to either solve the problem, or otherwise reestablish psychological homeostasis; and,
3. The distress engendered by the crisis has yielded some evidence of functional impairment."

He continued with a review of the biology of extreme and traumatic stress with a focus on "the most common signs and symptoms that serve to predict poor mental health outcomes if no intervention is provided" and concludes with a list of 10 signs and symptoms to consider. Another suggestion for a disaster behavioral health triage came from Pynoos [12] when he suggested a more "clinical triage protocol" for children. His guidance included assessing the following: level of traumatic exposure, both objective and subjective: loss; acute difficulties the child is experiencing; ongoing adversities the child is facing; existing traumatic reminders; traumatic exposure or extreme loss; and current level of distress.

Early focus on psychological triage has been based on psychiatric interventions in the emergency room.[9,10] However, these are typically focused on individuals with serious and persistent mental illnesses and do not translate well to the field of disaster behavioral health. A psychiatric approach to disaster/trauma triage is based on Advanced Trauma Life Support (ATLS) and advocates that psychiatrists who expect to be conducting disaster work be certified in ATLS as well as Advanced Cardiac Life Support (ACLS). [13] This triage system focuses "on those psychiatric conditions that would most likely adversely affect medical-surgical outcome" and utilizes a formalized assessment starting with a Mental Status Examination, complete history, and an assessment of biological responses based on ATLS and ACLS medications. Roberts [14] presents the Assessment, Crisis Intervention and Trauma

Treatment or ACT model for early intervention and includes triage as a part of that model. Within the ACT model triage is a screening tool to be used "in gathering and recording information about the initial contact between a person experiencing crisis or trauma reactions, and the mental health specialist". The suggested components of this tool include demographics, perception of the event, coping skills, presenting problems, safety issues, substance use, psychiatric history, support network and suicide/homicide ideation or risk. Roberts goes on to define psychological triage as the decision-making process determining lethality and referral.

At the 2005 National Disaster Medical Systems conference Dr. Lawrence Hipshman's suggested model, Behavioral Health Disaster Triage (BHDT), [15] focused on those medically triaged individuals rated as "green". The model's goal is "to restore psychological and social functioning of individuals and communities and limit the occurrence and severity of adverse impacts of disaster related mental health problems". Hipshman notes that the triage method used should be simple with priority status given to safety, then function and finally comfort as assessed utilizing that DSM-IV Axis V Global Assessment of Functioning (GAF). From these three domains, a further assessment of the person's arousal, behavior and cognition is done to determine severity and category levels.

One of the newest behavioral health triage tools being developed as a system and written about in current literature is the PsySTART Rapid Mental Health Triage and Incident Management System. [16-18] The system is intended to facilitate the determination of behavior health needs in disasters. The system uses a Field Triage Tag that requires the responder to ask eleven different questions. Should the individual being assessed "express thought/intent to seriously harm self and/or others"; the site supervisor is to be contacted immediately. Second level events include "family members missing; death of a family member, friend, schoolmate, pet; saw/heard death or serious injury to others" and require the assessor to contact Disaster Mental Health as soon as possible. Other items on the Field Triage Tag that can be checked off and indicate referral to mental health are: "felt they (or loved one) almost died; received physical injury or self/loved one is physically ill; received medical treatment (self/loved one); separated from family member; child separated from parent; and home not livable". It is noted in the American Red Cross participant's manual[19] that the Field Triage tag questions are not meant to be asked of every person, but by listening to people telling their stories, the assessor might hear something that would be checked as "yes" on the card. The PsySTART Triage system requires collecting information through listening to stories. This gives quality information and looks at the portion of the event the person experienced. It is based on dose response and was used for assessing children in Thailand after the 2004 Tsunami.

A key theme in all of these approaches to behavioral health triage is the emphasis on *assessment*, diagnostics and intervention. These models are resource intensive versus resource efficient. Each of the above models requires the disaster behavioral health professional spend significant amounts of time with survivors, listen to experiences, question responses and assess functioning based on past and current responses to stress. Based on experience, we believe these methods are *not* viable models for MCI- immediate, behavioral health triage. They are useful models of *assessment* that can be utilized as behavioral health resources are more plentiful and as the community moves into the recovery phase.

In contrast we believe that a strong, functional model of disaster behavioral health MCI triage includes the following elements:

- Clear guidance on prioritizing behavioral health casualties who need immediate attention in order to maintain their own safety and the safety of others during the *response* phase.
- Based on objective signs and symptoms of severe distress and dysfunction.
- Based on low levels of interaction.
- Simple to implement.
- Reduces chaos and provides the greatest good for the greatest number of people.

We propose the Mass Casualty Behavior Triage (MCBT) as a model that fits the above criteria and fills a gap in the disaster behavioral health intervention toolbox. The following is not an attempt to replace models such as PsySTART, but to be used as a precursor to an assessment when casualties are many and resources few. The proposed model provides a first step triage tool used prior to more time intensive assessment. The model is intended for mass casualty, but can be used for most any situation where the need or potential need for disaster behavioral health services is greater than the onsite resources can handle.

Mass Casualty Behavior Triage (MCBT)

The Mass Casualty Behavior Triage (MCBT) is a model to address triage of psychological needs in the immediate aftermath of a MCI. MCBT was conceptualized during the response to Hurricane Katrina when approximately 22,000 individuals sought shelter at the Astrodome in Houston. A medical team that included three behavioral health professionals screened thousands of individuals for admittance to the shelter, which during the early stages, resulted in over 900 people per day triaged for medical concerns. An on-scene Physician's Assistant, Tom Pedigo, realized that the team could not meet the medical needs of all the people encountered. He created a priority list of needs that warranted further investigation: Geriatrics, Altered Mental Status and Pediatric, which became known as the Pedigo - GAP triage method. This was not to say that other populations did not warrant care, it simply provided a focal point for the team's limited capacity to provide care.

It became evident that the behavioral health needs of Katrina evacuees were so great the team urgently needed a system to correctly prioritize resources. A goal of the behavior health staff was to determine who was struggling to maintain emotional equilibrium and who needed urgent/immediate behavior health intervention. A list of obvious signs and symptoms was created and the mission of the behavioral health staff became to identify those who were most in need. Every person had a story to tell and a need, it was critical not to get sidetracked by each one. Eye contact needed to be avoided in order to continue the work of determining the most urgent needs of the crowd. This approach was an effective form of triage.

Lessons learned from this experience indicate a standard tool and common language is needed for mass casualty behavior health triage. The MCBT model sets a standard and operationalizes what responders in Louisiana and Texas as well as multiple states across the nation, were attempting to do. The MCBT is a tool that helps determine need and direct resources for severe behavioral health casualties. When resources are scarce it helps those working in the response system identify those needing immediate care (red), those needing urgent care- delayed (yellow) and which needs can be delayed and addressed later (green).

The MCBT tool is to be used as part of a stepped system of care, in the immediate aftermath of a MCI but before a brief assessment is completed. The duty of triage is identification, not intervention. Frequently, behavioral health personnel ask questions and want to do a "verbal check" with survivors, but a key skill for response personnel utilizing MCBT is an ability to assess and remain relatively verbally disengaged. During the often-chaotic early phase of a response, the use of visual assessment technique of behavioral indicators can save time and allocate scarce resources efficiently. If a triage officer stops to engage in conversation he or she may miss the critical issues of individuals deeper in the crowd who need immediate attention. An example of the MCBT tool is illustrated below. (See figure 1)

Mass Casualty Behavior Triage Tool

This is the proposed tool that field staff could use for determining urgency of need for behavior health intervention. If this is used as a tracking tool, a clinician can put their name on it, designate if the person seen was adult, child or a staff/responder and the date. The cards can be collected and information tallied at the end of a shift. The back of the card identifies common stress reactions that are usually normal reactions in a catastrophic event. The degree that the reaction is interfering with functioning may indicate an immediate need for care.

Front of Card

<table>
<tr><td rowspan="3">BH Triage & Tracking Form
Name of clinician ___________
Adult___ Child___ Staff___
Date___________</td><td>Red - Immediate Take to advanced care</td><td>Suicidal, homicidal, child/ elder abuse
Aggressive behavior</td><td>Unable to understand and follow directions</td><td>Unable to care for self or children</td></tr>
<tr><td>Yellow Delayed needs intervention</td><td>Difficulty understanding and following directions</td><td>Stress reaction interfering with functioning</td><td>Unable to self soothe</td></tr>
<tr><td>Green give coping information</td><td>Stress reactions</td><td></td><td></td></tr>
</table>

Back of Card

Common Stress Reactions

Physical: Stomach upset/ sleep disruptions since the event/ exhaustion/pounding heart/ rapid breathing/ headache/ sweating/excess smoking, alcohol, drugs, food/ vague aches and pain

Emotional: Crying/ nervous/ fearful/ irritable/ easily upset/ negative view of self or others/ being over controlling/ withdrawal/ misinterpreting others intent as hostile/ exceedingly worried/ hopeless about the future/ trouble concentrating/ constantly alert/ edginess

Figure 1: Mass Casualty Behavior Triage card

The MCBT tool is designed for use by the response triage staff to determine the criticality of casualties. Crisis counselors or therapists may see this model as too simplistic, but in the midst of chaotic and potentially on-going dangerous situations, the critical duty is to get help to those with the greatest need. This system uses current behavior and functioning status descriptors versus the person's exposure level at an event. In triaging the needs of people during a response or rescue phase we are trying to get the most urgent, life threatening, needs met first. In behavior triage the focus is primarily on response safety; issues such as those disruptive individuals, non-functioning individuals and/or those who are a danger to themselves or others. This tool provides descriptions of primary behavioral indicators that coincide with the level of care designated as a color- red, yellow or green.

Criteria for *Red* MCBT include any one of the following:

- Individuals have shown or indicated suicidality or homicidality
- Signs of child abuse (perpetrator or victim of)
- Signs of elder abuse (perpetrator or victim of)
- Aggressive/threatening behavior toward others
- Inability to understand and follow directions
- Inability to care for themselves or for their children.

Criteria for *Yellow* MCBT include any one of the following:

- The person does not meet any of the criteria for *Red*
- Difficulty understanding and following directions
- A *serious* stress reaction interfering with functioning
- Inability to self soothe

Those designated as Red or Yellow usually exhibit behaviors that are disruptive to those around them. By selecting these individuals for immediate intervention, the tension level of the group drops.

Criteria for *Green* MCBT include:

- Do not meet the criteria for Red or Yellow
- Affected, but functioning.

These are the majority of people at disaster sites. They may exhibit a wide range of behavioral functioning, cognitive functioning, emotion, and mood. A common assumption is that no one who experiences a disaster is untouched by it 20 and depending on the circumstances people have different reactions to the event.

Using the MCBT tool

During the triage process, those who meet the criteria for *Red* are to be routed to behavioral health resources as soon as is possible for an assessment using a tool such as PsySTART. Psychological First Aid is the suggested method of intervention as a first line of stabilization. It is an evidence informed way of helping people in the aftermath of a disaster designed to reduce distress and foster adaptive functioning. [21] Those who meet the criteria for *Yellow,* are to be seen by behavioral health after the Red designees or immediately if there are no affected people who meet the Red criteria. Those who do not meet the criteria for Red or Yellow fall into the Green category of minor or absent disruptive behavioral indicators. If there are sufficient resources for assessing the Red and Yellow designees and staff are available, information on coping can be distributed to those meeting the Green criteria.

Mass Casualty Behavior Tracking

Tracking use data is important for providing an adequate response, allocating resources, requesting additional resources and funding for the recovery period following the disaster. A tracking form for response activities and situation acuity is included as part of the MCBT triage model (See Figure 2). It provides a simple tally sheet for those conducting and monitoring the response. The tracking sheet can be forwarded to a collection point such as Operations, Planning or the state mental health authority. This form can be filled out at the end of each shift by a designated team lead and faxed or brought to the agency collecting the data. Figure 2 (on the next page) is an example of a tracking form for estimation of resources to deal with casualties.

Next steps – use and research

With any new tool, a period of use, research and reporting is necessary. Some of the early problems in the field may stem from improper use of concepts and constructs, improper training and as a result poor outcomes in research. The MCBT is a new concept for the field. It should be used in specific situations with specific populations for a period of time associated with research support and reporting of outcomes. Therefore, we suggest that the next steps for the MCBT should be:

a. Field test the tool in exercises and live incidents
b. Develop an objective training system for professionals and paraprofessionals on how to best use the MCBT.
c. Develop a research program to assess:
    - The effectiveness of the MCBT for identifying individuals most in need
    - The effectiveness of the MCBT on impacting the efficiency of the response

- The impact of the MCBT on lessening chaos in disaster affected populations due to intervening with the most urgent needs

With these questions answered, the MCBT could have a tremendous impact on the field and on early behavioral health interventions. The main intent of this system is not to mitigate downstream behavior health consequences such as PTSD or trauma so much as it is intended to provide a way to identify those who pose a danger to themselves or others. This is not to minimize the effects of trauma, but it can be dealt with more effectively after the dust has settled and providers are more abundant.

Conclusion

The MCBT system is intended to reduce the chaos in a mass casualty incident by providing a simple and efficient method to triage behavior health casualties. Homeland Security Presidential Directive #21 regarding Public Health and Medical Preparedness outlines the need for a mass casualty care response that is rapid, flexible, scalable, sustainable, exhaustive, comprehensive, integrated and coordinated, and finally –appropriate. [22] The MCBT system has the potential to assist in addressing these capabilities through standardizing MCI behavior health triage and filling a gap that currently exists for behavior health triage.

Figure 2: MCBT Daily Tracking Form

Daily Tracking Form Behavioral Health Date________________________

Name of person filling out form ____________________________________

Location ____

Tally Total

Red **Needs Immediate Intervention**	Suicidal, homicidal, child or elder abuse Aggressive behavior	Unable to understand and follow directions	Unable to care for self or children		
Yellow **Delayed needs intervention**	Difficulty understanding and following directions	Stress reaction interfering with functioning	Unable to self soothe		
Green Needs information about coping	Stress reactions				

Comments:

____

____

____

____

____

References

1. Born, C.T., Briggs, S.M., Ciraulo, D.L. et al.: Disasters and mass casualties: I. general principles of response and management. *Journal of American Academy of Orthopedic Surgeons* 2007; 15(7): 388-396
2. Myers, D. Weapons of mass destruction and terrorism: Mental Health consequences and implications for planning and training. Presented at the Weapons of Mass destruction/terrorism orientation pilot program. Clara Barton Center for Domestic Preparedness, Pine Bluff, Arkansas, 2001; August 15-17.
3. Stein, BD., Tanielian, TL., Eisenman, DP., et al.: Emotional and behavioral consequences of bioterrorism: Planning a public health response. *The Milbank Quarterly: A Multidisciplinary Journal of Population Health and Health Policy,* 2004; 82(3).
4. Smithson, A. Ataxia: * the chemical and biological terrorism threat and the US response. *Rethinking the lessons of Tokyo.* 2000; 35, (3) page 95.
5. Reference cards created by Jack Dunn. Based on Simple Triage and Rapid Treatment (START) program developed by Newport Beach Fire Department.
6. Predicting Casualty Severity and Hospital Capacity: predicting triage severity. CDC: http://www.bt.cdc.gov/masscasualties/capacity.asp . Accessed December 31, 2007.
7. Murdoch, S., Cymet, T. C. Treating the victims after disaster physical and psychological effects. *Comprehensive Therapy* 32 (1), Spring 2006, 39-42.
8. Everly, G. S. Jr. Mitigating posttraumatic stress. *Personality Guided Therapy for PTSD.* 2004; (9), 143-159.
9. Smart, D., Pollard, C., Walpole, B. Mental health triage in emergency medicine. *Australian and New Zealand Journal of Psychiatry,* 1999; 33: 57-66.
10. Brasch J.S. and Ferencz J.C., Training Issues in Emergency Psychiatry. Psychiatric Clinics of North America, 1999; 22(4): 941-954.
11. Everly, G. S. Jr. Toward a model of psychological triage: who will most need assistance? *International Journal of Emergency Mental Health,* 1999; 3, 151-154.
12. Pynoos, R.S., Goenjian, A.K., Steinberg, A.L. A public mental health approach to the postdisaster treatment of children and adolescents. *Child and Adolescent Psychiatric Clinics of North America,* 1998; 7(1), 195-210.
13. Rundell, J.R. Psychiatric issues in medical-surgical disaster casualties: A consultation-liaison approach. *Psychiatric Quarterly,* 2000; 71(3), 245-258.
14. Roberts, A.R. Assessment, crisis intervention, and trauma treatment: The integrative ACT intervention model. *Brief Treatment and Crisis Intervention,* 2002; 2: 1-21.
15. Hipshman, L. Behavioral health triage in disaster settings. Presented at the 2005 National Disaster Medical Systems Conference, 2005.
16. Gurwitch, R.H.., Kees, M., Becker, S.M.., Schreiber, M., Pferrerbaum.B. When disaster strikes: Responding to the needs of children. *Prehospital and Disaster Medicine,* 2004; 19(1): 21-28.
17. Schreiber, M. PsySTART rapid mental health triage and incident management system. *The Dialogue,* 2005

18. Pynoos, R.S., Schreiber, M.D., Steinberg, A.M., and Pfefferbaum, B. The impact of terrorism on children. In:, Saddock, B. and Saddock, V., Lippincott, Williams and Wilkins. (eds): *Comprehensive Textbook of Psychiatry*, New York, NY, 2005; (8) pp. 3551-3564.
19. American Red Cross. *Psychological First Aid: Helping Others in Times of Stress.* DSCLS206A Sept. 2006.
20. SAMSHA - *Field Manual for Mental Health and Human Service Workers in Major Disasters*, DHHS Publication No. ADM 90-537 Substance Abuse and Mental Health Services Administration Printed 2000.
21. Brymer, M., Jacobs, A., Layne, C. et al: Psychological First Aid: Field Operations Guide, 2nd edition. July 2006. Available on: www.nctsn.org and www.ncptsd.va.gov. Accessed December 31, 2007.
22. Homeland Security Presidential Directive/HSPD-21. Public health and medical preparedness. Available at: www.whitehouse.gov/news/releases/2007/10/20071018-10.html. Accessed October 18, 2007.

ABOUT THE AUTHORS:

Ms. P.J. Havice-Cover, MA LPC CACIII CEM® is a Mental Health/Public Information Officer for a US HHS disaster response team, employed by the Colorado Medical Society as an Emergency Manager, and has 15 years of experience in public health. Some of her recent publications are: a field guide on "Pandemic Influenza – Behavioral Health Considerations" accepted as a best practice document by the Centers for Disease Control, "First Responders and Workforce Protection" in the Disaster Management Handbook (2008), "Care for the Caregiver" in Veterinary Disaster Response (in press) and an after-action report on volunteers post Katrina. Her current efforts are in developing and refining a mass casualty behavior health triage system and working to optimize physician disaster response. Field Response - Presentation http://www.cddbhc.com/library/documents/Field%20Response%20-%20Havice-Cover.ppt

Curt H Drennen is a licensed psychologist with the Colorado Department of Human Services Division of Behavioral Health. He has worked in disaster response since 2002 and is the Colorado Behavioral Health Disaster Response Coordinator and Program Manager for the Disaster Behavioral Health Planning and Response Section. He has 17 years of experience in the field with an emphasis in Public Psychology and Administration, Emotional Intelligence, Servant Leadership, Systems and Systems Conflict Management as well as Crisis Intervention and Behavioral Health Disaster Management.

In The Dark Times: The Use of Dramatic Reenactment and Authentic Witnessing in the Treatment of Trauma

Jamie Egolf, MSW, LCSW and Chavawn Kelley, MA

Abstract

The method of dramatic reenactment (theatre) and authentic witnessing (poetry) presented here by the authors was created for the purpose of training responders, counselors, and others who work with persons traumatized by war, natural disaster, sudden death or other tragedies or to work directly with trauma victims. The authors created the method to treat trauma using techniques that elevate trauma to the imaginal level, thereby allowing new neural pathways to be created. Although the memory of the trauma will remain, the goal of treatment is for the all-consuming pain to subside, therefore allowing the participant to begin the healing process and pursue a healthy life.

Authentic witnessing is a significant component of the treatment because both the traumatized person and the situation are acknowledged by empathic practitioners and participants who are engaged in the treatment. To heal from trauma, victims must deal with emotion and image above all and "stand beside themselves" in an "ecstatic" observation. Only then can new neural pathways be forged. The art that is created not only stands in witness of the individual and the traumatic event but also as an external vessel that may hold a portion of the traumatized person's pain. This paper is a document of the workshop presented at the conference. Confidentiality is maintained by the disguise of participants.

The setting for this workshop was the 7th Annual Rocky Mountain Disaster Mental Health Conference in Laramie, Wyoming, November 6-8, 2008 and the workshop was the last one scheduled. Threatening weather suggested the wisdom of early starts to long drives home. The presenters arranged a circle of chairs, wondering if anyone would come. The participants arrived, tired but attentive. The room was cold. The view out the window was winter gray. Before the conference closed, however, trauma met art and participants, now energized, entered the early evening dark, having come together in exploration, participation, and revelation.

The method presented by the authors, dramatic reenactment and authentic witnessing, was created for the purpose of training responders, counselors, and others who work with persons traumatized by war, natural disaster, sudden death or other tragedies or to work directly with trauma victims. Dramatic reenactment is Egolf's term for working in a psychodramatic setting. She has introduced the term, believing that it is more easily accepted by contemporary participants than the term "psychodrama." Descriptions of workshop participants and their situations documented here have been modified to ensure confidentiality.

It has been shown that trauma can be resolved through participation in theatre groups and that working with image and emotion are key to the release of trauma (van der Kolk, 1987). Neuroscientific research has shown that talking about trauma without utilizing other treatment measures engages only the left side of the brain and is likely to cause retraumatization, since the situation that must be treated is lodged in the right side of the brain.

The authors have strived to create an effective method to treat trauma using techniques that elevate trauma to the imaginal level, thereby allowing new neural pathways to be created. Although the memory of the trauma will remain, the goal of treatment is for the all-consuming pain to subside. Authentic witnessing is a significant component of the treatment because both the traumatized person and the situation are acknowledged by empathic practitioners and participants who are engaged in the treatment.

The art that is created not only stands in witness of the individual and the traumatic event but also as an external vessel that may hold a portion of the traumatized person's pain. The authors believe that whether undertaken on an inpatient or an outpatient basis, this method should only be attempted with willing participants who by their own assessment are "ready" to deal with trauma.

In the dark times,
will there also be singing?
Yes there will be singing
About the dark times.

Berthold Brecht

As Berthold Brecht's poem, "In the Dark Times," suggests, when we consider the "dark times," our memory is influenced by the way we think about them. If we think about them in a way that is paired with the idea of singing, they feel different than the raw experience of the dark times, whether the dark times are concerned with war, sudden death, natural disaster, or other tragedy. Again, the memory of the event will always remain, but the pain can be relieved by elevating the experience to one that is paired with poetry or other forms of creativity.

To heal from trauma, the victim must deal with emotion and image above all. Healing does not happen by engaging the intellect alone, although, of course, intellect is critical to understanding both the event and the process of healing. If healing could occur from intellect alone, then simply reading about it would suffice to produce healing. Instead, participating with practitioners and other "witnesses" in an experiential, "ecstatic" event facilitates healing. Literally, ecstasy comes from the root *ek stasis*, meaning outside the center. Participants must get outside them- selves, stand beside themselves, in order to see themselves in a different way. Robert Johnson, in his book *Ecstasy* stated, "To stand outside oneself means that [we] are filled with an emotion too powerful for our bodies to contain or our rational minds to understand. [We are] transported to another realm in which [we are] able to experience ecstasy." (Johnson, 1989, p 14) Dramatic reenactment and authentic witnessing provide this experience, as can other art forms, such as poetry, prose, music, and the visual arts.

In the 1940s, Psychiatrist Joseph Moreno, who was a student of Freud, stated, "Anything we can act, we can heal." (Moreno, 1947) Moreno later developed the technique of psychodrama. By reenacting the event that we keep responding to in an unhealthy manner, we can begin to have an emotional catharsis in conjunction with what the Buddhists call *satori*—the "aha" experience, with resulting relief and a heightened sense of hope and resiliency. The traumatic event means something different now; it can now be understood and reintegrated. It is a memory of the dark times, but now it is "sung." It no longer exists as a force that re-wounds us. (Or at least its power is dissipated.)

Stated another way, participating in theatre has the effect of the "translation of life under its universal and immense aspect, and the ex- traction of images from life, in which we desire to find ourselves again" —Antonin Artaud, poet and theatre critic. (Pastlewait and McConachie, 1989, p. 30).

In her book *Against Forgetting: Twentieth-Century Poetry of Witness,* Carolyn Forché compiled poetry about atrocities beginning with the Armenian Genocide (1909-1918), and including World War I, World War II, the Holocaust (the *Shoah*), the Korean and Vietnam conflicts, and ending with the struggle for democracy in China in the 1970s. She found her study evolving into a "repository of what began to be called 'poetry of witness.'" (Forché 1993, p. 30) As a poet and a human rights activist, she concentrated on poetry and politics and eventually found herself documenting "extremity" in the works she chose, including works by Federico Garcia Lorca, Ezra Pound, e.e. cummings, André Breton, Gertrude Stein, Boris Pasternak, Etheridge Knight and others.

Some of the poems in Forché's collection are the only evidence that an event occurred. An example is poet Miklos Radnóti's final notebook entry in October of 1944. His concentration camp was evacuated, and he and others volunteered to march home rather than wait in the camp as other prisoners did. The march was a trick, and all of the volunteers were shot. He wrote:

I fell beside him; his body turned over,
Already taut as a string about to snap,
Shot in the back of the neck.
That's how you too will end,
I whispered to myself; just lie quietly.
Patience now flowers into death.
Der springt noch auf, a voice said above me.
On my ear, blood dried, mixed with filth.

(Forché 1993, p.32)

As this poem demonstrates, the poem itself becomes a manifestation of trauma just as the event was a trauma. "And in an age of atrocity, witness becomes an imperative and a problem; how does one bear witness to suffering and before what court of law?" Forché asks. (Forché 1993, p. 33) The poet tells the story of those who have been tortured, raped, and murdered. Much of the poetry Forché includes in the book is composed of brief, incomplete sentences, staccato verse. Nonsense.

Psychiatrist Dore Laub has characterized the "oral testimony of survivors of the Shoah as fragmented as the victim approaches the core of the trauma." Thus again, the "narrative of trauma is itself traumatized, and bears witness to extremity by its inability to articulate directly or completely. Because institutionalized suffering has been globalized," she states, "fragmentation might also be global." (Forché, 1993, p. 43)

Indeed, has not our own American society become fearful, mistrustful, and almost paranoid as a society? Another witness to this condition can be seen in the enormous collection of horror/torture/psychopathic slasher/ murder films readily available to us in the rental market. In the language of psychology, this indicates that the culture has become involved in a repetition compulsion, where trauma repeats over and over until the individual, or in this case the culture, can come to terms with it and resolve it.

Forché concludes that "the poetry of witness is itself born in dialectical opposition to the extremity that has made such witness necessary; in the process it restores the dynamic structure of dialectics." Once again language, in the form of poetry, mirrors the healing process.

The number of suicides documented among soldiers returning from Iraq and those still based in Iraq is alarming. Domestic violence has been reported among a majority of returnees. (Matthieu and Hovmand, 2008) Problems adapting—to spouses, children, and regular life—seem to be universal. van der Kolk (1987) has shown that for soldiers and other war participants involved in treatment, interventions that target symptom reduction in group settings help participants heal more quickly than individual counseling only.

This training in dramatic reenactment and authentic witnessing is constructed to aid those who help, as well as the victims of traumatic events. Responders and others who assist trauma victims must keep themselves psychologically healthy in order to continue doing their jobs effectively and living harmoniously.

At the 7th Annual Rocky Mountain Disaster Mental Health Conference in Laramie, Wyoming, Jungian Psychotherapist Jamie Egolf and Writer and Poet Chavawn Kelley, joined by conference participants from a variety of back- grounds, began by talking about the poetry of atrocity after reading poems from Forché's collection. Two are represented here.

White Wedding Slippers

Anna Swir[1]

At night
my mother opened a chest and took out
her white silk wedding slippers.
Then she daubed them
a long time with ink.

Early in the morning
she went in those slippers
to the street
to line up for bread.
It was ten degrees,

---

1 Anna Swir survived execution by the Nazis in her native Warsaw where she served as a military nurse in 1939; she was unable to write about her experiences until 1974.

she stood
for three hours in the street.

They were handing out
one quarter of a loaf per person.

(Forché, 1993 p. 277)

The Last Lie

Bruce Weigl[2]

Some guy in the miserable convoy
raised up in the back of our open truck
and threw a can of C rations at a child
who called into the rumble for food.
He didn't toss the can, he wound up and hung it
On the child's forehead and she was stunned
Backwards into the dust of our trucks.

Across the sudden angle of the road's curving
I could still see her when she rose,
waving one hand across her swollen, bleeding head,
wildly swinging her other hand
at the children who mobbed her,
who tried to take her food.

I grit my teeth to myself to remember that girl
smiling as she fought off her brothers and sisters.
She laughed
as if she thought it were a joke
and the guy with me laughed
and fingered the edge of another can
like it was the seam of a baseball
until his rage ripped
again into the faces of children
who called to use for food.

(Forché, 1993, p 706)

Egolf, in her role as facilitator or "stage director," asked participants to talk about their work with traumatized groups or individuals. Very quickly Donna volunteered, describing events in her life that were colored by the psychological wounding and physical illness of her husband who was a Vietnam War veteran.

---

[2] Bruce Weigel is an award winning author of several books of poetry, including *Voices of Napalm*. He served in the first Air Cavalry in 1967 and 1968 in Vietnam.

Two other participants described their work with traumatized veterans. Nora, a counselor in a hospital setting, described a veteran client who would not talk to her. His intent was to "check in" regularly and keep his benefits going. Egolf's hunch was that this vet had a hidden agenda that arose from suppressed trauma, which had not surfaced yet. This client seemed to be a poster child for the generalized difficulty of talking about trauma among traumatized persons. Kelley, in her role as witness, did not participate in discussion but worked swiftly and silently, chronicling participants' statements and reassembling them into poetic bursts. Here, she characterizes the angry, uncooperative client.

The vet is a leaden cloud.
For eight minutes
his wordless grenade ticks.
The vet is a client
maintaining his rating.
The cloud sighs
the fingers twitch.

Because of his military background, Kevin, a participant, is familiar with many serious trauma cases. He related the story of a suicidal veteran in a small, closed community. Again Kelley witnesses his story.

The Postmistress and her Porn Addict Husband

She delivered the mail
He received oxygen and pity
The pinball exploded
The gunshot delivered his brains
express throughout town
Dead mail his neighbors
returned unopened.

Arlene, a family therapist, brought up a difficult situation she works with in which the mother is dying and the father, who is remarried, is carrying hostility toward her, the therapist. Kelley wrote

Dying Mother

The dying, divorcing mother
the children deathly quiet
the stepmother holds the husband's ear
the family dying a quiet death.

Last, Bruce, an author, described his losses as minor in comparison with those of his research subjects and the other participants who had spoken. Kelley witnessed Bruce minimizing the grief of losing his own parents to natural causes.

The Scribe

Observes, listens, records
survivors of the Holocaust,
is slow to open his own book

to forgive himself.
His losses are small.

Egolf then led "dramatic reenactments" of the situations. The authors have added a *Dramatis Personae,* or cast of characters, as a guide to aid the reader in following the series of workshop events.

Dramatis Personae (Cast of Characters)

Donna – a nurse. Her late husband was a Vietnam War veteran. She played the roles of (1) a traumatized vet and (2) herself, the wife of a veteran.
Nora – a counselor. She played the roles of (1) herself as counselor to a veteran and (2) wife of a traumatized veteran.
Kevin – a veteran and veteran's advocate. He played the roles of (1). Donna's husband and (2) a traumatized veteran.
Arlene – a family therapist. She mirrored the role of the counselor.
Bruce – an author. He (1) mirrored the role of Donna's husband and (2) played the role of the priest.

The first participant, Donna, was asked to begin by enacting the role of Nora's patient as described above. In the enactment, we referred to the downcast, uncooperative man as Eeyore, but she began playing herself. Later, after some shifting of roles and role confusion, Donna was asked to play her ill and dying husband. Egolf's intent was to allow Donna to become distanced enough from her own situation to come to terms with it.

Nora also became confused by the changing of roles and began to react to a composite of the challenging situations enacted. The room was chilly, and Nora reported being cold. She began to shiver. Egolf commented that for many of the veterans she works with their trauma is "frozen." Arlene, the family therapist, was a "double" for Nora. That is, she stood beside Nora and observed and occasionally filled in for her at Egolf's direction. Arlene's double character became very tired. The tiredness and shivering, besides being natural responses to a cold room and demanding conference agenda, suggested physical manifestations of the trauma they were dramatizing.

Kevin played several roles that evidenced violence and splitting. He eventually played Donna's husband, huddled in the basement with his firearm waiting for "them to come." This provided Donna with greater perspective on her deceased husband's behavior, and it allowed Kevin to reveal some of his own wartime trauma.

In one scenario, Bruce portrayed a priest who was to offer forgiveness to Donna's husband (still played by Kevin), but he turned the tables and attempted to convince Kevin's character to forgive (and come to a church picnic and pay money the priest believed he owed the church).

In the last dramatic reenactment, Egolf directed Kevin to play himself and Nora to play his wife. Kevin then dropped his guard and Nora warmed up to him. She moved her chair nearer. Kelley witnessed the following exchange.

"You're in my space," he objected as she moved closer.
She responded, "I'm your wife, not your counselor."

She offered her open palms and spoke in a gentle tone. After the reenactment, Kevin responded to Nora's kindness by giving her a small gift that had meaning for him. Members of the group responded to this surprising gesture of grace.

Kelley read the results of her witnessing of the entire workshop, which included the following poem. "To Raise a Family" witnesses not only events of Donna's marriage, but also insights offered by Kevin. The poem evolved to give voice to all the members of the family: Donna, her husband and their two children.

To Raise a Family

We left Michigan
to move west to make a home.
It was a good place to raise a family.
He painted houses. The years went on.

He drank, he said, to steady his hands
for those he had to sew. The quiet medic,
he cared for his brothers
blasted open.

We were always strapped. I was a nurse.
I taught other people's families how to cope
while he cared for the kids at home.
They adored him.

Seven years sick.
He smoked.
He never let up. He drank
like a badge he had earned.

She thinks she knows how I feel.
I sit here painting this train
this tiny train to nowhere.
I switch the channels when she walks in.

The years went on.
The children grew quiet.
He wore his oxygen.
The cord hung from his chin.

I don't know what's coming.
I let her think since Vietnam
Jack Daniels drives the train
but I hold the remote control.

I'm his daughter. I cut my skin.

Without chopper blades coming in
I cannot bleed. I make straight A's.
I cut again.

I'm the son. Our war at home
was never enough for him
so I'm off to California.
I've cut the cord.

Our father, your combat held
no place for us. You created our world.
You shielded yourself by the door
waiting to take communion.

You climbed that hill and smoked
your final cigarette. Mother has etched
the sign of Christ on her wrist
and tries to remember the two of you dancing.

Forgive us, father. The years go on.

After hearing Kelley read, Donna became tearful and soft. She asked for a copy of the poem, and Kelley promised to send it. Egolf's impression is that the group coalesced quickly because they had shared with great honesty the experiences weighing on them and had fully embraced the roles they were asked to play.

Dramatic reenactment and authentic witnessing provide a tool for the release of trauma. Image and emotion provide awareness and focus that are critical to healing. Our group, which began as a collection of strangers, hugged one another as we said our goodbyes. Through poetry and drama and without knowing what to expect, we had joined in singing the dark times.

References

Forché, C. 1993. *Against Forgetting: Twentieth Century Poetry of Witness.* New York, NY: Norton and Company, Inc.

Johnson, R.. 1989. *Ecstasy.* New York, NY: Harper and Row.

Levine, P. & Frederick,A. (1997). *Waking the tiger: Healing trauma.* Berkeley: North Atlantic Books.

Matthieu, M., & Hovmand, P., December 18, 2008. *Combat Veterans, PTSD, and Domestic Violence—A Sometimes Deadly Combination.* Caring for the Caregivers, Washington University in St. Louis.

http://www.healingcombattrauma.com/recent_research/

Moreno, J. 1947. *Theatre of Spontaneity.* New York: Beacon House.

Pastlewait, T. and McConachie, B. (1989). *Interpreting the Theatrical Past.* Iowa City: University of Iowa Press.

van der Kolk, B. (1987). *Psychological Trauma.* Washington, D.C.: American Psychiatric Press, Inc.

About The Authors

Jamie Egolf is a Jungian Psychotherapist and Consultant, in practice for 38 years, now practices in Laramie, Wyoming, received the MSW at Catholic University of America, Washington, DC; studied art at Purdue University; was trained by the Interregional Society of Jungian Analysts; and in Psychodrama and Creative Writing. She began The Magic Theatre of Life (workshops in psychodrama and drama therapy,) co-authored the Pre-Marital Inventory; presented "Dreaming Superman" at the University of Melbourne's Superhero Conference, 2005, published in *Superheroes: From Hercules to Superman* by New Academia Press in 2007; presented" Desire and Sensuality in the Music and Relationships of Claude Debussy: A Look at the Split in the Archetypal Feminine" at the 2007 Creativity and Madness Conference in Santa Fe with Pianist Gary Smart. She presented "Geysers, Grizzlies, and Paint Pots: Finding the Deep Self in the Yellowstone/Wyoming Wilderness and the Wilderness of the Psyche" at the Foundation for Mythological Studies Nature and Human Nature Conference, 2007. Accepted for publication. "Flyboy's Daughter" was presented at the 2007 Disaster Mental Health Conference; conference proceedings have subsequently been published. Her paper "Image, Symbol, and Story in The Medieval and Contemporary Tapestry and the Comic Strip" was presented at the San Francisco Jung Institute's Art and Psyche Conference in May, 2008.

Chavawn Kelley has spent her career exploring questions of effective human communication. She is the corporate communications manager for Western Research Institute in Laramie, Wyoming. She earned her Master of Arts degree in American Studies from the University of Wyoming and has given presentations for the Wyoming Humanities Council throughout the state since 2004. Her short stories, essays and poems have been published in literary journals, and she has been awarded fellowships and grants from the Wyoming Arts Council, the Wyoming Historical Society, the Ucross Foundation, the Ludwig Vogelstein Foundation, and Can Serrat International Arts Center.

Planning for Pandemic - Quarantine, Isolation and Social Distancing: Behavioral Health Concerns

P.J. Havice-Cover, LPC, CACIII, CEM and Curt Drennen, PsyD, RN

Abstract

Gearing up for a yet-to-occur event such as pandemic influenza requires recognition that this is a likely if not inevitable scenario (Patriarca and Cox, 1997; World Health Organization, 2005). Planning for the cascading affects of pandemic at the local, state or Federal level requires a diverse group to be at the table with public health as the lead agency. A flash-bang event such as the Oklahoma City Bombing or the events of September 11 have been the genre of "planned for" scenarios, but the protracted response of pandemic requires different strategies. Pandemic is likely to come in waves that brings commerce and civilization as we now know it to a slow crawl or possibly to a halt (HHS Pandemic Influenza Plan, 2005). In the Proposed Guidance for Alterations in the Healthcare System During an Influenza Pandemic (Colorado Department of Public Health and Environment, draft, 2008) the creation of altered standards of care for emergency medical surge capacity compels us to ask the hard questions such as "who gets the ventilator when there is a limited supply and we have to choose?"

The behavioral health consequences of having to institute such a triage system to decide who is most likely to benefit from scarce medical resources and who may be excluded can erode the resiliency of medical staff, family members and the community according to a study by Bonanno, Galea, Bucciareli, & Vlahov (2007). Communities who face dealing with quarantine, isolation, social distancing, shortages of or an absence of vaccine and prophylaxis and medical surge that overwhelms the system will need to rely on a volunteer workforce (ASPR, Pandemic All Hazards Preparedness Act, 2006). Inclusion of trained behavior health assets can positively impact the resilience of responders and communities affected by a long-term public health response.

Quarantine, Isolation and Social Distancing: Behavioral Health Concerns

The threat of pandemic influenza has caused concern worldwide. Currently there is no evidence of pandemic influenza, but health officials warn that the possibility exists. Historically, the world has experienced three major outbreaks in the last century; 1918-1919

Spanish Flu which killed over 20 million worldwide—550,000 in the U.S., 1957-1958 Asian Flu which killed over 70,000 in the U.S., and 1968-1969 Hong Kong Flu which killed over 34,000 in the U.S. The outbreaks do not occur at predictable intervals, but if the past is any indication of future events, another pandemic may be on the horizon. One strain of influenza that the World Health Organization, the Center for Disease Control (CDC) and U.S. Public Health are watching closely is the H5N1- Avian influenza virus. Individual liberties restrictions may need to be enforced to protect the public. These restrictions should be proportionate, necessary and relevant to the situation. They should also use the least restrictive means necessary to ensure protection, and be applied equitably.

Three main disease control methods are recommended: quarantine, isolation and social distancing. Quarantine refers to compulsory physical separation, including restriction of movement, of populations or groups of healthy people who have been potentially exposed to a contagious disease, or to efforts to segregate these persons within specified geographic areas. Quarantine does not have to be just a legal restriction. It can also be a strongly suggested voluntary restriction of activities of people exposed to a communicable disease. Isolation refers to separating an individual with a specific infectious illness from those who are healthy and restricting their movement to stop the spread of illness. It allows for the delivery of specialized health care and protects healthy people from getting sick. And finally, the method that will ultimately need to be instituted is social distancing. This is a voluntary, recommended limitation of physical contact. It can be as simple as maintaining a three-foot distance and not shaking hands to the more complex; staying home and avoiding public places and events. If more aggressive measures are required, schools may close and call "snow days", businesses may be asked to temporarily close or have employees work from home, travel restrictions may be necessary and social events canceled.

As the index case for the onset of a pandemic is identified and isolated in a community, a series of events begins and has a natural progression. The source of the contagion is identified and an investigation to locate and identify the people who had direct contact with the contagious person is launched. Prior to this event, people were able to maintain some psychological distance from the illness; it had been a terrible event that was happening to others elsewhere in the country. The hallmark of this stage is that an announcement has been made that the communicable agent presents a public health crisis. This can be called the "why" stage. People want to know why things have to be different now. Some people may become angry and want to take it out on someone. Anger can be reduced during the initial stages of an incident by giving out accurate information that includes the reasons for the containment. If the message is crafted to reflect a community protection, harm reduction type of announcement, most people will be receptive toward the measures taken to protect *them*.

Communication continues to reduce anger as the incident progresses and people become impatient with restrictions. If it is possible, a probable end time limit should be given, however if the restrictions are not lifted by that date, the anger may escalate. When the first local case is identified, it will be crucial to have a press conference. As the first group is quarantined, the community needs to know what actions they can take such as staying home when they are ill and being personally prepared in case the event escalates. When the first death from pandemic influenza occurs, information should be exchanged with the Center for Disease Control (CDC) on lethality of the disease noting high-risk groups. A press statement from the local public health department that alerts the community without causing alarm using sensitivity toward the deceased that doesn't minimize or sensationalize the death. The age and health of the fatality may be significant. The death of a formerly healthy child or youth can create panic to get antivirals. As cases are identified and isolation and quarantine of exposed populations implemented, enforcement may become unmanageable. "Modern Quarantine" (US HHS) or "Public Health Containment – Social Distancing" (US DHS) become the next step. This strategy involves disease containment measures and relevant decisions at the community level with support from State and Federal Governments. Initially, the least socially intrusive measures allow people to maintain normalcy, but more aggressive measures may be required.

The following are interventions with increasing psychosocial impact: For the initial, basic, and low cost with minimal effort an individual spatial separation of one-yard and increased business use of teleconferencing. As there is an increase of disease spread, cancellations of non-essential gatherings and travel restrictions are more likely. When more restrictive measures are needed for high intensity and greater economic cost in order to reduce disease transmission, "Snow Days" (recommended or mandated) to close schools and businesses, directing people to remain at home and maintain a greater social distance. Finally, if the above measures do not provide the disease containment needed, the highest level of social intrusion may be implemented. A *Cordon Sanitaire* is a geographic quarantine involving isolation (by force if necessary) of a specific area. This may be used to contain an outbreak or as a reverse quarantine to keep disease out of an uninfected area. Any or all of these steps may be necessary; however, with a price. Economic impact tops the list, but impact on community resilience as well as individual effect with increases in fear/anxiety, boredom, loneliness and anger.

One of the most important components included in the management of a pandemic is the communication of information. An initial reaction of disbelief quickly turns to fear as information, misinformation and rumors emerge. Fear becomes the dominant emotion. Some people will become fearful, afraid of the implications and the ways the changes will affect their daily lives. In ideal conditions, fear is an adaptive behavioral function as a response to perceived danger that protects us from injury or harm. Several factors such as previous experience, assessment of an opportunity to escape, and the perceived extent of a threat influence the intensity of a fear response. A high level of fear can elicit a fight, flight, freeze or faint response. While each of these responses has an adaptive, survival function, they can be problematic for disease containment. Those who react in fight mode typically do not trust that their best interests are being addressed and may challenge authorities. Those who choose to flee risk spreading the infection. The freeze or faint responses cause people to cease productive activities and become hopeless. An assessment to determine the type of message needed should be proportionate to the event and it is determined by the public's attitude toward the situation. If the consensus is that people are scared and worried, the message should reflect concern for their well being and reassure them that measures are being taken to manage the problem. They are probably being cautious at this point. If the people are taking a casual approach, they may need a stricter warning to alert them to the seriousness of the situation. A certain amount of uneasiness can facilitate a more responsive group.

Rumors are created out of misinformation or the lack of information. Rumors grow in a climate of ambiguity; can be unstable and difficult to stop. The best approach to minimizing rumors is to give frequent updates and provide accurate information. Rumor surveillance decreases the potential for misinformation and misunderstanding. It is the process of identifying and actively seeking out rumors from media reports, professional groups, and the public, while investigating the validity of the information. Rumor control becomes a mental health issue when people are becoming distressed by and possibly acting on unfounded information. The best way to combat rumors is to continually send out the correct information in order to minimize the impact of the rumor. This can be done through word of mouth, public service announcements, written materials such as handouts or flyers, the media, emails and by having neighborhood meetings. In the case of a large scale event, it may be best to have a trusted, public official give a press briefing that is broadcast on all affected area channels. When people feel that they have been given the whole dark picture, they are unlikely to come up with anything worse to explain their anxiety.

Fear is the characteristic emotion of pandemic. Many people in the community will become fearful and concerned about their health, safety, jobs, finances and families. People may also experience fear of exposure to the disease, enforcement actions, and the premise of death. If the fear becomes too much to handle, it can immobilize and lead to depression or it may incite some to act out. There are some who will overreact and avoid *any* activity even remotely connected to a threat of contagion. They may choose to stay home or engage in unwarranted precautionary behaviors such as wearing a mask and gloves even when they are alone. Medical facilities may be avoided out of the fear of becoming infected. Discriminatory fear may emerge if a certain group has a higher rate of symptoms than others.

As a public health agency, some suggestions for dealing with this are to remind the community of *reasonable* measures of protection and to educate people on the importance of self-care. People may neglect other medical concerns. Are there identified facilities that are *not* treating the flu where people can be seen for other concerns? Assess which populations are affected and address the fears with logical, factual information. Allow choices for location of quarantine if possible. Remind people that precautions have been implemented to protect them and others in the community. Voice appreciation for those in quarantine or isolation (Q & I) for keeping the community safe. Decide if publicizing mortality rates is helpful because, perspective on rates may help reduce panic. Fear is a normal response to a potentially dangerous situation especially one that involves extraordinary circumstances. The fear can work in your favor to get people to self-quarantine, or it can work against you if people are afraid and panic to get help. A balanced approach to administering a quarantine and isolation is the key to a well-orchestrated operation. In other words, people must understand the severity of the spread of the contagion and the necessity during a pandemic, but they must also be able to remain calm and trust that the system is doing the best they can in taking the necessary precautions.

Anxiety is the brain's reaction to fear. A moderate amount of anxiety along with a realistic view of the risks associated with the Q & I event is healthy and makes people more likely to take precautions. However, some people will get overly anxious when faced with the challenge of a pandemic. They are unable to stop worrying about the "what ifs" of the situation. The anxiety of "fear of contagion" can be immobilizing and cause an increase in calls for medical advice and an inability to carry on regular activities. In those who are quarantined, anxiety can cause undue worry and hypervigilance. In those who are ill and isolated, anxiety can aggravate the medical problems by interfering with sleeping, eating and fears that they will die. Anxiety reduction may include things such as preparing patients emotionally for isolation by providing educational materials to explain the strategy and the duration and setting up a hotline and have the media announce the contact numbers to handle questions and concerns and offer continually updated information on a website.

Good information increases compliance. The way risks are managed affects the mental health of the community. An atmosphere of trust is evident when the community feels that safety issues are being adequately addressed through obvious actions being taken. Mistrust occurs when citizens are not convinced that their best interests are being considered. Successful disease containment includes assessing and managing the risks associated with a Q & I. It is essential to communicate accurate, easily understood messages that increase compliance and decrease panic. Speaking with one voice and giving consistent messages for all involved agencies helps to echo increases in comprehension and builds trust.

If people are prepared for a crisis they feel as if they are more in control of their lives. Recommendations for public health are to schedule daily press briefings (6 AM, 11 AM, 4 PM, 9 PM) even if you have no new information. Build trust by giving honest information. When you don't know the answer to questions, say "I don't know the answer to your question" and "I can try to find out." And have an answer for the next press briefing. People want to know what to do for their symptoms so ensure that you distribute information on symptom management. If there is no medication, say so. If medications are available, give specific information about the use, availability, location, cost and side effects. Use a de-escalation strategy in briefings, while reinforcing the need to take precautions. Normalize responses such as frustration with the changes to daily life and promote self-care and caring for family members at home. Use a call-to-action type of message in briefings that emphasizes the seriousness of the situation, without using scare tactics.

Public health, medical and public behavior health staff needs training to deal with a Q & I event. They need information for themselves, families, and community. The workforce may be absent and affected by as much as 1/3 due to the illness. Train *all* staff so that they can give information to the community. Receptionists, maintenance, and all levels of staff from these agencies represent the organization and their friends and neighbors will ask them for news knowing they work there. Ensure that staff has Incident Command Systems training. At a minimum they should have taken ICS 100 & ICS 700 http://www.fema.gov/emergency/nims/index.shtm. In providing workforce protection, determine staffing needs and establish predictable schedules, limit overtime, educate staff on necessary precautions, ensure that staff has put together a family safety and communication plan, and remind staff to change clothes before entering their homes as a precaution and as a way to psychologically close the work day.

Being prepared for a disaster means several things, including having supplies on hand to stay put if it becomes required. Six categories of items you should stock in your home suggested by preparedness experts are: (www.ready.gov)

- Water for drinking, cooking or sanitation
- Food
- First Aid Supplies
- Clothing, Blankets and Sanitation Supplies
- Tools such as a manual can opener, flashlights, candles, matches and batteries

- Special Items- such as medications, pet food, baby supplies etc

Personal Protective Equipment (PPE) such as respirator type of masks (N-95) will most likely be used as a barrier to the airborne influenza virus. Several issues with PPE cause stress in health care personnel. In a pandemic situation, the staff needs training to deal with a Q & I event. In order to help staff adjust to the precautions, address PPE issues with staff such as it is uncomfortable, requires frequent change of gloves and masks, it is difficult to recognize coworkers. Additionally, speaking through a respirator mask creates communication difficulties and one size does not fit all. Some companies have been on International backorder for purchasing respirator masks. Other items to consider having on hand are alcohol-based hand sanitizer and a spray disinfectant for commonly touched surfaces. Finally, by developing a "we will get through this" mentality, confidence is built in the staff that is caring for the community. Measures to control the spread of the disease such as wearing gloves and masks can be cumbersome and interfere with speaking to and understanding others. A study on healthcare workers in Toronto during the SARS outbreak showed that those living with children might worry more than those who don't.

Public schools may be the first to close, requiring parents to stay home with their children. Provisions for childcare will help maintain the workforce. Supervisors may have a decreased level of concern about their safety due to having a measure of control (actual or perceived) in the event. Part time or contract employees are more likely to experience emotional distress. They often get less current information and have fewer supports at work. There is a perception among healthcare workers that the scope of the event is larger than it actually is since they see a constant influx of affected people. There is also an increased need for family and personal support as well as psycho-educational information for staff. Addressing the psychosocial needs of response staff helps maintain effectiveness during a response. An occupational hazard is vicarious traumatization from hearing traumatic stories from their patients and having empathy. A good workforce support plan builds resiliency, which delivers the best response possible. To mitigate some of the stress, have supervisor or peer led daily briefings. Promote teamwork, stress reduction and morale building activities. Encourage staff to use a buddy system and do stress reduction exercises such as breathing deeply and discussing situations with a friend. The number of hours staff can work should be limited to necessary time on the job and allow for down time to improve productivity and to decrease worker burnout. Leaders should give direction and model healthy behaviors. For example, they should take breaks, wear appropriate personal protective equipment and also have a family communication plan.

To improve the outcome of a catastrophic event and gain the community's cooperation in a pandemic, ensure an understanding of the culture and diversity of your community. Culture provides strength and resilience, but can be a barrier for people with varying ethnic backgrounds and socioeconomic status levels. Cultural competence is a skill that should be considered when planning for pandemic. It is critical that all populations receive reasonable information, and are accommodated, in consideration of any special needs. Information should be available and distributed in other languages spoken in your community i.e. Spanish, Korean, German... Bicultural, bilingual staff are very valuable assets to assist with hotlines and front desk to give information. If a certain race, gender or age group of the population is harder hit than others; they may feel as if it is a discriminatory issue. Services to diverse groups must be strategically located for optimal access.

Pediatric, geriatric and those with chronic medical conditions are usually at higher risk for complications during a contagious disease outbreak. However, during the 1918 Pandemic, formerly healthy young adults had the highest mortality rates. It will be critical to know who are the high-risk populations in a pandemic. Specific ages may be affected and need information regarding special precautions. Children should be given limited, age appropriate information and reminded to wash their hands and cover a cough. Pediatric populations need to feel safe and know that someone will care for them. Their caregiver's reactions and coping skills directly reflect upon the children's ability to deal with the stress. A child who is quarantined with familiar family members will probably be fine and may actually enjoy the family being "stuck at home" together. An isolated child may show symptoms of separation anxiety if he or she is not with their caregiver.

Geriatric populations need to know that they can depend on others to meet their needs. They need to know the specific details of what they can and can't do. How will they get basic supplies such as food, water and medications? Providing information can alleviate much of their anxiety. An isolation event may require them to be out of their familiar surroundings and without the supports that they have drawn on in the past.

Some of the reasons for noncompliance with quarantine, isolation and social distancing are that people have reactions to the event based on their perceptions of how the event personally affects them. Specifically, they don't understand the seriousness of the event, they don't understand what to do, they don't have the resources to comply, and they don't want to be inconvenienced by changes in routine. Others haven't been personally affected and many don't believe or trust the government. Economic barriers may cause some to be in noncompliance. Economic concerns may interfere with quarantine compliance. Many in the community will need financial assistance to remain at home. Additionally, economically disadvantaged and self-employed workers may be prone to violating a quarantine or isolation order. It will be essential to identify resources or the lack of as the case may be. Some of the needed resources may be food assistance, help with rent, mortgage deferments and utility assistance. Other issues affecting compliance include where someone is quarantined, social stigma, accessing healthcare and medications and being exposed to someone who is ill. If possible, quarantine at home will be best as hospitals and medical facilities will be overwhelmed. An order releasing someone from quarantine or isolation needs to be given so that the individual may return to work or other functions. The release statement should be issued as signed, dated, revocable documentation of completion of quarantine. This does not guarantee that they are disease free, but that they did not develop symptoms during the recommended incubation period.

Several factors can interfere with individuals following the directives of a quarantine and isolation research on the SARS incident in Toronto shows that the two populations most likely to break a quarantine or isolation order are teenagers and healthcare workers. For teens, addressing the "that won't happen to me" mentality and encourage distanced communication through the Internet or text messaging on phones. For health care workers, proactively monitoring their status by disallowing them to come to work if ill or exposed. Healthcare workers may minimize or distort the fact that they were exposed, because if they admit to being exposed, they will need to be quarantined too. However, if they do not take the responsibility for their exposure they may be spreading the contagious agent. If we can determine reasons for noncompliance, we are likely to find solutions to help people comply with orders. We should also note populations who *are* complying with orders to see what factors contribute to their status.

During a pandemic, people are placed in quarantine or isolated in order to contain a contagious disease. Their freedom is restricted, causing considerable distress. The community may avoid individuals and their families identified as exposed, contagious or ill, long after they have been medically cleared of any concerns. Those placed in restrictions may suffer the additional burdens of anger; depression, anxiety, loneliness, fear and/or grief and the reactions may last long after the orders are lifted. Although these are normal reactions, they are distressing and can interfere with recovery and daily functioning. Healthcare workers may be subject to additional stress due to their involvement in the event. They may be concerned about their health and the health of their families, including fear of contagion, safety for those working in healthcare, loneliness, demanding expectations, anger, anxiety and uncertainty related to stress of the event. A balanced response from public health and community leaders, based on an accurate situational assessment has a direct impact on the psychosocial aspect of the community. Overreaction or under reaction leads to mistrust and breeds fear.

Stress is a reaction to physical, emotional, or intellectual demands. Extreme stress triggers the brain to use survival mechanisms including "Fight/Flight/Freeze/Faint" reactions. The causes of stress can be external or internal. *Eustress* (good stress) increases performance and response.

Distress (bad stress) impairs our ability to perform and respond. During times of high stress, our ability to function at an optimal level is diminished. Managing stress is an art form. You must actively implement and practice those activities that help you. In adults, those at highest risk for mental health problems think that they are uncared for by others, have little control over what happens to them, or lack the capacity to manage stress.

A feeling of helplessness can lead to depression. During a pandemic people may feel as if they are powerless to deal with such a large-scale event. Some may go so far as to proclaim it to be the end of the world or a punishment. Situational depression is a sense of helplessness and gloom or irritability, trouble sleeping, fatigue and/or a change in eating habits. It is usually self-limiting; it lifts when the situation changes. There are steps one can take to alter the course such as getting exercise; regular meals and developing a positive attitude that "this too shall pass" all contribute to a more balanced outlook on life along with a personalized plan for beating the blues. A more serious depressive episode that includes suicidal thoughts needs immediate mental health intervention. When the stress of a pandemic begins to wear people down, they may have short tempers or problems sleeping. They can become overly sensitive and snap at one another. Worry and doubt crowds their thoughts and it can be difficult to turn off the noise when it's time to go to sleep. When a community is dealing with pandemic many will turn to using the phone or the Internet, but it may not be a viable option. Not only are technical and social activities curtailed at the community level, family interactions and physical contact may be restricted in order to maximize their safety. Schools may be closed; children may be separated from friends. Normal activities may be cancelled leaving people to entertain themselves, often at home. Reminders that this is temporary can help people to maintain hope for the future.

When people are forced to change their daily habits, some adapt to the changes and some get angry that their routines are interrupted. Anger can be a side effect of feeling scared and out of control. Blame may get assigned in an attempt to make sense of the situation. Paranoia may emerge if the person is assigning blame and is also fearful. Anger reduction requires normalizing the reactions to the event and acknowledging the anger. Information regarding the event must be continually updated and circulated in order for people to process the new data and have a sense of control over the situation. An event that triggers quarantine or isolation can cause people to feel out of control. Most people are used to having some degree of control over where they go and with whom they can socialize. In a community-wide containment of a communicable disease, freedoms that are taken for granted may be curtailed in favor of safety.

Choices become important in allowing people to have a measure of control. For example, by allowing them to either shelter in place, at work, school or home and avoid contact with others, they have participated in making a decision that concerns their location and well being. Generally, people will be more receptive to comply with the orders if they have some say in the matter. Those who have been under a restrictive order may be subjected to stigmatization in people avoiding them. An unfounded fear can be the driving force. Minimize the distress by educating the public about the incubation period and provide specific, factual information about what indicates a non-transmissive state. Publishing a timeline for disease transmission using the most conservative figures available to ensure community safety and build trust.

A pandemic will likely produce significant losses in the community. It is the loss of innocence and a sense of living in a safe world where events like this don't happen to us and it will take time to bounce back. There is also a certainty that there will be fatalities as a result of the disease. Grief and sadness change the social fabric of the community, and the nation. There may be feelings of helplessness and powerlessness, survivor guilt, dealing with many shocking deaths, unanswered questions and a violation of their belief in a world of safety and meaning. These factors may impact people's ability to resolve grief. According to Dr. Elisabeth Kubler-Ross's theory on how people process the loss of a significant person or a life-changing event, there are overlapping stages of grief and recovery from grief. The process of grieving often fluctuates between the stages rather than progressing in a linear fashion. Sometimes people go from anger to acceptance to depression and back again. As people work through grief the goal is to experience the loss, accept the reality; adjust to the loss, and to re-connect emotionally in life. Community memorial services and symbols of hope and remembrance will be useful in bringing back a sense of balance to the community. The magnitude of people affected by the losses can directly affect the intensity of the grief. When large numbers of people are involved as with a pandemic, people's ability to offer support to others may be limited, because of the magnitude of the situation. On the other hand, large-scale events may allow survivors to bond and grieve together as a collective community sense of sadness. They may find support in knowing that there are others who understand the devastation of their loss.

The bereaved person may suffer from "survivor guilt," wondering why they survived when others have died and may believe that they could have or should have done more to prevent the tragedy.

Resilience is the ability to bounce back and adapt to changes after a crisis. The threats to psychological well being that outbreaks pose can be overcome with the skills of resilience, which can serve as a kind of emotional vaccine. Research shows that most people will be able to carry on and rebuild their lives. Although most people will bounce back after a traumatic event, they still experience emotional distress, and recovery can be a painful process. Being resilient does not provide immunity to problems or stress but it is important in recovering from a crisis situation.

People deal with change in their lives through a process called resilience. The degree of resilience that people have directly affects the outcome of the event and the speed at which they recover. Helping others can contribute to one's resilience as a sense of being needed and being useful provides the bridge that connects us to others. The skills needed for resilience can be developed through the nurturing of thoughts, behaviors and actions that promote the fortitude to pick up the pieces and go on. While there are several factors that increase one's resiliency, the key factor to maintaining it is having concerned, supportive relationships with family and friends. Additionally, the ability to plan and follow through, having a positive self image and confidence, good communication and problem solving skills, and the capability to handle strong feelings and impulses all contribute to being able to adjust to and rise above adverse situations. Resilience can be fostered in communities by instituting a strong sense of self-reliance through preparedness. A strong community is willing to help each other out in a crisis and is optimistic about the future of their community. When people are at risk, they tend to find new ways of responding when the old ways are inadequate, often discovering creative solutions. In responding to a pandemic, it may benefit the community to mobilize and use volunteers in the community to assist with disease containment. Traditional disaster relief involved sending aid to those affected, and it is a noble plan. However, recent research into community resilience offers suggestions for determining strengths, talents and services in the community, and asking the community what would be the most useful for them in their situation. This helps reduce the burden of unwanted or useless donations i.e. winter coats to tropical climates or high heels to people who have lost their transportation capabilities and are walking. A resilient community is more likely to voluntarily cooperate with a quarantine and isolation order and enact social norms that support enforcement.

Eventually, the restrictions will be lifted. The community will be allowed to return to normal activities. Some people will run out and resume their lives; some will exercise caution. Both are normal responses. Most people will bounce back quickly; however, if there have been a number of fatalities, recovery may be slow.

It is tempting to look at all of the bad things that come out of an event, and it may be difficult to see that something positive emerged as a result of it. An investigation into the research from the SARS outbreak in Toronto showed that being isolated is not always a negative experience. Some people welcomed the solitude, privacy and a chance to get a good night's sleep. A new awareness of disease transmission was also noted and hand washing took on new significance. Medical staff reported an increased awareness of disease control and group cohesion due to spending a great deal of time together. It was a chance to put into practice some little used procedures and test their effectiveness. Families who are quarantined at home may welcome a chance to spend time together. People are offered the chance to solve unique problems. In dealing with the losses, people may have a new appreciation for life and for the freedoms they may have taken for granted prior to the event.

Information in this document was a compilation of the Colorado Disaster Mental Health Response System "Pandemic Influenza: Quarantine, Isolation and Social Distancing Toolbox for Public Health and Public Behavioral Health Professionals". This field manual offers guidance for public health and behavioral health workers dealing with the stress of a quarantine and isolation event. In the event that this manual is not needed, we are grateful. If an event such as this does occur, we hope you will find the information in these pages useful.

References

Information contained in this document was compiled from several sources. The following is a list of the major sources of reference materials.

Allport, G.W., & Postman, L. (1947). The Psychology of Rumor. In Maccoby, E. E., Newcomb, T.M. & Hartley,E.L. (Eds.) *Readings in social psychology* (3rd ed.). London:

ASPR, Pandemic All Hazards Preparedness Act, 2006. http://www.hhs.gov/aspr/opsp/pahpa/index.html

Blendon R.J., DesRoches C.M., Cetron M.S., Benson J.M., Meinhardt T., Pollard W. Attitudes toward the use of quarantine in a public health emergency in four countries. 2006; Health Affairs, Datawatch: Quarantine. Web exclusive www.healthaffairs.org

Blendon R.J., Benson J.M., DesRoches C.M., Raleigh E., Taylor-Clark K. The public's response to severe acute respiratory syndrome in Toronto and the United States. *Clinical infectious disease 2004*; 38:925-927.

Bonanno, G. A., Galea, S., Bucciareli, A., & Vlahov, D. (2007). "What predicts psychological resilience after disaster? The role of demographics, resources, and life stress. *Journal of Consulting and Clinical Psychology, 75(5),* 671-682.

Colorado Department of Public Health and Environment. Proposed Guidance for Alterations in the Healthcare System During an Influenza Pandemic. Draft, 2008.

Colorado Department of Human Services. "Colorado Mental Health Disaster Response System: Field Response Training", Division of Mental Health, 2005.

Department of Health and Human Services, Substance Abuse and Mental Health Services Administration, Center for Mental Health Services "Communicating in a Crisis: Risk Communication Guidelines for Public Officials", U.S., 2002.

The community resilience project team. (1999) "The Community Resilience Manual", Making Waves, 10(4). 10-14.

"Developing Cultural Competence in Disaster Mental Health Programs", Guiding Principles and Recommendations, U.S. Department of Health and Human Services, Substance Abuse and Mental Health Services Administration, Center for Mental Health services, 2003.

Hawryluck, L., Gold, W.L., Robinson, S., Pogorski, S., Galea, S., Styra, R., (2004) "SARS Control and Psychological Effects of Quarantine, Toronto, Canada", *emerging infectious diseases*, 10(7), 1206-1212.

Davies H., Rees, J. (2000) Psychological effects of isolation nursing: mood disturbance. *Nursing standard,* 14(28), 35-38.

Heyman D. *Model operational guidelines for disease exposure control.* Pre-publication draft. The Center for Strategic & International Studies Homeland Security Program. 11/2005.

"HHS Pandemic Influenza Plan", U.S. Department of Health and Human Services, November 2005. http://www.hhs.gov/pandemicflu/plan/

National Child Traumatic Stress Network and National Center for PTSD, *Psychological First Aid: Field Operations Guide,* September, 2005.

"National Strategy for Pandemic Influenza –Implementation Plan". Homeland Security Council May 2006. http://www.whitehouse.gov/homeland/nspi_implementation.pdf

Nickell,L.A., Crighton, C., Al- Enazy, H., Bolaji, Y., Hanjrah, S., Hussain, A. et al. Psychosocial effects of SARS on hospital staff: survey of a large tertiary care institution. *CMAJ* 2004; 170(5) 793-798.

Patriarca PA, Cox NA. Influenza pandemic preparedness plan for the United States. J Infect Dis 1997;176:S4-7.

Public Health Guidance for Community-Level Preparedness and Response to Severe Acute Respiratory Syndrome (SARS) Version 2. (2004) "Severe Acute Respiratory Syndrome-Supplement: Community Containment Measures, Including Non-Hospital Isolation and Quarantine". Department of Health and Human Services, Center for Disease Control and Prevention.

"The Road to Resilience" 2004. American Psychological Association. http://www.apahelpcenter.org/featuredtopics/feature.php?id=6

Robertson., Hershenfield, K., Grace, S.L., Stewart, D.E., (2004) "The Psychosocial effects of Being Quarantined Following Exposure to SARS: A Qualitative Study of Toronto Health Care Workers". Canadian Journal of Psychiatry, 49(6), 403-406.

Substance Abuse Mental Health Services Administration (SAMSHA) Disaster Technical assistance Center. http://www.mentalhealth.samhsa.gov/dtac/

"The Public/Private Response to Sudden Disease Outbreak - Final Report", (2005). Institute for Public Health Law, CDC Foundation.

World Health Organization, 2005. Avian flu the next pandemic? http://www.cbc.ca/news/background/avianflu/

Young, B.H., Ford, J.D., Ruzek, J.I. Friedman, M.J., Gusman, F.D., "Disaster Mental Health Services: A Guidebook for Clinicians and Administrators", National Center for Post Traumatic Stress disorder, Department of Veterans Affairs.

ABOUT THE AUTHORS:

P.J. Havice-Cover, MA LPC CACIII CEM®

Ms. Havice-Cover is a Mental Health/Public Information Officer for a US HHS disaster response team, employed by the Colorado Medical Society as an Emergency Manager, and has 15 years of experience in public health. Some of her recent publications are: a field guide on "Pandemic Influenza – Behavioral Health Considerations" accepted as a best practice document by the Centers for Disease Control, "First Responders and Workforce Protection" in the Disaster Management Handbook (2008), "Care for the Caregiver" in Veterinary Disaster Response (in press) and an after-action report on volunteers post Katrina. Her current efforts are in developing and refining a mass casualty behavior health triage system and working to optimize physician disaster response. Field Response - Presentation http://www.cddbhc.com/library/documents/Field%20Response%20-%20Havice-Cover.ppt

Curt H Drennen, Psy.D., R.N.

Curt H Drennen is a licensed psychologist with the Colorado Department of Human Services Division of Behavioral Health. He has worked in disaster response since 2002 and is the Colorado Behavioral Health Disaster Response Coordinator and Program Manager for the Disaster Behavioral Health Planning and Response Section. He has 17 years of experience in the field with an emphasis in Public Psychology and Administration, Emotional Intelligence, Servant Leadership, Systems and Systems Conflict Management as well as Crisis Intervention and Behavioral Health Disaster Management.

Part II:
Returning Military and Families

Invisible Wounds: Treating Military Service Members and Their Families

Adele D'Ari, Ed.D.

Abstract

The war in Iraq and Afghanistan has had many unintended consequences for service-members and their families. This paper outlines the major mental health consequences to the service-member and the effect these consequences have on the family. Of the three prevalent mental health conditions that have been identified--Post-Traumatic Stress Disorder, Depression, and Traumatic Brain Injury--this paper will primarily focus on Traumatic Brain Injury as it is the least understood in this population.

• • •

There are 23.8 million veterans in the U.S., and since October 2001 over 2 million U.S. troops have been deployed for Operation Enduring Freedom and Iraqi Freedom (OEF/OIF). Approximately one third of these troops have served multiple deployments. As of November 2008 there have been 4,191 deaths and 32,772 wounded (DOD website, 2008). Twenty-five percent of the wounded have filed for a disability. The Department of Defense is creating a holistic and family-centric approach to recovery and integration of these veterans back into society that includes a recovery coordinator, a recovery plan, and a national resource directory (Davis, 2007). The coordinator develops a long-term relationship with the veteran and develops a web-based plan that is a comprehensive "life map" to identify all the necessary goals and support the needed transitions across care settings. The national directory connects veterans to appropriate resources, which can be organized by diagnosis, geographic region of the veteran, and by type of service needed (Davis, 2007). Recently, the Defense Center for Excellence specifically set themselves up to work with veterans with brain injuries and post-traumatic stress disorder.

Give an Hour is just one of the many organizations set up to provide services to veterans and their families. Give an Hour strives to develop a national network of volunteers capable of responding to both acute and chronic conditions that arise within our society. The first target population is the U.S. troops and families who are affected by the current military conflicts in Afghanistan and Iraq. Give an Hour is asking mental health professionals nationwide to literally give an hour of their time each week to provide free mental health services to military personnel and their families. Research will guide the development of additional services needed by the military community, and appropriate networks will be created to respond to those needs. Individuals who receive services will be given the opportunity to give an hour back in their own community. Give an Hour volunteers are ready to work with families, including extended families, as well as the veteran individually. There are many hidden consequences of combat deployment and Give an Hour is developing an ongoing network to be available to those in need.

Being deployed to a combat situation has a huge effect on families. Forty percent of the National Guard and Reservists troops (Segal, 2005) have a mean age of thirty-five years and are the ones most likely to have career and family when they deploy (Veterans Benefits Administration, 2005). Forty-eight percent who serve are about twenty-five years of age or under and many are just out of their teens and leaving home for the first time (Department of Defense, 2006). Fifteen percent of those serving are women (Swords to Plowshares, 2007). More mothers are leaving home to participate in this combat situation than ever before.

More than 2 million children have had one parent deployed to Iraq or Afghanistan and 40 percent of those children are younger than five (*Washington Post,* Chartrund, Dec. 2008). Over 27,000 service members have filed for divorce, which is a significant increase since 2001. PTSD is associated with interpersonal deficits and emotional intimacy, and is associated with a greatly elevated divorce rate. Children are also impacted by their parent's deployment and many have struggled with multiple deployments. Active grief is another issue for military families. Half of all children who have lost a parent are under the age of ten. That number grows monthly. Given this situation, children of military families are at an increased risk for psychological disorders.

A recent study indicated that children age 18 months to 5 years old have significantly higher scores on measures of externalizing and overall behavior problems than children of the same age without a deployed parent (*Washington Post,* Chartrund, 2008). This study was based on perceptions of the non-deployed parent and the results were still significant even after controlling for the parental stress and depressive symptoms. Family relationships were the focus of some studies after the Vietnam War. Generally these studies looked at veterans and their families who reported problems with parenting and parental satisfaction after returning home from their tour of duty in Vietnam. Some findings suggest that veterans with PTSD, who may already have a heightened reactivity level due to their PTSD, would tend to avoid emotional experiences of any kind, including positive emotions evoked in parent-child relationships (Rand, 2008). To the extent that post-combat mental disorders go untreated, these disorders are likely to have a long-term effect on the development of their children (Rand, 2008).

Military families are affected by stress, anxiety, and fatigue, even before the deployment occurs. During a parent's deployment, family members may feel isolated, unsupported, and anxious (Henderson, 2006). Once the deployment begins these children live in single parent families with the same family demands that existed prior to the parent's deployment. There is often financial stress in addition to the anxiety of having a family member away from home in a dangerous situation. Additionally, there is significant increase in stress and worry about the service member's safety while being deployed. While their family member is away, they are aware of the news coming from Iraq/Afghanistan and they will often know another family who has lost a person (Henderson, 2006). These deployments disrupt parental roles and can lead to confusion for children. Parents often feel unable to talk with their children about changes in their family due to multiple deployments, combat injuries in a parent, death, or disorders like post-traumatic stress (Cozza, 2008). There are no stress free days for these families.

There is much discussion about the negative effects on children and families from combat deployment of a parent, especially multiple times. The military and some mental health organizations have begun to focus on information and programs that will help families during these transitions (APA fact sheet, 2008; Armstrong, 2006; Henderson, 2006; NCPTSD pamphlet, 2008). Families will be able to cope better and have more resilience if they have the education and support they need. The military is addressing the psychological needs of the troops and their families through a variety of programs that provide many services pre-deployment, during the deployment, and post deployment. They are also overwhelmed by the level of deployment demands and cannot provide all the mental health services needed for families. Unfortunately, the tremendous number of people affected makes it impossible for the military to respond adequately to all the mental health needs in its greater community. It is also important to remember that the majority of families and veterans reintegrate well and are resilient despite difficult times. There are, however, always individuals and families who are missed and we need to find ways to help all families who need service.

Organizations like Give an Hour are created to provide services as needed to families whenever they are needed by just contacting the organization through the website. Families will be provided with what services are needed if there are not easily available in their community. Preventing problems from developing is an important goal of this organization and should be a national priority. By providing services that are separate from the military establishment, we offer an essential option for men and women who might otherwise fail to seek or receive appropriate services. We are also offering services to parents, siblings, and unmarried partners who are not entitled to receive mental health benefits through the military. Although these individuals may have access to mental health services through other means, they are less likely to seek the help they need and deserve if that help is difficult to find or costly.

Our goal is to provide easy access to skilled professionals for all of the people affected by the current war. The participating mental health professionals offer a wide range of services including individual, marital, and family therapy; substance abuse counseling; treatment for post-traumatic stress disorder; and counseling for individuals and their families with traumatic brain injuries. Whether it is a young military wife who is anxious because her four-year old has had nightmares since her husband's deployment, or a father who is struggling to cope with the loss of his son's leg as a result of an explosion in Iraq, they will receive the assistance they need to move through their experience. The healthier the support system for the returning troops, the lower the risk of severe or prolonged dysfunction within these military families. Our primary focus will always be to attend to those in need by linking them to individuals in our society best equipped to respond effectively. In addition, we will develop research and educational programs to further promote the value and importance of a new kind of volunteerism. We hope to encourage an increase in shared responsibility for those citizens who are suffering.

Silent Wounds

Although PTSD has been long identified and understood as a reaction to trauma and in this case, combat trauma, treatment and diagnosis are still being actively developed (Friedman, 2006; Ochberg, 1988; Walser, 2007). Depression is also being diagnosed more in combat veterans and their families. Finally, traumatic brain injury (TBI), a consequence of blast exposure or other head injury, is the least well documented because it has increased dramatically during this conflict due to the new nature of warfare and the newer technologies. These invisible wounds, which remain invisible to the other service members, family members, and society, affect an individual's mood, thoughts, and behavior. Without a more comprehensive understanding of TBI, these effects will go unrecognized and unacknowledged (Rand, 2008). The effects of traumatic brain injury are the least understood leaving a large gap in knowledge related to how extensive the problem is and how to handle it. Traumatic Brain Injury and PTSD will be the primary focus of this paper.

Post Traumatic Stress Disorder

A traumatic event is defined as exposure to a catastrophic event and the experience of emotional distress due to the exposure to the event. In combat one can witness an event and not necessarily be in danger and still be vulnerable to PTSD. PTSD is defined by seventeen symptoms that reflect profound disturbances in cognitive, behavioral, and physiological functioning (Friedman, 2006). Although PTSD can only be diagnosed one month after an individual has been exposed to trauma, many individuals can experience acute, post-traumatic reactions immediately that would be considered an Acute Stress Disorder (DSM-IV Diagnostic Manual, 200. The most researched criterion and therefore the basis of the diagnosis used in the Diagnostic Manual DSM-IV are 1) Re-experiencing symptoms, which is a persistence of thoughts, feelings, and behaviors specifically related to a traumatic event, 2) Avoidance and Numbing, and 3) Hyperarousal. Researchers suggest that trauma (especially combat trauma) exerts its most etiologic effect on the development of re-experiencing symptoms. For combat trauma, exposure alone can be the cause for the development of PTSD. Most people who experience combat trauma do not develop PTSD but it is helpful to understand who is at risk for developing this disorder through combat exposure. A solider going to war who is younger than twenty-five is the most at risk for having PTSD. Women are twice as likely to be at risk than men. Individuals who have been exposed to childhood traumas and experience an adverse life event prior to deployment are also more at risk for developing PTSD. Studies have also indicated that soldiers with more than a high school education are at less risk for developing PTSD.

Re-experiencing is a symptom that involves intrusive recollections, traumatic nightmares, PTSD flashbacks, trauma-related, stimulus evoked psychological distress and physiological reactions. Daytime recollections and traumatic nightmares often evoke panic, terror, dread, grief, or despair. Sometimes an individual is exposed to a trauma and is then suddenly thrust into a psychological state called a flashback.

Avoidant and numbing symptoms have a profound effect on the individual as well as individuals close to them. The soldier with PTSD might avoid certain thoughts and feelings, along with certain activities, places, or people to ward off distress caused by re-experiencing symptoms. The soldier may experience a diminished interest in life activities, and feel detached or estranged from those around them. They can have a sense of a foreshortened future and amnesia for the trauma-related memories. Psychic numbing suppresses all feelings in order to block out intolerable ones. So the individual has to anesthetize positive loving feelings as well as the intolerable ones. Avoidance and numbing symptoms in a veteran with PTSD have the most negative effect on his relationships with the family (NCPTSD, 2008).

Symptoms of hyperarousal are manifestations of physiologic arousal that is part of the PTSD syndrome. The major symptoms are insomnia, irritability, difficulty concentrating, hyper-vigilance, and an exaggerated startle response (Friedman, 2006). A veteran can have only one or many of these symptoms. When the PTSD is at its worst these symptoms can look like panic disorder or a generalized anxiety disorder.

Since PTSD has been identified and treated for many years there are many treatments and combination of treatments that have proven to be effective for the veteran themselves. Cognitive exposure and cognitive restructuring are one of the most validated PTSD treatments (Friedman, 2006). Cognitive restructuring is designed to help the patient review and challenge distressing trauma-related beliefs. This treatment involves education about the relationship between thoughts and emotions and exploring common negative thoughts held by trauma survivors. The treatment involves the identification of personal negative beliefs and the development of alternative interpretations or judgments. Homework assignments and real world practice using what has been learned in personalized PTSD treatment is central to effective treatment (Friedman, 2006). Exposure therapy is different as it is set up to help the veteran directly confront the trauma-related emotions and painful memories. In most settings exposure is delivered as part of a more comprehensive treatment that could include; traumatic stress education, coping skills training, and cognitive restructuring. Exposure therapy can help correct faulty perceptions of danger, improve perceived self-control of memories and accompanying negative emotions, and strengthen adaptive coping responses under stress.

Eye Movement Desensitization and Reprocessing Therapy (EMDR) has also begun to be used for the treatment of PTSD. The individual is instructed to imagine a traumatic memory and an associated negative cognition. Then the veteran is asked to articulate an incompatible positive cognition (e.g. personal worth, trustworthiness). The veteran is then asked to focus on the rapid movement of the clinician's finger while visualizing the traumatic memory. There is conflicting research results about the importance of the eye movement in the resolution of trauma but the efficacy is clearer as studies have indicated that between 50 to 77 percent of those receiving EMDR no longer meet the criteria for PTSD (Friedman, 2006). There are a number of single case studies using EMDR to treat combat trauma, such as traumatic amputation-related phantom limb pain (Russell, 2008) and are being published in journals like the Journal of EMDR Practice and Research.

The psychological assessment of veterans returning from Iraq is likely to be complicated and clinically challenging. The assessment process must include the possible stressors and unique difficulties that may be associated with service in Iraq (Litz & Orsillo, 2008). It is important to provide referrals for acute needs, and to provide some normalizing, psycho-educational information to veterans and their families. Family therapy has been suggested by the National Center for PTSD as a means of treating these important relationships that have been disrupted by PTSD (Friedman, 2006).. Family treatment helps to integrate the service member back into the family post deployment and it is important to assist families to understand what the service member is experiencing. The returning parent may avoid emotional experiences that are an important part of a parent-child relationship if they are struggling with symptoms of PTSD or TBI. There is also a new cognitive behavioral treatment that helps the couple understand the negative effects PTSD has on their relationship and they learn ways to fight those effects together (Journal Clinical Psychology, 2008).

There are some "mindfulness" based treatments that are starting to be used in VA clinics (personal communication) such as Acceptance and Commitment Therapy (Walser & Westrup; 2007). John Briere also has a relational therapy model that incorporates "mindfulness" (online video lecture 2008). His treatment focus is to try and change the service member's relationship to psychological pain. They learn to experience pain but to not feel overwhelmed by the experience. Mindfulness exercises including yoga, reiki, meditation, acupuncture, and qi qong also have been helpful to treat PTSD, especially the hyperarousal symptoms of veterans with PTSD (A Soldier's Mind, 2007).

Traumatic Brain Injury

Traumatic Brain Injury (TBI) occurs when the brain has been injured by an external force and usually nerve tracts and neurons are effected so when these parts are damaged the messages the brain sends to the rest of the body is dramatically altered (West Point Wounded Warriors Program, Handbook, 2007). This contributes to a combination of changes in personality, behavior, motor skills, and cognitive thinking. These changes can be temporary or permanent and can affect communication, judgments, perception, reading and writing skills, memory, and decision-making, to name some of the most significant. A TBI can affect the five senses, motor coordination, balance, and speech. Little is known about what happens to the brain as a result of a bomb blast, as opposed to civilian brain injuries acquired by sports concussions and car crashes. These blasts throw off energy waves that change the atmospheric pressures and are absorbed by the body/brain, and may be different than blunt force trauma to the head (Alvarez, 2008).

A TBI can cause cognitive deficits that effect attention, concentration, distractibility, memory, speed of processing information, confusion, perseveration, impulsiveness, language processing, and executive functioning (Wounded Warriors Program, 2007). Often times these deficits are subtle and are only evident under certain conditions. It is often difficult for the individual to remember what they were like before their deployment. However these deficits, individually and together, can affect academic tasks, work performance, and impacts interpersonal relationships.

Speech and language can also be affected by having a TBI and can affect the understanding of the spoken word (receptive aphasia), slurred speech, speaking very fast or very slow, difficulty speaking or being understood (expressive aphasia), and problems with reading and writing skills. Often times individuals are not aware of their abilities so cannot determine if they have changed or decreased in any way. There can also be sensory difficulties that affect the interpretation of touch, temperature, movement, limb position, and fine discrimination. The perceptual difficulties may include the integration or patterning of sensory impressions into psychologically meaningful data. There can be hearing deficits that involve increased sensitivity to sounds, ringing in the ears (tinnitus), and decrease in hearing. These vision weaknesses may involve blurred vision, problems judging distance, involuntary eye movements (nystagmus), intolerance of light (photophobia), weakness of eye muscles, double vision (diplopia), and partial vision loss. Some of the brain changes can affect the sense of smell (anosmia) and the sense of taste. A TBI can affect physical changes and can cause chronic pain, loss of stamina, regulation of body temperature, appetite changes, sleep disorders, control of bowel and bladder, and menstrual difficulties. When the assault to the brain is more significant there can be physical paralysis and seizures.

Soldiers who have a TBI often have what the neurologists and neuro-psychologists call a "mood disorder". It is a much more common and serious aspect of a TBI than was previously recognized. Individuals can have a change in motivation, can become irritable or aggressive, and can exhibit more dependent behaviors. An individual with a TBI can have times of disinhibition, which involves making poor or impulsive decisions; saying things "without thinking" that may hurt others feelings; increase in impulse buying; getting violently angry over little things; and flying "off the handle" without sufficient cause to do so. There are often feelings of depression that involve "survivor's guilt." They can experience loss of emotional control and these are often important areas to treat (Wounded Warriors Handbook).

Overall 2,726 service members have been diagnosed with a TBI (Rand, 2008). Of those 2,094 are mild and 632 are from moderate to penetrating head injuries. It is believed the number of undiagnosed TBI's are significant. In Rand's review of the research there is evidence to indicate that diagnosis has been difficult in the past when the injury is caused by exposure to blasts. The few studies published used different criteria to define a TBI making it difficult to extrapolate from the findings. Today more mild TBI's are managed in theater (Drake , 2007). There is generally a brief loss of consciousness (30 seconds to 30 minutes) with negative results on a CT/MRI scan. The return to duty rate varies and a service member can remain in theater. These mild TBI's have varying effects on their return to duty, work performance, family stress, and they are at more risk for discipline problems (Drake, 2007).

Until September 2007 there was no consistent post deployment screening for TBI exposure, but now it is part of each service members annual yearly physical. As of May 2008, service members who deploy longer than 30 days undergo neuropsychological screening before leaving to determine baseline functioning (Alvarez, 2008). Fort Carson, is an example of a post that spent time screening one hundred percent of returning soldiers for an extended period of time. They found a higher number of soldiers who reported symptoms several months after returning home. This suggests a possible interaction between the subtleties of the symptoms, the lack of awareness the individual might have of the symptoms, and the euphoria about returning home. The symptoms may be more apparent to self and family several months after an individual returns home and is in their previous routine.

Sixty to eighty percent of mild TBI injuries resolve over time without medical intervention. Education materials for the family and service member are extremely helpful in these situations (Rand, 2008). Those who go undiagnosed and untreated tend to be at risk for substance abuse and other negative health compromising behaviors. Although there is little current research there is indication that treatment reduces the severity of symptoms (Miller & Mittenberg, 1998; Rand, 2008). Substance abuse is a significant problem in the military and those who have untreated mental health conditions are at the highest risk of self-medication. In 2006, 9,000 veterans were treated for substance abuse (McCanna, 2007). TBI and substance abuse co-morbidity are specifically associated with military discharge (Rand, 2008). Veterans with a TBI are at great risk for substance abuse and the long term consequences for the military and the individual have been well documented over the years.

It is important, but extremely difficult, to accurately diagnosis TBI. Dr. Ibokja Cernak, a doctor at Johns Hopkins University, who conducts research into "blast injuries", indicated that soldiers can develop symptoms up to two years post exposure to a blast and that these veterans have more significant symptom severity than civilians with a TBI (Alvarez, 2008). Diagnosis is difficult as many of the symptoms overlap with other mental health disorders, especially depression and PTSD. For example, difficulty with anger, diminished interest in activities, and problems with concentration can be indicative of all three disorders. It is also important for the individual to have accurate diagnosis so they can utilize extended services while on active duty and then later through the Veterans Administration.

In PTSD, the most common neurocognitive functions that are weakened are verbal memory, attention, working memory, and diverse executive capacities. TBI injury can be different because the most consistently observed deficit is marked slowing of mental processing (Felmingham et el, 2004). This reduced speed of mental processing impacts the coding of information, verbal comprehension, and adaptive responding to novel tasks and situations, as well as attention (Tombaugh et el, 2007).

TBI, depression, and PTSD have many similarities and affect service members and their families in similar ways. Often the presence of one disorder predicts the likelihood that the person will have another diagnosis. Some studies indicate that up to sixty-five percent of individuals with PTSD have at least one other mental health condition. The relationship between TBI and depression is often indirect, resulting from stress, poor coping, and personal isolation. Most research is from the civilian population and does not account for the unique situation of combat and deployment away from home. All three conditions increase the risk of suicidal ideation and attempts (Rand, 2008). Individuals diagnosed with any of the three conditions have higher rates of unhealthy behavior such as smoking, overeating, and unsafe sex (Rand, 2008). These individuals can miss more days of work, can be less productive, and are more likely to be unemployed. The consequences of the disorders become more severe if untreated. Severe TBI injuries often contribute to anxiety and substance abuse. There is less clinical research on depression and TBI. Most of the research on PTSD comes from the Vietnam War, although there are exceptions (Hoge et al, 2004), which involves a large-scale study, using an anonymous survey filled out by military personnel before and after deploying to Iraq and Afghanistan. This study documented the increase in rates of PTSD post deployment. These rates were highly related to the amount of combat exposure, and focused on the access to services and stigma of mental health disorders in this population. In addition to difficulty diagnosing TBI and PTSD there is a social stigma to needing mental health services that prevent service members from receiving appropriate treatment.

It is important to understand the invisible wounds of war-the mental, emotional, and cognitive injuries sustained during deployment to Iraq and Afghanistan both to the individual service member and to their families and friends. Although PTSD, major depression, and TBI are conceptually distinct conditions, with different etiologies, symptoms and recommended treatments, these three conditions and their developmental trajectories affect lives in similar ways. 71 percent of the service members injured are under thirty and most of those are low ranking (E-4 and below) (Fryar, 2005) and this is just one of the many statistics that indicate this is the population at most risk for PTSD and TBI. Loss of productivity due to these conditions that go undiagnosed and untreated have a huge effect on the individual and their family and also are more expensive to the military/VA systems. The importance of information and accurate assessment of mental health conditions along with providing evidence-based treatment is clear. It also is important as it may reduce the downstream costs stemming from unemployment, need for disability programs, and public assistance in the future (Rand, 2008). It is impossible to estimate the costs of homelessness, domestic violence, and substance abuse to our society, yet we know these are also unintended consequences of these untreated conditions.

References

Alvarez, L. (2008), "War Veterans' Concussions are often overlooked", The New York Times.

American Psychological Association (2008), APA Task Force on Resilience in Response to Terrorism, Fact Sheet and The Road to Resilience pamphlet.

Armstrong, Keith (2006) *Courage after the fire*, Ulysses Press, Berkley, CA.

Briere, John (2007) PTSD Treatment. You Tube Video UCLA, CA.

Chartrand, M. Ph.D. (2008) Behavioral Problems in young children .Archives of Pediatric and Adolescent Medicine reported. Washington Post December 2008.

Cognitive Behavioral Study on Iraqi Vets with PTSD, Journal of Clinical Psychology, 2008.

Cozza, S. MD (2008) Experts watching mental health of army children. Army Military News October 16, 2008 reported by Elizabeth Collins.

Davis, L. (2007) Emergent Population with Disabilities: Veterans and Returning Veterans, US Dept of Defense.

Department of Defense Demographics Report, (2005), PBS "More Women Soldiers Dying in Iraq", News Hour with Jim Lehrer. December 18, 2007.

Diagnostic and Statistical Manual of Mental Disorders, (1994), 4th Edition, American Psychiatric Association.

Drake, A. Ph.D,. (2007, Power Point) "Traumatic Brain Injury and Post Traumatic Stress Disorder", Defense and Veterans Brain Injury Center and Defense Center of Excellence.

Felminghan KL, Baruley IJ, Green AM., (2004), Effects of diffuse axonal injury on speed of information processing following severe traumatic head injury. Neuropsychology. 18(3): 564-71.

Fryar, D.K. (2005), "Variables affecting the financial and emotional stability of families of service members wounded in action", Research Troy University.

Friedman, M. (2006) 4th Ed. Post-Traumatic and Acute Stress Disorders: The Latest Assessment and Treatment Strategies, Compact Clinical, Kansas City, MO.

Henderson, Kristen, (2006) While They Are At War: The True Story of American Families on the Homefront, Houghton Mifflin, NY

Hoge, C., Castro, C., Messer, S., McGurk, D., Cotting, D., and Koffman, R., (2004), "Combat Duty in Iraq and Afghanistan, Mental Problems and Barriers to Care". New England Journal of Medicine. 351(1): 13-22.

Litz, P. & Orsillo, S. (2007) The Returning Veteran of the Iraq War: Basic Issues and Assessment Guidelines. National Center for PTSD. Factsheet

McCanna, Shaun. (2007), "It's easy for soldiers to score heroin in Afghanistan." Salon Magazine. August 7.

Miller & Mittenberg (1998), " Brief Cognitive Behavioral Interventions in Mild Traumatic Brain Injury", Journal of Applied Neurology, 5(4): 175-82.

Monson, C.M., Fredman, S.J., & Adair, K.C., (2008), "Cognitive-Behavioral Therapy for Posttraumatic Stress Disorder: Application to Operation Iraqi Enduring Freedom and Iraqi Freedom Veterans", Journal of Clinical Psychology: 64(8), 958-971 (2008).

National Center for PTSD (2008), Returning from the War Zone a Guide for Families of Military Members, Available www.ncptsd.va.gov

Ochberg, F. Ed., (1988), Post Traumatic Therapy and Victims of Violence, Brunner/Mazel, NY.

Russell, M.C. (2008) "Treating traumatic amputation-related phantom limb pain: a case study utilizing EMDR within the armed services", Clinical Case Studies,7(1), 136-153.

Segal, David, and Segal M.R. (2005), "US Military Reliance on Reserves", Population Reference Bureau, Available http://www.prb.org/Articles/2005/USMilitarysRelianceontheReserves.aspx.

Sword to Plowshares, Iraq Veteran Project, (2007), "Risk and Protective Factors for the Global War on Terrorism Veterans". Powerpoint Presentation

Tannielian, T. and Jaycox, L., Eds. (2008), Invisible Wounds of War; Psychological and Cognitive Injuries, and Their Consequences and Services to Assist Recovery, Rand Corporation Center for Military Health Policy Research

Terri (July 2008) "Army Chief of Staff: Ft Bliss PTSD Program Should Be Replicated", A Soldier's Mind

Tombaugh TN, Rees L, Stormer P, Harrison AG, Smith A., (2007), The effects of mild and severe traumatic brain injury on speed of information processing as measured by computerized tests of information processing (CTIP). Archives Clinical Neurology, 22(1): 25-36.

Veterans Benefits Administration, (2005), "VA Benefits Activity: Veterans Deployed to the Global War on Terrorism".

Walser, R., & Westrup, D., (2007) Acceptance and Commitment Therapy for the Treatment of Post-Traumatic Stress Disorders & Trauma-Related Problems: A Practioner's Guide to Using Mindfulness & Acceptance Strategies, New Harbinger Publications, Oakland, CA.

West Point Wounded Warrior Mentor Program (2008), Walter Reed Army Medical Center TBI Handbook.

About the Author

Adele D'Ari, Ed.D. is a founding board member of Give an Hour, an organization which links licensed mental health professionals and pastoral counselors with service members and affected others who may be un-served or underserved by existing programs. She is a licensed clinical psychologist who has been practicing in Virginia and the District of Columbia for twenty years. She specializes in working with children and families affected by traumatic loss. She is also a clinical member and approved supervisor of the American Association of Marriage and Family Therapy and founded the Northern Virginia Reflecting Team. Other areas of expertise include couples therapy and work with divorcing families. She is a co-chair of the Collaborative Professionals of Northern Virginia, a practice group of collaborative divorce professionals. She received her doctorate in counseling psychology from Northeastern University in 1988.

Gender, Personality, and Coping: Unraveling Gender in Military Post-Deployment Wellbeing (Preliminary Results)

LCDR Alan L. Hensley, USN (Ret.), BCETS, FAAETS

Abstract

The vast majority of Department of Defense, Service, and Veterans Health Administration study results and statistics regarding the wellbeing of the veterans of Operation Iraqi Freedom (OIF) and Operation Enduring Freedom (OEF) deployment find no statistically significant gender-related differences. Unfortunately, virtually all these studies use the term, gender, synonymously with biological sex. This practice disregards a wide body of empirical data that gender is, in fact, the amalgamation of biology, psychology, and sociology. Consequently, biological sex is the sole differentiating variable. This study investigates post-deployment wellbeing, both in terms of biological sex and biopsychosocially-derived gender. The study then explores gender, personality, and ways of coping in relationship to the *Primary Traumatic Event* (PTE), PTSD symptomology, trauma-related guilt, and level of distress using a battery of proven valid and reliable self-report instruments. Findings are presented and recommendations are then made for a new *Military Wellbeing and Assessment Protocol* (MWAP) that will provide military planners and medical and mental health practitioners with information necessary to make better-informed troop deployment decisions, better assessment of troop/unit wellbeing, as well as potential biopsychosocial consequences of troop-deployment.

Introduction

Since the beginning of Operation Iraqi Freedom (OIF) in 2003, the US Army Office of the Army Surgeon General has periodically deployed *Mental Health Assessment Teams* (MHATs) to assess the wellbeing of Soldiers and Marines deployed to Iraq. Since inception, five MHATs have been conducted. The MHAT IV (USA OSG, 2007), the foundation of the present investigation, purported to anonymously assess the wellbeing of 1,320 Soldiers and 447 Marines in-locus from August and October 2006. However, several sampling, methodological, and procedural errors are apparent, which potentially bring arguments regarding differences between male and female Soldiers into question.

The MHAT IV assessment protocol was conducted using the *Land Combat Study of the Walter Reed Army Institute of Research* (Castro & Hoge, 2005). Specifically, the MHAT IV addressed: a) environmental risk factors (e.g., Service branch; length of deployment; combat proximity, intensity, and duration; and unit composition); b) protective/prophylactic factors (e.g., training, education, and leadership; and c) behavioral health status and wellbeing (e.g., anxiety, angry hostility, and depression). Intake was accomplished by self-report Soldier/Military Wellbeing survey.

Methodologically, the MHAT IV endeavored to identify differences in the wellbeing based upon three levels of combat intensity—*low, medium,* and *high.* Consequently, the researchers categorized participants in terms of these three categories. Unfortunately, the MHAT IV deviated from stated study goals; thereby, becoming enmeshed in a disappointing sociopolitical agenda. The report writers made assertions regarding the suitability or viability of female soldiers in combat that were not supported by study sampling, conduct, or findings. The Army sample population consisted of 1,118 (86%) male Soldiers and 188 (14%) female Soldiers. The Marine sample population consisted of 408 (93%) male Marines and 30 (7%) female Marines. The MHAT (USA OSG, 2007) incorrectly worded the demographic composition of females in low, medium, and high combat conditions to a level that would have rendered correlation and differentiation mathematically impossible.

Correctly worded, however, 29 percent of the sampled Soldiers in low combat conditions were female. Twelve percent of the sampled Soldiers in the medium combat condition were female. Three percent of the Soldiers sampled in the high combat condition were female. The female Marine sample (n=30) was of such diminutive size that they were discarded from analysis from the onset. Thus, in reality, 188 female Soldiers (11%) were compared to 1,118 male soldiers and 408 male Marines (1,506 males; 89%). Despite this asymmetry, the report writers asserted, overall, there were no significant differences in anxiety, depression, or acute stress observed between male and female soldiers. However, in the low combat conditions, significant differences between males and females did exist. Specifically, while nine percent of the males screened positive for any mental disorder in the low combat condition, 17 percent of the females screened positive. Given the earlier assertion, then, females in the low combat condition, either: a) experienced traumatic or stressful events in the low-combat condition not experienced by male persons; b) assigned greater meaning to events than males occurring in the low combat condition; or, c) exhibited less adaptive coping strategies than their male counterparts in the low combat condition. Unfortunately, the researchers, seemingly, disregard the significance of this observation in future research and analysis.

The report writers (USA OSG, 2006), themselves, argue the number of women reporting high combat conditions (n=11; 5.85% of all female participants) was so insignificant that no further inferences or analysis could be drawn regarding the mental health of women in combat. However, in the summary section of the report, the writers assert that female soldiers were no more vulnerable than male Soldiers in how combat can affect their wellbeing. A seemingly negative correlation exists among females in relationship to combat intensity, suggesting alternative explanations should be explored. Unfortunately, the sociopolitical agenda of the MHAT IV becomes overtly obvious in the final statement (USA OSG, 2006; p. 79), *"When discussing the role of the female Soldier in combat, the focus needs to move away from weakness and vulnerability, to one of strength and accomplishment."* This assertion is, not only an obtuse statement of sociopolitical origin detracting from the objectiveness of empirical research, it disregards a large body of knowledge that personality and ways of coping rely not only upon biology, but also upon social learning for development and maintenance (Pervin, 2004; Lazarus & Folkman, 1984).

Consistent evidence is evident in examination of the existent body of empirical data that early socialization experiences influence outcome of life experiences. Macoby and Martin

(1983), for example, find parenting style can be correlated to academic, behavioral, and biopsychosocial outcome. Another example found that while children with *authoritarian* parents—those parents who are demanding and repressive—tend to perform moderately well in school and exhibit low levels of problematic behavior, he or she also tends to have poorer social skills, have lower self-esteem, and suffer higher levels of depression than children with *authoritative* parents—parents who are demanding, yet responsive. Authoritative parents nurture children in a rational, issue-oriented manner. Children of authoritative parents also generally tend to demonstrate academic and social competence, and present less problematic behavior than children of permissive parents (Holmbeck & Wandrei, 1993; Strage & Brandt, 1999).

Permissive parents are non-restrictive and are less demanding of academic achievement and adherence to acceptable sociocultural morals, ethics, values, rules, policies, and procedures. They tend to be ambivalent to their child's needs; neither distinctly indulging, nor neglecting their child's needs. Thus, the children of permissive parents must be largely self-motivated and self-disciplined or are, alternatively, guided by peer pressure. Unfortunately, children of permissive parents are highly susceptible to diminished academic performance and problematic or antisocial behavior (Condry & Simon, 1974; Steinberg, 1987). However, children of permissive parents frequently have higher self-esteem, more highly developed social skills, and lower levels of depression than children from authoritarian parents (Strage & Brandt, 1999). Thus, childhood parenting style presents lifelong benefits and challenge; especially male children reared to be the sociocultural epitome of maleness and girls reared as subservient unequals, who are not permitted to experience the more adventurous perils traditionally the exclusive domain of males (e.g. tree-climbing).

Competence, achievement-striving, and self-discipline, discussed as outcomes of parenting styles, are underlying facets of the *Conscientiousness* domain of the Revised NEO Personality Inventory (Costa & McCrae, 1992). Similarly, anxiety, angry hostility, impulsiveness, and depression are integral facets of *Neuroticism* (N) in the Five-Factor Model of Personality, as conceptualized by Costa and McCrae (1992). Many of the NEO-PI-R domains and facets, in fact, reflect the outcome of biology, learning, and experiences amalgamated during childhood and adolescence.

Ways of coping, likewise, also reflect biological, psychological, and sociological (biopsychosocial) strategies developed through learning and experience. These factors provide potential predictors of perception, cognition and response to life events, and life event outcome, such as *post-traumatic stress disorder* (PTSD), *trauma-related guilt* (TRG), and distress.

A corollary, then, potentially exists that predeployment prophylactic training and education, intra-deployment intervention and post-deployment treatment could benefit from additional insight of the relationships between sex, gender roles, personality, ways of coping, traumatic history, locus of control, PTSD, trauma-related guilt, and distress. However, no evidence exists in the body of research related to post-combat deployment that the Department of Defense (DOD), military Services, and the Veterans Health Administration (VHA) have considered or integrated these factors into past, current, or future research.

While substantial research has been conducted in the typical sociocultural and socio-environmental circumstances, a dearth of empirical research is available to correlate the effects of childhood/adolescent experiences on post-deployment outcome; especially the post-deployment wellbeing of veterans deployed as *emerging adults* (18-25; Arnett, 2000). Consequently, this investigation endeavors to explore the relationship between sex, gender role, personality domains and facets, ways of coping, locus of control, trauma history, primary traumatic event (PTE), PTSD, trauma-related guilt, and distress. To address the omissions of the MHAT IV, this study specifically addressed the relationships between biological sex, gender roles, personality, locus of control, ways of coping, the primary traumatic event (PTE), PTSD symptom severity, trauma-related guilt, and distress. Because of small sample size, however, correlation to prior traumatic history was not accomplished as planned.

METHOD

Participants

The sample population for this investigation consisted of 61 Army and Air Force veterans of deployment in support of Operation Iraqi Freedom (OIF) and Operation Enduring Freedom (OEF). The sample population, which was largely Caucasian, consisted of 35 (57%) males and 26 (43%) females. With respect to age, seven (11.5%) participants were between the ages of 18 and 25, 20 (32.8%) participants were between the ages of 26 and 35, 19 (31.1%) participants were between the ages of 36 and 42, and 15 (24.6%) were 43 or older. Respecting ethnicity, 51 (83.6%) participants were Caucasian, four (6.6%) participants were African American, three (4.9%) participants were Asian, two (3.3%) participants were Hispanic, and one (1.6%) participant was Other. Forty-four participants (72.1%) were current or former Air Force. Seventeen (27.9%) persons were current or former Army. Twenty-seven persons (44.3%) were Active Duty, 21 persons (34.4%) were Reserve, and 12 persons (19.7%) were National Guard. One person was a civilian.

Instruments

Demographic information was acquired by a researcher-developed demographic questionnaire.

Gender Role. Gender role, the amalgamation of biology, psychology, and sociology was ascertained using the *Bem Sex Role Inventory* (BSRI; Bem, 1974, 1981). Using a Likert methodology, this 60-question self-report inventory identifies the extent to which the respondent believes he or she identifies with Western European/American male and female characteristics presented in the inventory. Quantitative measurement provides an indication of the participant's proclivity to masculine, feminine, undifferentiated, or androgynous gender roles. Undifferentiated persons have neither strong masculine, nor feminine characteristics. Androgynous persons, alternatively, have both strong masculine and feminine characteristics.

The *Bem Sex Role Manual* (Bem, 1978) reports internal consistencies between .75 and .90. Test-retest reliabilities for the masculinity and femininity scales for the original BSRI used in the present investigation were .89 and .76 for males and .82 and .94 for females.

Locus of Control. Perceived locus of control influences benefits and risks of action or inaction; roles, responsibilities, and expectations; resources and impediments; decision-making, and perception, cognition, and response to event outcome. Although a number of other scales have been developed purporting to measure the respondent's perceived position on the continuum from internal to external attribution, the 23-item forced response Rotter I-E

Locus of Control Scale (LOCS) (Rotter, 1966) dominates literature. The LOCS measures the extent to which the respondent attributes outcome of life events to his or her own action/inactions or, alternatively, to the actions/inactions of or powerful others, or even with acceptable validity and reliability. Among a group of Australian students, for example, researchers (Lange & Tiggemann, 1981) found test-retest reliability of the LOCS to be .61; which is better than chance.

Personality. The 240-question Revised NEO Personality Inventory (NEO-PI-R; Costa & McCrae, 1992) measures the five personality domains (neuroticism, extraversion, openness, agreeableness, and conscientiousness) and six supporting facets for each domain using the Five-Factor Model of personality. The NEO-PI-R self-report (S) is answered using a five point Likert scale ranging from *Strongly Disagree* to *Strongly Agree.* In a sample of n=1,539, internal consistency of the NEO was: N= .92, E= .89, O= .87, A= .86, C= .90. Test retest reliability of the NEO PI-R is also good. The test retest reliability reported in the manual of the NEO PI-R over six years was N= .83, E= .82, O= .83, A= .63, C= .79.

Ways of Coping. The Ways of Coping Questionnaire (WCQ; Folkman and Lazarus, 1988) was used to discern the differences in dominant short-term adaptive/long-term adaptive and short-term adaptive/long-term maladaptive coping strategies between males and females, and across the four gender roles. The self-report 66-question WCQ is rated on a 4-point Likert scale, in which 0 reflects *Does not apply or not used* and 3 denotes *Used a great deal.* A higher score indicates more frequent use of a strategy to cope with stress. The internal consistency alpha for each of the eight coping strategies included in the WCQ is 0.73 for Confrontive Coping (CC), 0.76 for Distancing (DI), 0.85 for Self-Control (SC), 0.78 for Social Support-Seeking (SS), 0.75 for Accepting Responsibility (AR), 0.81 for Escape-Avoidance (EA), 0.80 for Planful Problem- Solving (PP), and 0.85 for Positive Reappraisal (PR). Rexrode, Petersen, and O'Toole (2008) found reliability across WCQ subscale scores to range from .60 to .75, with SC demonstrating the most reliability, and PR demonstrating the least.

Traumatic History. Several instruments were considered to intake potentially traumatic experiences occurring during childhood and adulthood. The 12-item self-reported Brief Betrayal Trauma Survey (BBTS; Goldberg & Freyd, 2004) was selected primarily because of its design emphasizing relationship between the perpetrator and victim and relationship between self and the victim of physical, psychological and emotional trauma. The BBTS has good test-retest reliability of 83% for childhood items and 75% for events that occurred during adulthood (Cromer & Freyd, 2007).

Primary Traumatic Event and Associated PTSD symptomology. The traumatic event for which a veteran is referred to medical or mental healthcare providers is not necessarily the primary traumatic event (PTE)—the event by which all other traumatic experiences are gauged. The PTSD Symptom and Diagnostic Scale (Kubany, 2004) was used in the present study to gather data regarding the participants' PTE, whether the outcome of that event met DSM-IV-TR (American Psychiatric Association, 2000) criteria for a diagnosis of PTSD, and the severity of any PTSD symptomatology. This instrument, in conjunction with the data gleaned from the BBTS, provided the researcher with the capability to place all traumatic events within proper context in the mind of the individual. The participant was asked to recall the most traumatic event occurring in his or her life—the event by which he or she evaluates all other types of trauma that have occurred, or will occur, in his or her life. This event was then referred to as his or her *Primary Traumatic Event* (PTE). The PTE was then placed into a hierarchical interval-level progression that considered proximity, intensity, duration, and closeness of the perpetrator and victim as recommended by Costa and McCrae, 1994). Additionally, this methodology considered whether the event was deployment-related and whether it was duty-related or non-duty related. The PSDS methodology provides for the capability to assess each of the DSM-IV-TR criteria for PTSD diagnosis.

Trauma-Related Guilt. The Trauma-Related Guilt Inventory (TRGI; Kubany & Haynes, 2004) continued to explore effects of the PTE. The TRGI consists of three major scales and three subscales. The major scales include *Global Guilt* (GG), *Distress* (DI), and *TGC.* While the GG and DI scales are self-supporting scales, the TGC scale reflects three subscales: *Hindsight Bias, Insufficient Justification,* and *Wrongdoing.*

Procedure

Participants were solicited verbally and via e-mail. Participants were informed that the goal of the study was to better understand the role of biological sex, socially learned gender role, personality domains and facets, locus of control, ways of coping, and prior traumatic or stressful experiences on post-deployment PTSD, trauma-related guilt, and distress. The participants were advised of the benefits and potential risks associated with participation. Participation was strictly voluntary. Each participant was free to discontinue participation at any time prior to assessment submission. They were informed that privacy and confidentiality would be protected to the full extent of the law. Each potential participant was required to sign a letter of Informed Consent prior to completing self-report assessment. In return, the participants were provided a summary/booklet (appendix 1) highlighting his or her individual personality domains and facets, LOC, gender role characterization, top three ways of coping, PTSD scores from the PTSD Symptoms and Diagnostic Scale (PSDS) and summary scores of trauma-related guilt (TRG) as requested/approved by military commanders. The booklet (Appendix A) provided participants with a comprehensive assessment of personality, ways of coping, and biopsychosocial wellbeing that focuses on the *why* of the journalistic *who, what, when, where, why* and *how* than the current intake (Appendix B). Participants were also offered completed study results. Participants completed assessments, both, in groups and individually as preferred/requested.

Each participant was required to read and sign Informed Consent prior to participating to signify his or her understanding of the goals of the study, time required, voluntariness, benefits and risks, privacy and confidentiality limitations, and recourse for researcher violation. Each participant was provided with the battery of self-report instruments, which were either completed in groups or individually depending upon the participant's availability and desires. Participants were offered the opportunity for individualized assessment analysis results (Appendix A).

Data was collected using a researcher developed demographic questionnaire, *Revised NEO Personality Inventory* (NEO-PI-R; Costa & McCrae, 1992), *Bem Sex Role Inventory* (BSRI; Bem, 1974), *Rotter Locus of Control Scale* (LOCS; Rotter; 1966), *Brief Betrayal Trauma Survey* (BBTS; Goldberg & Freyd, 2006), *Ways of Coping Inventory* (WOC; Folkman & Lazarus, 1988), *PTSD Symptom and Diagnostic Scale* (PSDS; Kubany, 2004), and the *Trauma-Related Guilt Inventory* (TRGI; Kubany & Haynes, 2004).

The NEO-PI-R (Costa & McCrae, 1992) assesses the five personality domains – *Neuroticism* (N), *Extraversion* (E), *Openness* (O), *Agreeableness* (A), and *Conscientiousness* (C) – as well as six supporting facets for each of the primary domains. Each participant was assessed to the facet level for the greatest specificity and personality correlation with other study variables. Data from the *NEO-PI-R Self-Report Form* was transferred to the *NEO-PI-R Inventory.* Observing the inventory, the *very low* range was assigned the interval level 1, the *low* range was assigned the interval level 2, the *average* range was assigned the interval level 3, the *high* range was assigned the interval level 4, and the *very high* range was assigned the interval level 5.

The Bem Sex Role Inventory (BSRI) provides the researcher/practitioner with a *feminine* score and a *masculine* score indicating degree to which the respondent possesses Western European/American gender role characteristics. Participants self-rate the degree to which he or she identifies with the item. Response choices range from 1 - *Never or almost never true* to 7- *Always or almost always true.* The masculinity and femininity scales are each comprised of 20 items. The Social Desirability Scale also consists of 20 items. Median masculinity (M) scale scores and femininity (F) scale scores determine gender role. In construction of the instrument, Bem (1977) suggests while above-median scores define androgyny, below-median scores indicate undifferentiation. During this study, the masculine score was subtracted from the feminine score to establish the relative strength of the dominant gender role. Table 2 of the *Bem Sex Role Inventory Manual* (Bem, 1981) was then consulted to derive a *t-score.* The following methodology was then used to classify the respondent as *masculine, feminine, undifferentiated* or *androgynous* (see Fig. 1 on next page). If the feminine score was 10 points or greater than the masculine score, the individual was classified as a predominantly feminine gender role person. If the masculine score was 10 points or greater than the feminine score, the person was classified as a predominantly masculine gender role person. If the feminine score minus the masculine score resulted in a score less than 10 (<+/-10) and the *t-score* was 50 (median score) or less, the person was categorized as undifferentiated (possessing neither strong masculine or feminine characteristics). If the feminine score minus the feminine score resulted in a score less than 10 (<+/-10) and the t-score was 51 or greater, the person was categorized as androgynous (possessing both strong masculine and feminine characteristics). The categorizations were then assigned a nominal value: 1 - *masculine,* 2 - *feminine,* 3 – *undifferentiated;* and 4 - *androgynous.*

The Rotter Locus of Control Scale (LOCS; Rotter, 1966) assesses the degree to which a person believes life event outcome results from his or her actions or inactions (highly internal) or, alternatively, the actions or inactions of powerful or influential others, or even serendipity (highly external). Raw scores on the Rotter Locus of Control were converted to five interval-level categories. The five interval-level categories included 1 - *highly internal* locus of control (1-5), 2 - *moderately internal* locus of control (6-11), 3 - *undifferentiated* (12-13), 4 -*moderately external* locus of control (14-19), and 5 - *highly external* locus of control (20-23).

Trauma related history from the BBTS was catalogued into previously determined categories developed by amalgamation of models developed by Erikson (1975); Goldberg and Freyd (2006); Young, Klosko, and Weishaar (2003); and van der Kolk, McFarlane, and Weisaeth (1996) and subsequently quantified by an algorithm developed by the researcher using these same models which considered: the intrusiveness (physical, psychological, both), age when trauma occurred, closeness perpetrator and victim, and repetitiveness.

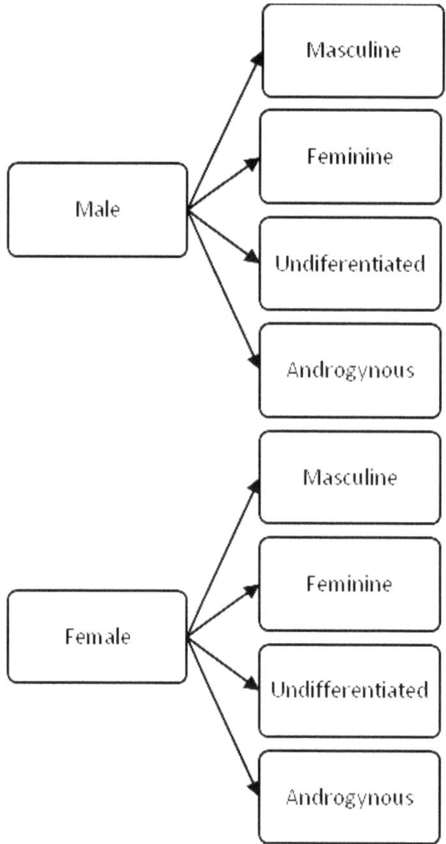

Fig. 1: Biopsychosocial Classifications

The PTE was cataloged according to pre-deployment, deployment duty- or non-duty-related, post-deployment; physical, psychological, or physical and psychological; and close or not close. *PSDS PTSD Score* was tabulated into four categories, 1 - *none to mild symptomology* (0-17), 2 – *mild to moderate symptomology* (18-39), 3 – *moderate to severe symptomology* (40-49), and *severe symptomology* (50-80).

TRGI raw scores were computed on the TRGI Autoscore Form and then transferred to the *TRGI Profile Sheet.* The TRGI Profile Sheet provides a hierarchical representation of the TRGI scores with t-scores ranging from <30 to >80. The researcher in the present study divided the t-scores into six categories: 1 - *No x* (<30-30), 2 - *Slight x* (31-40), 3 - *Mild x* = (41-50), 4 – *Mild to Moderate x*, 5 – *Moderate to Severe x* (51-60), and 6 – *Severe x* (61+). The scores were entered into the database as interval-level variables.

RESULTS

Preliminary analysis

Prior to engaging in further SPSS analysis, the global Gender Role (SR) variable was syntactically divided into four individual gender roles: 1-masculine gender (mgen), 2-feminine gender (fgen), 3-undifferentiated gender (ugen), and 4-androgynous (agen) gender. Sex remained nominally categorized as 1-male and 2-Female.

The first analytical process was then undertaken to investigate whether males were inherently masculine and females were inherently feminine. Logically, the null hypothesis argued males would be inherently masculine and females would be inherently feminine.

Consequently, no differences would exist upon exploration. Hypothesis *H0,* however, hypothesized that men would not be inherently masculine and women would not be inherently feminine. In multivariate analysis (MANOVA), with sex as the independent variable and mgen, fgen, ugen, and agen as the dependent variables and the Bonferonni set at .05, statistical significance was achieved: $F(4, 56)= 5.602$, Wilks' Lambda= .714, $p=.001$. partial eta squared= .286. Examination of the Tests of Between-Subjects Effects reveals all four gender roles are statistically significant positive predictors: mgen $F(1, 61)= 4.852$, $p= .032$, partial eta squared= .076; fgen F(1, 61)= 8.839, $p= .004$, partial eta squared= .130; ugen $F(1, 61)= 5.330$, $p= .024$, partial eta squared= .083; and agen $F(1, 61)= 3.772$, $p= .057$, partial eta squared= .060. In examination of the means, important differences were noted. Substantially more males than females were observed to be masculine. More females than males were observed to be feminine. More males than females were observed to be undifferentiated. More females than males were observed to be androgynous (Table 1).

Table 1: Sex and Gender Role

Gender Role	*Male*	*Female*	*Total*
Masculine	16	5	21 (33.3%)
Feminine	3	10	13 (21.7%)
Undifferentiated	13	3	16 (26.7%)
Androgynous	3	7	10 (16.3%)
Total	35 (58%)	25 (42%)	60 (100%)

Regressions

Hierarchical regressions were conducted to examine the relationship(s) between personality domains and facets, PTSD symptom severity, global guilt, total guilt cognitions, and distress (See Figure 2):

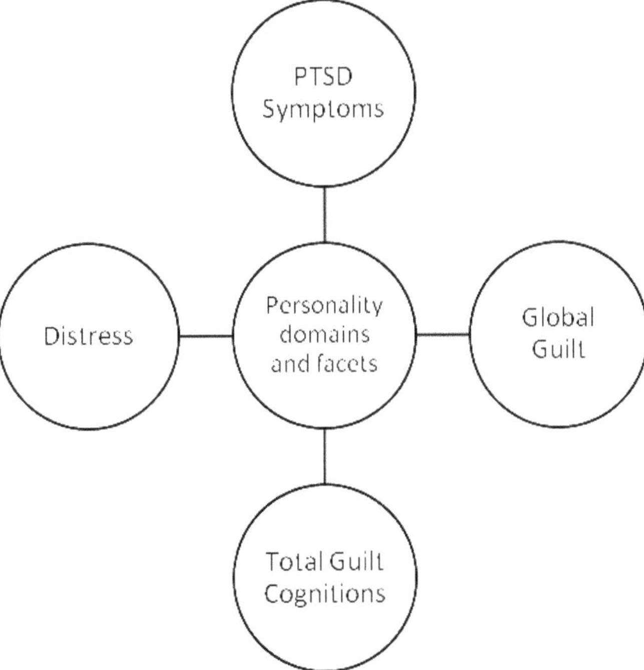

Fig. 2: Personality and PTSD, trauma-related guilt (TRG), and distress

In multivariate analysis (MANOVA), with biological sex and gender role as independent variables and the five personality domains—N, E, O, A, and C—as dependent variables, biological sex did not reach statistical significance. However, gender role did reach statistical significance F(15, 133)= 1.926, Wilks' Lambda=.581, p=.026, partial eta squared= .166. The *sex*gr* term did not reach statistical significance. Examining the means, the mean score for neuroticism (N) for masculine males was 3.25/5.0 (n=16; SD=.775). Alternatively, the mean score for feminine females was 3.9/5.0 (n=10; SD=1.287). Feminine females (n=10) presented a higher mean score (3.9/5.0) for neuroticism than masculine (n=5; mean=3.00), undifferentiated (n=3; mean-3.33), and androgynous (n=7; mean=2.27) counterparts. Feminine males (n=3) reported the highest mean score for neuroticism (mean=3.67; SD=1.528) among males. In both males and females, androgynous persons (male n=3; female=7) reported the lowest mean score of neuroticism (*M* mean=3.00/SD 2.00; *F* mean= 2.57/SD 1.272). Thus, gender role appears to be a more valid predictor of N than biological sex.

In regression analysis, however, with biological sex in block 1; mgen, fgen, ugen, and agen in block 2; and with neuroticism (N) as the dependent variable, neither the combined nor the independent variables reached statistical significance. When investigating at the supporting facet level, self-consciousness (N5) the combined variables of sex and gender role neared statistical significance: R^2=.174, Adj. R^2=.099, R^2 *Ch.*= .167, *F Ch.*=2.788, *F*=2.325, *p*=.055. Examined separately, none of the individual variables were statistically significant. Impulsiveness approached statistical significance: R^2=.165, Adj. R^2=.08, R^2 *Ch.*= .151, *F Ch.*=2.481, *F*=2.17, *p*=.070. Sufficient inferential evidence is presented regarding the distinction of biological sex and biopsychosocially derived gender in relationship to neuroticism to continue with examination of the relationship between biological sex, gender role, personality, locus of control ways of coping, PTSD symptom severity, trauma-related guilt, and distress.

The next question investigated the differences in ways of coping between males and females, and persons of the four gender role types. The null hypothesis, that which would support the MHAT findings, was that no significant difference would exist between males and females. H0 argued androgynous persons would possess the most highly evolved short-term adaptive/long-term adaptive coping strategies by virtue of his or her biological, psychological, and sociological adeptness. H1 argued masculine males would engage greater confrontive coping reliance than their androgynous, feminine, and undifferentiated counterparts. H2 argued undifferentiated males and females would report the least arsenal of long-term adaptive coping strategies; relying instead on emotional short-term adaptive/long-term maladaptive coping strategies. H3 argued sex/gender-role congruence among females would result in greater short-term adaptive/long-term adaptive coping strategy reliance. The results are presented in the following table (Table 2):

Table 2: Ways of Coping Means

Coping Strategy	male	female	mgen	fgen	ugen	Agen
Confrontive	1.1658/ .66235	.9787/ .45200	1.1229/ .49256	1.0618/ .58267	1.2493/ .72694	.8460/ .51863
Distancing	1.0426/ .69672	1.0355/ .70387	.9838/ .60020	1.1382/ .97060	.9751/ .64708	1.1960/ .58039
Self-Control	1.5219/ .54844	1.4089/ .47312	1.3833/ .53540	1.4581/ .37920	1.3509/ .59824	1.9107/ .28004
Social Support-Seeking	1.3904/ .73240	1.2924/ .79439	1.0690/ .69291	1.5551/ .83390	1.3977/ .85753	1.6243/ .50158
Accepting Responsibility	.8529/ .83284	.8877/ .57492	.7857/ .62393	1.0577/ .81108	.7053/ .87786	1.0250/ .61745
Escape/Avoidance	.8782/ .51666	.7476/ .90716	.7476/ .90716	.8262/ .40601	.7437/ .77421	.8120/ .59486
Planful Problem-Solving	1.7115/ .63414	1.4088/ .67003	1.6052/ .76110	1.7623/ .49068	1.3713/ .61070	1.7130/ .64165
Positive Reappraisal	1.0304/ .74868	1.0137/ .74619	.7317/ .76480	1.1738 .63577	1.1017/ .75770	1.3530 .70527

In examination of H0, while feminine persons presented the highest level of planful problem-solving (figure 3), androgynous persons reported substantially greater deftness than their masculine and undifferentiated counterparts. Androgynous persons, however, reported the most highly evolved reliance upon social support-seeking. Androgynous persons also reported the highest reliance upon positive reappraisal. Thus, H0 is satisfied.

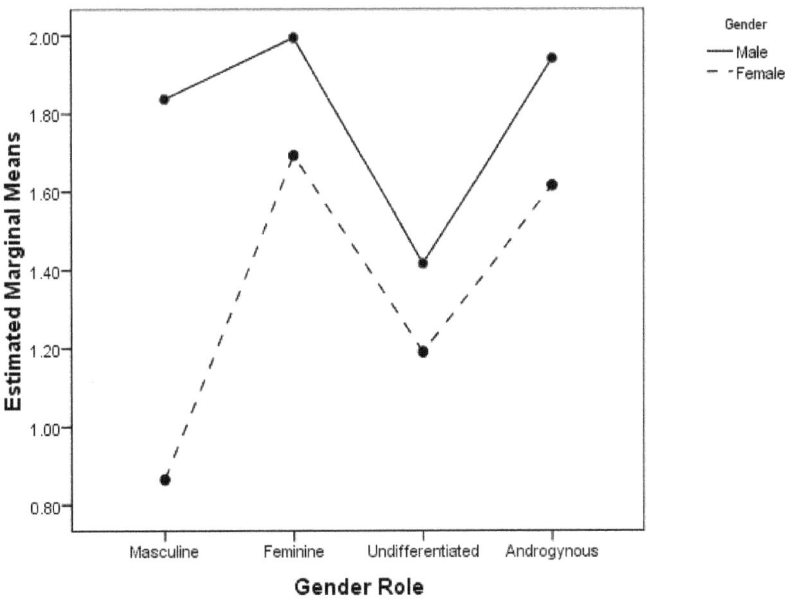

Fig. 3. Gender role means adeptness of planful problem-solving.

In examination of H1, undifferentiated male gender role oriented persons presented the greatest reliance upon confrontive coping (See Figure 4), followed by masculine male persons. Androgynous male gender role persons, followed by undifferentiated female persons, reported the least reliance upon confrontive coping. While the null hypothesis was refuted, it was, in fact, undifferentiated male persons who rely most highly on confrontive coping. Thirteen of the 35 males (37%) in this study are categorized as undifferentiated. Masculine males, however, report the second highest reliance upon confrontive coping. Sixteen of the 35 males (47%) are categorized as masculine.

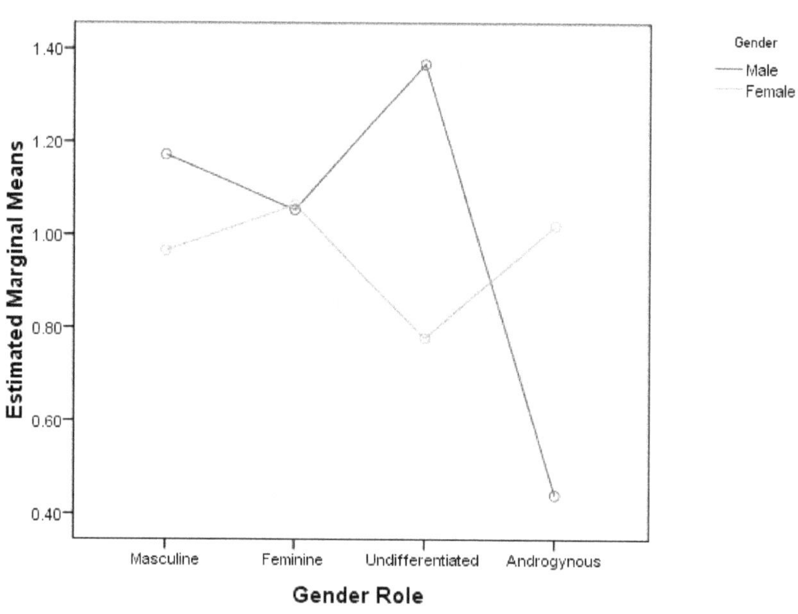

Figure 4. Gender role adeptness of confrontive coping.

In examination of H2, undifferentiated persons reported the least adeptness in planful problem-solving. However, the masculine gender role reported less reliance than the undifferentiated gender role in social support-seeking and positive reappraisal. When short-term adaptive/long-term maladaptive coping strategies are observed, however, both masculine and feminine gender role persons demonstrated greater deftness in distancing; undifferentiated persons reported decidedly less deftness in self-control; undifferentiated persons reported the least responsibility acceptance; and undifferentiated persons reported less escape/avoidance than both masculine and feminine gender roles.

In examination of H3, feminine females reported greater deftness in self-control (See Figure 5) than their masculine female counterparts, greater adeptness in social support-seeking, and greater planful problem-solving abilities.

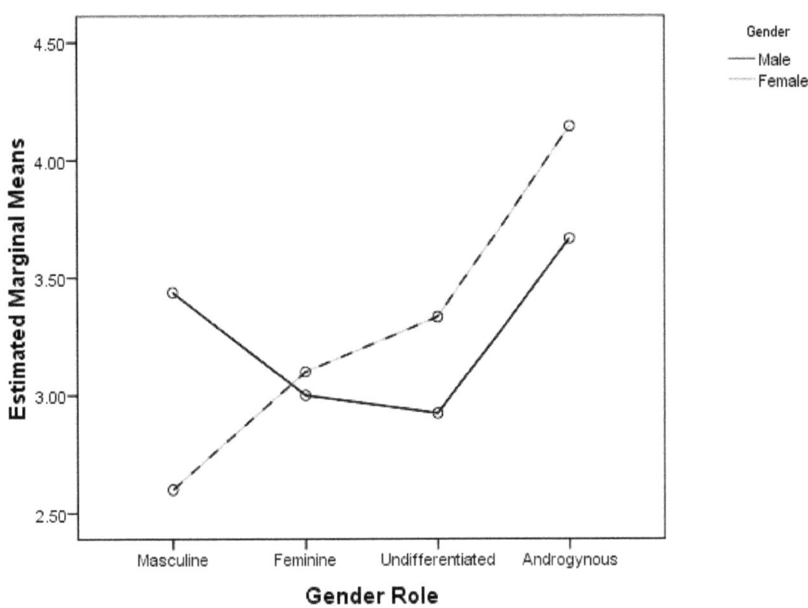

Fig. 5: Gender role adeptness at self-controlling coping.

No statistically significant observations are made regarding sex, gender, and locus of control.

In exploration of the relationship(s) between the personality domains and PTSD symptom severity, trauma-related guilt, and distress, neuroticism (N) was a statistically significant positive predictor of PTSD symptom severity (Table 3), global guilt (Table 4), total guilt cognitions (Table 5), and distress Table 6). Persons scoring high in neuroticism (N) are generally anxious, apprehensive, and prone to worry.

Table 3: N Facets and PTSD Symptom Severity

Model	R^2	*Adj.* R^2	R^2 *Change*	*F Change*	*F*	*F Sig.*
1	.022	.004	.022	1.253	1.253	.268[a]
2	.037	-.055	.016	.211	.405	.843[b]
3	.383	.236	.346	4.298	2.599	.012[c]

a. Predictors: (Constant), Biological sex

b. Predictors: (Constant), Biological sex, agen, ugen, fgen, mgen

c. Predictors: (Constant), Biological sex, agen, ugen, fgen, mgen, Angry Hostility, Impulsiveness, Depression, Self-Consciousness, Vulnerability, Anxiety

d. Dependent Variable: PTSD Symptoms

Table 4: N Facets and Global Guilt

Model	R^2	*Adj.* R^2	R^2 *Change*	*F Change*	*F*	*F Sig.*
1	.028	.010	.028	1.577	1.577	.214[a]
2	.057	-.036	.029	.393	.616	.688[b]
3	.326	.162	.269	2.997	1.981	.054[c]

a. Predictors: (Constant), Biological sex

b. Predictors: (Constant), Biological sex, agen, ugen, fgen, mgen

c. Predictors: (Constant), Biological sex, mgen, agen, fgen, ugen, Anxiety, Self-Consciousness, Impulsiveness, Angry Hostility, Depression, Vulnerability

d. Dependent Variable: Global Guilt

Table 5 N Facets and Total Guilt Cognitions

Model	R^2	*Adj.* R^2	R^2 *Change*	*F Change*	*F*	*F Sig.*
1	.038	.021	.038	2.185	2.185	.145[a]
2	.107	.019	.068	.976	1.217	.315[b]
3	.329	.164	.222	2.480	2.002	.051[c]

a. Predictors: (Constant), Biological sex

b. Predictors: (Constant), Biological sex, agen, ugen, fgen, mgen

c. Predictors: (Constant), Biological sex, mgen, agen, fgen, ugen, Anxiety, Self-Consciousness, Impulsiveness, Angry Hostility, Depression, Vulnerability

d. Dependent Variable: Total Guilt Cognitions

Table 6 N Facets and Distress

Model	R^2	*Adj.* R^2	R^2 *Change*	*F Change*	*F*	*F Sig.*
1	.001	-.017	.001	.077	.077	.783[a]
2	.023	-.073	.022	.282	.240	.943[b]
3	.410	.266	.387	4.915	2.841	.007[c]

a. Predictors: (Constant), Biological sex

b. Predictors: (Constant), Biological sex, agen, ugen, fgen, mgen

c. Predictors: (Constant), Biological sex, mgen, agen, fgen, ugen, Anxiety, Self-Consciousness, Impulsiveness, Angry Hostility, Depression, Vulnerability

d. Dependent Variable: Distress

The combined Agreeableness (A; Table 7) facets reached statistical significance in relationship to PTSD. Agreeable persons generally trust others and assume well-meaning motivation. Agreeable persons are generally sincere. They tend to place the needs of others before himself or herself. He or she is generally proud of himself or herself and his or her accomplishments. He or she is often viewed as hard-headed and opinionated. His or her opinions often reflect pragmatism.

Table 7. A Facets and PTSD Symptoms

Model	R^2	*Adj.* R^2	R^2 *Change*	*F Change*	*F*	*F Sig.*
1	.022	.004	.022	1.253	1.253	.268[a]
2	.037	-.055	.016	.211	.405	.843[b]
3	.518	.402	.480	7.632	4.488	.000[c]

a. Predictors: (Constant), Biological sex

b. Predictors: (Constant), Biological sex, agen, ugen, fgen, mgen

c. Predictors: (Constant), Biological sex, agen, ugen, fgen, mgen, Straightforwardness, Trust, Modesty, Altruism, Tender-Mindedness, Compliance

d. Dependent Variable: PTSD Symptoms

Examination at a greater level of specificity, specifically at the domain supporting facet level, revealed depression (N3), altruism (A3), and modesty (A5) were significant positive predictors of PTSD symptom severity. Of note, depression on the NEO-PI-R does not denote the presence of clinical depression at the time of survey. Rather, it measures the predisposition towards depressive affect. Persons scoring high in the depression (N3) scale are more prone than low scorers are to feelings of guilt, sadness, hopelessness, and loneliness. Highly altruistic persons have an active concern for the welfare of others. Persons scoring low in altruism, conversely, are self-centered and reluctant to become involved in the problems of others. High scorers in modesty tend to be humble and self-effacing. High scorers, alternatively, tend to be seen as arrogant and conceited by others. Extremely low scorers are the basis for a diagnosis of narcissism.

Gregariousness (E2), positive emotions (E6), straightforwardness (A2), compliance (A4), and deliberation (C6) were significant negative predictors of PTSD symptom severity. The positive emotions scale assesses the tendency to experience such positive emotions as joy, happiness, love, and excitement. Persons scoring high in positive emotions are generally cheerful and optimistic. Persons scoring low are not necessarily unhappy; however, they experience less happiness and joy in their life. Straightforward individuals are blunt, sincere, and ingenuous. Persons scoring low in straightforwardness are more prone to manipulate others through false praise, flattery, or deception. Compliance refers to the reaction to interpersonal stress or conflict. High-scorers tend to defer to the opinion of others as a means to avoid conflict. Low scorers are aggressive, competitive, and readily express anger or displeasure. Deliberation refers to the tendency to analyze the task at hand, consider options, create a plan, identify resources, assess risk, and plan for adverse outcome. Low scorers tend to be impetuous and often speak or act without considering consequences.

The combined facets of neuroticism (N; Table 8), extraversion (E; Table 9), and openness (O; Table 10) were significant positive predictors of global guilt (GG).

Table 8: N Facets and Global Guilt

Model	R^2	*Adj.* R^2	R^2 *Change*	*F Change*	*F*	*F Sig.*
1	.028	.010	.028	1.577	1.577	.214[a]
2	.057	-.036	.029	.393	.616	.688[b]
3	.326	.162	.269	2.997	1.981	.054[c]

a. Predictors: (Constant), Biological sex
b. Predictors: (Constant), Biological sex, agen, ugen, fgen, mgen
c. Predictors: (Constant), Biological sex, mgen, agen, fgen, ugen, Anxiety, Self-Consciousness, Impulsiveness, Angry Hostility, Depression, Vulnerability
d. Dependent Variable: Global Guilt

Table 9: E Facets and Global Guilt

Model	R^2	*Adj.* R^2	R^2 *Change*	*F Change*	*F*	*F Sig.*
1	.028	.010	.028	1.577	1.577	.214[a]
2	.057	-.036	.029	.393	.616	.688[b]
3	.343	.183	.286	3.267	2.137	.037[c]

a. Predictors: (Constant), Biological sex
b. Predictors: (Constant), Biological sex, agen, ugen, fgen, mgen
c. Predictors: (Constant), Biological sex, mgen, agen, fgen, ugen, Gregariousness, Excitement-Seeking, Activity, Positive Emotions, Warmth, Assertiveness
d. Dependent Variable: Global Guilt

Table 10: O Facets and Global Guilt

Model	R^2	*Adj.* R^2	R^2 *Change*	*F Change*	*F*	*F Sig.*
1	.028	.010	.028	1.577	1.577	.214[a]
2	.057	-.036	.029	.393	.616	.688[b]
3	.321	.155	.264	2.916	2.137	.037[c]

a. Predictors: (Constant), Biological sex
b. Predictors: (Constant), Biological sex, agen, ugen, fgen, mgen
c. Predictors: (Constant), Biological sex, mgen, agen, fgen, ugen, Feelings, Ideas, Actions, Values, Fantasy, Aesthetics
d. Dependent Variable: Global Guilt

Modesty (A5) was a significant positive predictor of GG. Gregariousness (E2), positive emotions (E6), [willingness to reexamine] ideas (O5), and straightforwardness (A2) were significant negative predictors of GG. Actions (O4) neared statistical significance. Gregariousness refers to the preference for the company of others. High scorers tend to enjoy the company of others. Low scorers, alternatively, tend to be solitary individuals, and loners.

The combined facets of Neuroticism (N; Table 11) and Agreeableness (A; Table 12) were significant positive predictors of total guilt cognitions (TGC).

Table 11: N Facets and Total Guilt Cognitions

Model	R^2	*Adj.* R^2	R^2 *Change*	*F Change*	*F*	*F Sig.*
1	.038	.021	.038	2.185	2.185	.145[a]
2	.107	.019	.068	.976	1.217	.315[b]
3	.329	.164	.222	2.480	2.002	.051[c]

a. Predictors: (Constant), Biological sex
b. Predictors: (Constant), Biological sex, agen, ugen, fgen, mgen
c. Predictors: (Constant), Biological sex, mgen, agen, fgen, ugen, Anxiety, Self-Consciousness, Impulsiveness, Angry Hostility, Depression, Vulnerability
d. Dependent Variable: Total Guilt Cognitions

The combined variables of openness (O) neared statistical significance. In the model exploring extraversion and total guilt cognitions, the undifferentiated gender role (ugen) was a significant positive predictor of TGC. Modesty (A5) was a significant positive predictor of TGC. Positive emotions (E6), [willingness to reexamine] ideas, and compliance (A4) were significant negative predictors of TGC.

The combined variables in the model exploring sex, gender roles, the O facets, and distress (Table 12) reached statistical significance.

Table 12: O Facets and Distress

Model	R^2	*Adj.* R^2	R^2 *Change*	*F Change*	*F*	*F Sig.*
1	.001	-.017	.001	.077	.077	.783[a]
2	.023	-.073	.022	.282	.240	.943[b]
3	.332	.169	.309	3.475	2.037	.047[c]

a. Predictors: (Constant), Biological sex
b. Predictors: (Constant), Biological sex, agen, ugen, fgen, mgen
c. Predictors: (Constant), Biological sex, mgen, agen, fgen, ugen, Feelings, Ideas, Actions, Values, Fantasy, Aesthetics
d. Dependent Variable: Distress

In examination of the coefficients in exploration of the E facets, biological sex was the sole significant predictor. In examination of distress, depression (N3) was also a significant positive predictor of distress. Positive emotions (E6), [openness to] feelings (O3), [opens to new] actions (O4), and [willingness to reexamine] ideas (O5) were significant negative predictors of distress.

Finally, in the exploration of sex, gender roles, and ways of coping in relationship to PTSD symptom severity, trauma-related guilt, and distress, the combined ways of coping failed to reach statistical significance in relationship to PTSD symptom severity. However, in examination of the coefficients, escape/avoidance (EA) was a statistical predictor of PTSD symptom severity.

In relationship to global guilt, the combined variables reached statistical significance (Table 13). In examination of the coefficients, biological sex reached statistical significance in relationship to GG. Positive reappraisal was a statistically significant negative predictor of GG. Confrontive coping neared negative statistical significance.

Table 13: Ways of Coping and Global Guilt

Model	R^2	*Adj.* R^2	R^2 *Change*	*F Change*	*F*	*F Sig.*
1	.024	.006	.024	1.322	1.322	.255[a]
2	.060	-.034	.036	.482	.640	.670[b]
3	.400	.214	.340	2.969	2.151	.031[c]

a. Predictors: (Constant), Biological sex

b. Predictors: (Constant), Biological sex, agen, ugen, fgen, mgen

c. Predictors: (Constant), Biological sex, agen, ugen, fgen, mgen, Distancing, Confrontive Coping, Escape-Avoidance, Positive Reappraisal, Accepting Responsibility, Planful Problem-Solving, Social-Support-Seeking, Self-Controlling

d. Dependent Variable: Global Guilt

In relationship to total guilt cognitions, the combined variables reached statistical significance (Table 14). In examination of the coefficients, biological sex was a significant predictor. Escape/avoidance approached positive statistical significance.

Table 14: Ways of Coping and Total Guilt Cognitions

Model	R^2	*Adj.* R^2	R^2 *Change*	*F Change*	*F*	*F Sig.*
1	.032	.014	.032	1.779	1.779	.188[a]
2	.112	.024	.080	1.133	1.266	.293[b]
3	.401	.216	.289	2.532	2.164	.030[c]

a. Predictors: (Constant), Biological sex

b. Predictors: (Constant), Biological sex, agen, ugen, fgen, mgen

c. Predictors: (Constant), Biological sex, agen, ugen, fgen, mgen, Distancing, Confrontive Coping, Escape-Avoidance, Positive Reappraisal, Accepting Responsibility, Planful Problem-Solving, Social-Support-Seeking, Self-Controlling

d. Dependent Variable: Total Guilt Cognitions

No statistical significance was observed in relationship to distress.

DISCUSSION

Erikson clearly defined eight phases of a person's psychosocial development from birth to late adulthood with general age approximations for each phase. Of salience to the present discussion, Young (in Young, Klosko, & Weishaar, 2003) theorizes that within each of these phases, persons develop schemas for interaction with life events based upon his or her existing and imminent needs, such as those elucidated in Maslow's hierarchy. Maslow argued persons ascend a hierarchy from basic physiological needs; through safety needs; needs for love, affection, and belonging; needs for esteem; and, finally, the need for self-actualization. Unlike Erikson's progression, however, Maslow argued need attainment and satisfaction is not perpetually guaranteed. In fact, a person might ascend and descend the hierarchy many times during his or her life. Likewise, no assurance is made that the pinnacle of self-actualization will ever be achieved. Traumatic or overwhelmingly stressful events might debase the individual and cause him or her to rapidly descend to the most foundational levels of physiological or safety needs, where he or she will remain until he or she perceives the level to, once again, be satisfied. The meaning and significance of this equilibrium-debasing event is self-determined, based upon innate and socially learned needs, morals, ethics, and values.

Unfortunately, some, if not many of the persons entering the contemporary military, as evidenced by delineation of traumatic history and identification of his or her primary traumatic event (PTE), do so as a venue to extricate themselves from adverse environments. Thus, his or her perch on Maslow's hierarchy is precarious at best. Additionally, Arnett (2000) argues persons within the age range from 18 to 25 are in a stage of life referred to as *Emerging Adulthood.* The researcher in the present study argues that it is during this phase that persons engage in development of psychological contracts (Rousseau, 1996)—perceived mutual perception of accepted morals, ethics, and values, and rules, roles, policies, and procedures—from which he or she views, understands, and responds to others in personal and professional relationships.

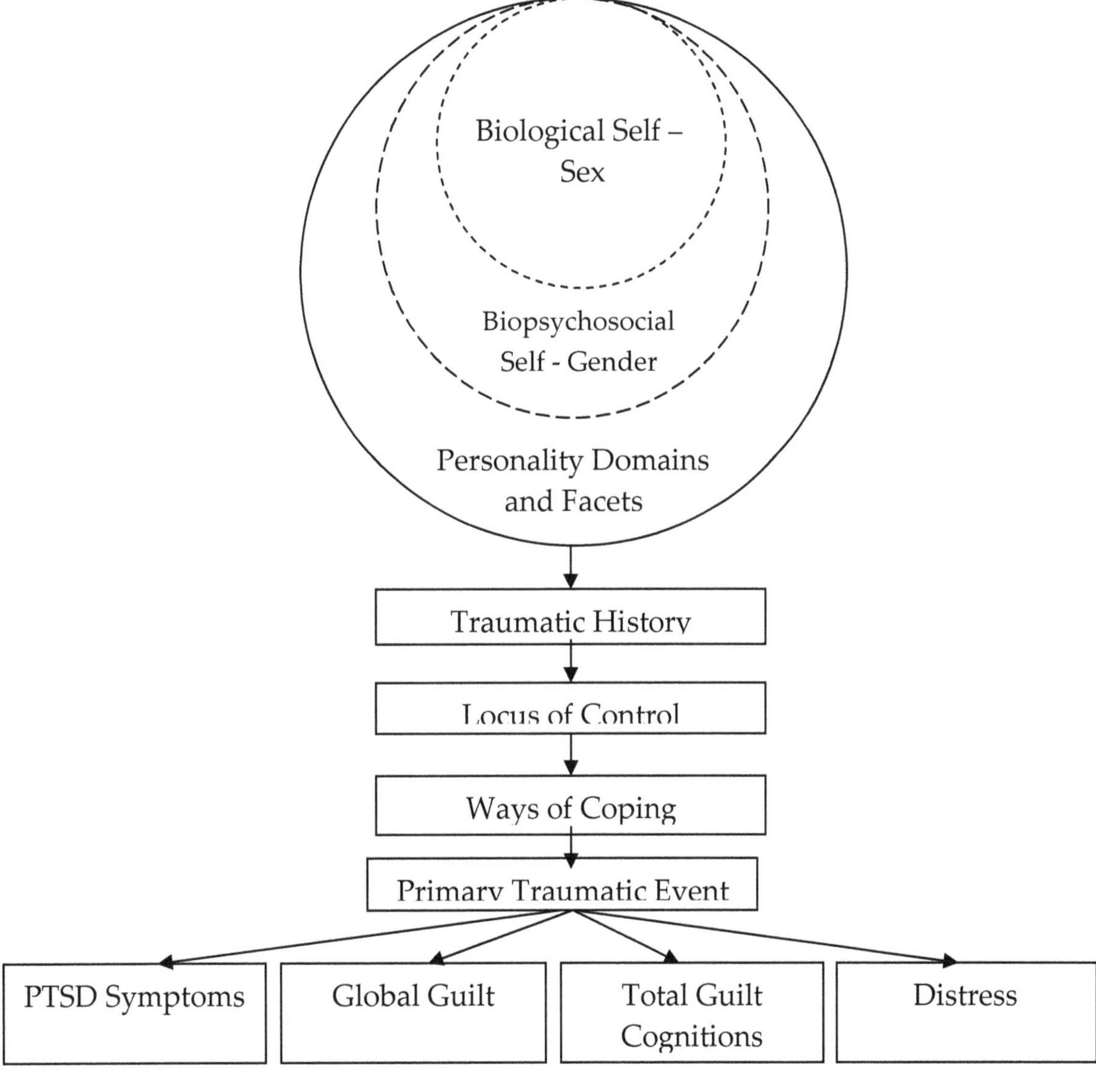

Fig-6: Revised Hensley Military Wellbeing Assessment Protocol

At the most basic level, this psychological contract is the foundation of internal and external attribution for life event outcome. At the more protracted level, this psychological contract serves as the basis for perception of self-efficacy or helplessness; equitability and fairness; and trust, distrust, and betrayal—pivotal to the establishment of PTSD, betrayal trauma, trauma-related guilt, and debilitating distress. In view of the empirical findings of this investigation, the researcher argues PTSD is not merely the consequence of sensory perception of blood, guts, and gore. Rather, PTSD, betrayal trauma, trauma-related guilt resulting in distress is the consequence of individual biopsychosocially-derived meaning of the event. Both independently and in combination, sex, gender role, personality, and ways of coping predict PTSD symptom severity, trauma-related guilt, and debilitating distress. The researcher proposes the Hensley Military Wellbeing and Assessment Protocol (MWAP; See Figure 6) as a viable solution to assess pre- and post-deployment-related wellbeing.

The MHAT IV (USA OSG, 2007) asserts no overall gender differences between men and women participating in the study. However, when the level of combat was considered differences emerged. Specifically, proportionally more women Soldiers in low-combat conditions presented mental health problems than male Soldiers. However, the study offers no potential explanations for this anomaly. Using the MWAP in the current investigation the researcher offers a plausible explanation.

Case 1 (Appendix C) provides a clinical assessment of a male Soldier who experienced extensive repetitive combat-associated trauma based exclusively on self-report using the previously identified study instruments. The veteran exhibits a profile supporting a diagnosis of Chronic PTSD in accordance with the criteria set forth in the DSM-IV-TR (American Psychiatric Association, 2000).

Case 2 (Appendix D) reflects a male veteran asserting to be afflicted with PTSD based upon generalized combat deployment. However, his assertions are not supported by his MWAP profile. Additionally, the Primary Traumatic Event (PTE) lacks the specificity to generate traumatic or stressful stigma, invariantly described by others meeting the MWAP profile for PTSD diagnosis.

Case 3 (Appendix E) reflects a female Soldier who would have been categorized as low-combat in the MHAT IV. In a pure sense, the MHAT IV assertions would have been literally valid in that her trauma comes not from combat exposure. Rather, her PTSD-evoking distress results from sexual assault/rape by a superior unit member, in which her psychological contract would have defined her perpetrator as a trusted individual necessary for survival in a gender role incongruent environment. Allard, Freyd, and Goldberg (2005) argue this psychological contract of trust predisposes the victim to higher levels of anxiety, depression, and dissociation than trauma caused by non-close persons. Her personality profile portrays a person with extremely high neuroticism (N) facets accompanied by stereotypical extremely low conscientiousness (C) facets. She also presents two highly developed short-term adaptive/long-term maladaptive coping strategies—escape avoidance and accepting responsibility, which predisposes her to such maladaptive self-soothing coping as promiscuity, alcohol and drug abuse, poor self-esteem associated behavior and peer-induced antisocial behavior.

Case 4 (Appendix F) reflects a female Soldier who would also have been categorized as low combat. This veteran's trauma, likewise, was not combat-related. Rather, she, too, was the victim of sexual assault/rape by a fellow unit member. Unlike the female soldier presented in Case 3, who self-reported a more prophylactic androgynous gender role orientation, this female soldier self-reports a decidedly masculine gender role orientation. Unfortunately, female soldiers with a masculine gender role orientation are unlikely to engage in social interaction or social-support-seeking with other female or male Soldiers. Additionally, females with masculine gender role orientation are unlikely to engage in short-term adaptive/long-term adaptive coping strategies. Using a median score of 1.5 on a 3.0 scale, this veteran possesses, overall, poor short-term adaptive/long-term adaptive and short-term adaptive/long-term maladaptive coping strategies. Specifically, her three most dominant coping strategies were: social support-seeking (1.16/3.00), confrontive coping (1.00/3.00), and distancing (1.00/3.00). The MWAP, then, provides the journalistic *who, what, when, where,* and *how* from which to assess, intervene, and treat her PTE; a cognitive dissonance evoking pursuit of why. This PTE would not have been apparent in the current assessment protocol. Thus, practitioners would be engaging in prolonged intervention based upon symptomology, rather than the insidious, endemic cause resulting from the PTE.

The combined cases presented identify, not only the strengths of the MWAP in assessment, but also personality variables that should be considered in intervention and treatment. The MWAP also provides probable impediments to treatment or intervention.

LIMITATIONS

The results presented in this paper are based upon preliminary results, which perhaps do not reflect analysis of final data. The outcome of the present investigation was greatly inhibited/impeded by the junior and senior leadership of many Army Reserve and National Guard Commands and units, as well as research staff at Midwestern Veterans Healthcare Administration Regional Offices. Additionally, several current active duty, Reserve, and National Guard military members declined to participate, citing their primary reason as fear that military commanders would obtain the information.

RECOMMENDATIONS

The present study provides a baseline insight into key factors that might be invaluable to development of preventative training and education, intra-deployment intervention, and post deployment assessment and treatment programs. The researcher in the current investigation intends to conduct similar investigations from which to contrast military and non-military populations. Additionally, one or more repeated measures studies assessing wellbeing prior to and following deployment would be invaluable to assess stability of personality, locus of control, and ways of coping variables during an often gender role incongruent deployment. Additionally, the MWAP might prove invaluable in assessing predispositional factors in crisis response, law enforcement, and similar personnel. An electronic assessment instrument is being developed by the researcher in this study to more accurately and succinctly address the observed relationships, while furthering the holistic relational understanding of such other factors as *heritance,* which is currently included in the PCL-M (Appendix B).

ACKOWLEDGEMENTS

The researcher in this study would like to thank the 61 anonymous study participants. Special appreciation is given to the three women and one man participating in this study who endured sexual assault/rape during deployment and others who experienced sexual assault prior to deployment for the invaluable added insight into your biopsychosocial dilemmas.

REFERENCES

Allard, C.B., Freyd, J.J., & Goldberg, L.R. (2005). *Are all traumatic events equal? Further research using the BBTS.* Poster presented at the 21st Annual Meeting of the International Society for Traumatic Stress Studies, Toronto, Ontario, Canada, November 2-5, 2005.

Aquilino, W.S. (2001). *Long-term effects of single versus multiple family disruptions on young adult well-being.* Rochester: The Annual National Council on Family Relations.

Aquilino, W.S., & Supple, A.J. (2001). Long-term effects of parenting practices during adolescence on well-being outcomes in young adulthood. *Journal of Family Issues, 22(3),* 289-308.

American Psychiatric Association. (2000). Diagnostic and statistical manual of mental disorders: dsm-iv-tr. Washington, DC: Author.

Arnett, J.J. (2000). Emerging adulthood: a theory of development from the late teens through the twenties. *American Psychologist, 55,* 469-480.

Bem S.L. (1974). The measure of psychological androgyny. *Journal of Consulting and Clinical Psychology, 42 -2,* 155-162.

Bem, S.L. (1981). Gender schema theory: A cognitive account of sex typing source. *Psychological Review, 88,* 354.

Castro, C.A. & Hoge, C.W., (2002). *Psychological impact of modern warfare: The WRAIR Land Combat Study Symposium.* American Psychological Association Annual Convention. Washington, D.C. August 18-21, 2005.

Condry, J. & Simon, M.L. (1974). Characteristics of peer- and parent-oriented children. *Journal of Marriage and the Family, 36,* 543-554.

Costa, P.T., Jr., & McCrae, R.R. (1992). *NEO PI-R professional manual.* Odessa, FL: Psychological Assessment Resources, Inc.

Cowan, P.A., Powell, D. & Cowan, C.P. (1988). Parenting interventions: a family systems Perspective. In W. Damon, I.E., Sigell, & K.A. (Eds.), *Handbook of Child Psychology, Vol. 4: Child Psychology in Practice* (pp. 3-72). NY: Wiley.

Cromer, L.D., & Freyd, J.J. (2007). *What influences believing child sexual abuse? The roles of depicted memory persistence, participant gender, trauma history, and sexism.* Psychology of Women Quarterly, 31(1), 13-22.

Deshler, D.D., Schumaker, J.B., & Lenz, B.K. (1984). Academic and cognitive interventions for LD adolescents: I). *Journal of Learning Disabilities, 17(2),* 108-117.

Erikson, E.H. (1975). Life history and the historical moment. NY: Norton.

Folkman. S., & Lazarus, R.S. (1988). *Manual for the Ways of Coping Questionnaire.* Palo Alto, CA: Consulting Psychologists Press.

Goldberg, LR. & Freyd, J.J. (2006). Self-reports of potentially traumatic experiences in an adult community sample: Gender differences and test-retest stabilities of the items in a Brief Betrayal-Trauma Survey. *Journal of Trauma & Dissociation,* 7(3), 39-63.

Hawley, G.A. (1988). *Measures of Psychosocial Development Manual.* Odessa: Psychological Assessments Resources.

Kimerling, R., Gima, K., Smith, M.W., Street, A., & Frayne, S. (2007). The Veterans Health Administration and military sexual trauma. *American Journal of Public Health, 97(12),* 2160-2166.

Klein, H.A., O'Bryant, K., & Hopkins, H. R. (1996). Recalled parental authority style and self-perception in college men and women. *Journal of Genetic Psychology, 157,* 5-17.

Lange, R.V, & Tiggemann, M. (1981). Dimensionality and reliability of the Rotter I-E locus of control scale. *Journal of Personality Assessment, 45(4),* 398-406.

Lazarus, R.S., & Folkman, S. (1984). *Stress, Appraisal, Coping.* New York: Springer.

Lefcourt, H.M. (1976). *Locus of Control: Current Trends in Theory and Research* (2nd Ed.). Hillsdale: Lawrence Erlbaum Associates.

McCombs, B. (1991). *Metacognition and Motivation in Higher Level Thinking.* Paper presented at the annual meeting of the American Educational Research Association, Chicago.

Pervin, L.A. (2004). *Personality: Theory and research* (9th ed.). New York: Wiley and sons.

Pervin, L., John, O.P., & Robins, R.W. (2008). *Handbook of personality* (3rd ed.). New York The Guilford Press.

Rexrode, K.R., Petersen, S., & O'Toole, S. (2008). *The Ways of Coping Scale.* Educational and Psychological Measurement, 68(2), 262-280.

Rotter, J.B. (1966). Generalized expectancies of internal versus external control of reinforcements. *Psychological Monographs, 80* (whole no. 609).

Rousseau, D.M. (1996). *Psychological Contracts in Organizations: Understanding Written and Unwritten Agreements*. Newbury Park, CA: Sage.

Steinberg, L. (1987). Single parents, stepparents, and the susceptibility of adolescents to antisocial peer pressure. *Child Development, 58,* 269-275.

Strage, A. & Brandt, T.S. (1999). Authoritative parenting and college students' academic adjustment and success. *Journal of Educational Psychology, 91(1),* 146-156.

Van der Kolk, B.A., McFarlane, A.C., & Weisaeth, L. (1996). *Traumatic stress: the effects of overwhelming experience on mind, body, and society.* New York: The Guilford Press.

Young, J.E., Klosko, J.S., & Weishaar, M. (2003). *Schema Therapy: A Practitioner's Guide*. New York: Guilford Publications.

APPENDIX A

Individualized Personality, Coping, and Wellness Survey Result Summary

Based upon the Hensley Model of Biological, Psychological, and Sociological (Biopsychosocial) Model of Military Wellbeing

Note: The results noted in this study are the result of self-report instruments and should not be considered to be a clinical assessment. This summary should be considered to be a tool to provide you and your clinical practitioner with diagnostic data, based upon psychological community-recognized instruments, from which to provide optimal preventative, interventional, and therapeutic assistance.

DEMOGRAPHIC INFORMATION

Confidential Research Code: __________________ **Date Survey Taken:** __________________

Gender: Male: _________ Female: _________

Age:
____ 1. 18-25
____ 2. 26-35
____ 3. 36-42
____ 4. 43-50
____ 5. 50+

Race/Ethnicity:
____ 1. African American
____ 2. Hispanic
____ 3. Asian
____ 4. Caucasian
____ 5. Other

Service Branch (if military):
____ 1. Army
____ 2. Air Force
____ 3. Navy
____ 4. Marines
____ 5. Coast Guard

Status:
____ 1. Active
____ 2. Reserves
____ 3. National Guard
____ 4. Civilian

Rank/Grade (if military):
____ 1. E1-E4
____ 2. E5-E6
____ 3. E7-E-9
____ 4. O1-O3
____ 5. O4-O5
____ 6. O6-O9
____ 7. W1-W2
____ 8. W3-W4
____ 9. W5

Occupational Specialty Code (Military): __________; **Occupation (if civilian):** ___________

Deployments (if military):
1. Location:________________________ Total months: __________ Combat Intensity __________
2. Location:________________________ Total months: __________ Combat Intensity __________
3. Location:________________________ Total months: __________ Combat Intensity __________
4. Location:________________________ Total months: __________ Combat Intensity __________
5. Location:________________________ Total months: __________ Combat Intensity __________

PERSONALITY DOMAINS AND FACETS

Domain or Facet	Very High	High	Average	Low	Very Low
NEUROTICISM					
1. Anxiety					
2. (Tendency to experience) Angry Hostility					
3. (Tendency for) Depression					
4. Self-Consciousness (Shyness/Social anxiety)					
5. Impulsiveness (Tendency to act on desires)					
6. Vulnerability (to stress)					
EXTROVERSION					
1. Warmth (Friendliness towards others)					
2. Gregariousness (Preference to companionship)					
3. Assertiveness (Forcefulness of expression)					
4. (Need for) Activity					
5. (Need for) Excitement-Seeking					
6. (Tendency to experience) Positive Emotions					
OPENNESS					
1. Fantasy (Receptive to imagination)					
2. Aesthetics (Appreciation of art and beauty)					
3. Feelings (Openness to experience inner emotions)					
4. Actions (Openness to new Experiences)					
5. (Willingness to reevaluate) Ideas					
6. (Willingness to reevaluate) Values					
AGREEABLENESS					
1. Trust (Belief in other's intentions and goodness)					
2. Straightforwardness (Frankness in expression)					
3. Altruism (Concern for welfare of others)					
4. Compliance (Response to interpersonal conflict)					
5. Modesty (Tendency to minimize own successes)					
6. Tender-Mindedness (Empathy/sympathy for others)					
CONSCIENTIOUSNESS					
1. Competence (Belief in own abilities)					
2. Order (Personal organization)					
3. Dutifulness (Need to fulfill self-perceived obligations)					
4. Achievement-Setting (Setting personal goals)					
5. Self-Discipline (Ability to follow through with tasks)					
6. Deliberation (Tendency to contemplate plans, actions, outcome, and consequences).					

GENDER ROLE

_____ 1. **Masculine** (Stronger masculine-associated Euro-American views and schemas)
_____ 2. **Feminine** (Stronger feminine-associated Euro-American views and schemas)
_____ 3. **Undifferentiated** (Weak masculine and feminine associated Euro-American views and schemas)
_____ 4. **Androgynous** (Strong masculine and feminine associated Euro-American views and schemas)

LOCUS OF CONTROL

_____ 1. **Strongly Internal** (Life-event outcome strongly dependent upon own action/inaction)
_____ 2. **Moderately Internal** (Life-event outcome somewhat dependent upon own action/inaction)
_____ 3. **Undifferentiated** (Life-event outcome equally dependent upon own action/inaction, influential others, and serendipity.
_____ 4. **Moderately External** (Life-event outcome somewhat determined by influential others or serendipity)
_____ 5. **Strongly External** (Life-event outcome largely determined by influential others or serendipity)

DOMINANT COPING STRATEGIES

______ **Confrontational** (Seeks to actively justify actions/inactions in perceptions of influential or judgmental others).

______ **Distancing** (Seeks to remove pain, distress, and stigma by removing self from social or environmental situation)

______ **Self-Control** (Seeks to consciously suppress adverse biological, psychological and sociological response)

______ **Social Support-Seeking** (Seeks to gather advice and strength from others)

______ **Accepting Responsibility** (Psychologically attributes negative outcomes and consequences to self)

______ **Escape/Avoidance** (Diverts conscious biological, psychological, and sociological distress by psychologically removing self from painful stimuli or environment)

______ **Planful Problem-Solving** (Develops thoughtful plan, envisions steps and obstacles, assesses risk, and envisions probable outcome)

______ **Positive Reappraisal** (Attributes adverse outcome to powerful or influential others; e.g., God's will, or pre-destiny. Diminishes distress by ascribing value of "lesson(s)-learned").

TRAUMATIC HISTORY (Most traumatic to least traumatic)

_____ 1. Childhood Physical - Self/Close
_____ 2. Childhood Psychological/Emotional - Self/Close
_____ 3. Adult Physical Job/Occupation-Associated - Self/Close
_____ 4. Adult Psychological/Emotional Job/Occupation-Associated - Self/Close
_____ 5. Adult Physical Non-Job/Occupation-Associated - Self/Close
_____ 6. Other – Self/Close (e.g. pet injury/death, catastrophic loss, natural disaster etc.)
_____ 7. Childhood Physical - Not Close
_____ 8. Adult Physical Job/Occupation-Associated - Not Close
_____ 9. Adult Physical Non-Job/Occupation-Associated - Not Close

_____ **Total** (Event Type x Number)

PRIMARY DEFINING PTSD EVENT (Most traumatic to least traumatic)

_____ 1. Childhood Physical - Self/Close

_____ 2. Childhood Psychological/Emotional - Self/Close

_____ 3. Adult Physical Job/Occupation-Associated - Self/Close

_____ 4. Adult Psychological/Emotional Job/Occupation-Associated - Self/Close

_____ 5. Adult Physical Non-Job/Occupation-Associated - Self/Close

_____ 6. Childhood Physical - Not Close

_____ 7. Adult Physical Job/Occupation-Associated - Not Close

_____ 8. Adult Physical Non-Job/Occupation-Associated - Not Close

_____ 9. Other – Self/Close (e.g. pet injury/death, catastrophic loss, natural disaster, etc.)

PTSD SYMPTOMOLOGY

_____ DSM-IV-TR Criterion A

_____ DSM-IV-TR Criterion B

_____ DSM-IV-TR Criterion C

_____ DSM-IV-TR Criterion D

_____ DSM-IV-TR Criterion E

_____ DSM-IV-TR Criterion F

PTSD Symptom Score

_____ 1. None – Mild (0-17)

_____ 2. Mild – Moderate (18-39)

_____ 3. Moderate – Severe (40-49)

_____ 4. Severe (50-80)

TRAUMA-RELATED GUILT

Global Guilt

_____ 1. No Guilt

_____ 2. Slight Guilt

_____ 3. Mild Guilt

_____ 4. Mild – Moderate Guilt

_____ 5. Moderate – Severe Guilt

_____ 6. Severe Guilt

Distress

_____ 1. No Distress

_____ 2. Slight Distress

_____ 3. Mild Distress

_____ 4. Mild – Moderate Distress

_____ 5. Moderate – Severe Distress

_____ 6. Severe Distress

Total Guilt Cognitions

_____ 1. No Guilt
_____ 2. Slight Guilt
_____ 3. Mild Guilt
_____ 4. Mild – Moderate Guilt
_____ 5. Moderate – Severe Guilt
_____ 6. Severe Guilt

Hindsight

_____ 1. No Distress
_____ 2. Slight Distress
_____ 3. Mild Distress
_____ 4. Mild – Moderate Distress
_____ 5. Moderate – Severe Distress
_____ 6. Severe Distress

Insufficient Justification(s)

_____ 1. No Distress
_____ 2. Slight Distress
_____ 3. Mild Distress
_____ 4. Mild – Moderate Distress
_____ 5. Moderate – Severe Distress
_____ 6. Severe Distress

Wrongdoing

_____ 1. No Distress
_____ 2. Slight Distress
_____ 3. Mild Distress
_____ 4. Mild – Moderate Distress
_____ 5. Moderate – Severe Distress
_____ 6. Severe Distress

DATA COLLECTION INSTRUMENTS

1. Confidential Identification Code Creation Sheet (Hensley, 2008)
2. Demographic Questionnaire (Hensley, 2008)
3. Revised NEO Personality Inventory (NEO-PI-R; Costa & McCrae, 1992)
4. Bem Sex Role Inventory (BSRI; Bem, 1978)
5. Revised Ways of Coping Checklist (WOC; Folkman & Lazarus, 1985)
6. Brief Betrayal Trauma Survey (BBTS; Goldberg & Freyd, 2006)
7. Rotter Internal-External Locus of Control Scale (LOC; Rotter, 1990)
8. PTSD Screening and Diagnostic Scale (PSDS; Kubany, 2004)
9. Trauma-Related Guilt Inventory (TRGI; Kubany, 2004)

Assessments administered and analyzed by
LCDR Alan L. Hensley (USN, Ret.), PhD Candidate, BCETS, FAAETS or his representatives

PTSD CheckList – Military Version (PCL-M)

Patient's Name: ____

Instruction to patient: Below is a list of problems and complaints that veterans sometimes have in response to stressful military experiences. Please read each one carefully, put an "X" in the box to indicate how much you have been bothered by that problem in ***the last month***.

No.	Response:	Not at all (1)	A little bit (2)	Moderately (3)	Quite a bit (4)	Extremely (5)
1.	Repeated, disturbing *memories*, *thoughts*, or *images* of a stressful military experience?					
2.	Repeated, disturbing *dreams* of a stressful military experience?					
3.	Suddenly *acting* or *feeling* as if a stressful military experience were happening again (as if you were reliving it)?					
4.	Feeling *very upset* when *something reminded* you of a stressful military experience?					
5.	Having *physical reactions* (e.g., heart pounding, trouble breathing, or sweating) when *something reminded* you of a stressful military experience?					
6.	Avoid *thinking about* or *talking about* a stressful military experience or avoid *having feelings* related to it?					
7.	Avoid *activities* or *situations* because *they remind you* of a stressful military experience?					
8.	Trouble *remembering important parts* of a stressful military experience?					
9.	Loss of *interest in things that you used to enjoy?*					
10.	Feeling *distant* or *cut off* from other people?					
11.	Feeling *emotionally numb* or being unable to have loving feelings for those close to you?					
12.	Feeling as if your *future* will somehow be *cut short?*					
13.	Trouble *falling* or *staying asleep?*					
14.	Feeling *irritable* or having *angry outbursts?*					
15.	Having *difficulty concentrating?*					
16.	Being *"super alert"* or watchful on guard?					
17.	Feeling *jumpy* or easily startled?					

Weathers, F.W., Huska, J.A., Keane, T.M. PCL-M for DSM-IV. Boston: National Center for PTSD – Behavioral Science Division, 1991

DEPLOYMENT HEALTH CLINIC - INTAKE FORM

Identifying Information:

Name: ____________________ **Date:** ____________________

Gender: ___male ___female **SSN:** (last 4) ____________________

Marital Status: ___single ___married ___separated **Age:** ____________________

___divorced ___widowed ___other:

Ethnicity: ___Caucasian ___African-American ___Hispanic/Latino ___Native American

___Asian/Pacific Islander ___Other:

Contact Phone#: ____________________ **Work Phone#:** ____________________

Residence: ___barracks ___on-base housing ___off-base housing (location/city:____________________)

Living with: ___wife/significant other ___roommate ___offspring(#:) ___alone

Rank/Rate: ____________________ **Branch of Service:** ___USMC ___USN ___Army ___USAF

Duty Station: ____________________ **Unit:** ____________________

Time in Service: ___years ___months ___continuous service ___broken service

EAS date (month/year): ____________________

Deployments: Dates (mo/yr to mo/yr) Location:

1) ________ to ________ ____________________

2) ________ to ________ ____________________

3) ________ to ________ ____________________

4) ________ to ________ ____________________

5) ________ to ________ ____________________

Mental Health History

Chief/Current Complaint:

1. Who referred you? ____________________

____

2. What brings you in today? ____________________

____

____

____

Mental Health History (cont.)

Ever had any:

Prior mental health therapy/counseling? ___Yes ___No When?______________ Why?____________________________

Prior psychiatric medications? ___Yes ___No When?______________ Why?____________________________

Prior psychiatric hospitalizations? ___Yes ___No When?______________ Why?____________________________

Please list past psych meds: ____

Prior mental health/psychiatric diagnoses given: ____

Any current psychiatric medications or therapy/counseling: ______________________________________

Biological family history of mental health diagnosis or treatment? ___Yes ___No ___Don't Know

Who (relationship)?	Diagnosis	Treatment (check all that apply):		
____________________	____________________	___Medication	___Therapy	___Hospitalization
____________________	____________________	___Medication	___Therapy	___Hospitalization
____________________	____________________	___Medication	___Therapy	___Hospitalization
____________________	____________________	___Medication	___Therapy	___Hospitalization

In the past, have you ever:

Thought of suicide? ___Yes ___No When? ____

Attempted suicide? ___Yes ___No How? ____

Thought of killing someone else? (non-combat situation) ___Yes ___No Who?_________________________

Tried to kill someone else? (non-combat situation) ___Yes ___No Who?_____________________________

How? ______________________ When? ___________________________________

Engaged in self-injury (cutting, burning yourself, etc.) ___Yes ___No When? ___________________________

Are you now:

Thinking of hurting yourself? ___Yes ___No How? ____

Thinking of hurting someone else? ___Yes ___No How? _______________________________________

Thinking of cutting/burning yourself? ___Yes ___No

What stops you from acting on thoughts of hurting others of yourself?

____

____

____

Current Physical Problems/Medical Conditions (please list): ____________________________________

____

History of Head Injury? ___Yes ___No Medication Allergies? ___Yes ___No

History of Seizures? ___Yes ___No If yes, to what? ______________________________

History of Blackouts? ___Yes ___No Problems with dizziness now? ___Yes ___No

Current Physical Problems/Medical Conditions (cont.)

Problems with headaches now? ___Yes ___No   Problems with ringing in ears now? ___Yes ___No

Current physical pain rating: from 0 (none) to 10 (excrutiating) = of 10

Current medications: ______________________________

Sleep problems? (circle) trouble getting to sleep   waking up at night   oversleeping

waking too early in the morning   excessive snoring   naps during the day

bothered by nightmares vivid dreams   restless legs

Eating problems? (circle) overeating   loss of appetite   binging&purging

Weight change in past month? ___None ___Gain ___Loss   of _____ lb.

Substance Use

Current number of times using alcohol per week: ______________________________

Current number of drinks per occasion: ______________________________

Past evaluation or treatment for alcohol abuse? ___Yes ___No   When?___________

Type: ___evaluation only ___inpatient/residential ___outpatient ___alcohol awareness classes

Ever had alcohol-related ticket/arrest/DUI? ___Yes ___No   When?___________

Current illicit drug use: ___Yes ___No   What? ___________ When? ___________

Past illicit drug use: ___Yes ___No   What? ___________ When? ___________

Family alcohol/drug history? ___Yes ___No   Who? ___________ When? ___________

Social History

Early Development:

Born where? ______________________ Rasied where? ______________________

Number of brothers: ________ Number of sisters: ________ Number of half/step-siblings: ________

Home discipline/enforcement of rules: ___strict ___lenient ___inconsistent ___absent

Raised by: ___biological parents ___mother&stepfather ___father&stepmother ___ grandparents

___foster care ___ adoptive parents ___single parent ___ institution

How would you describe your childhood? ______________________________

Exposure to Trauma/Abuse/Neglect:				***How old were you?***
Emotional/psychological abuse:	___Yes	___No	___unsure	______________
Physical abuse:	___Yes	___No	___unsure	______________
Sexual abuse/molestation	___Yes	___No	___unsure	______________
Neglect/abandonment:	___Yes	___No	___unsure	______________

Social History (cont.)

Winessing Domestic Violence ___Yes ___No ___unsure ____________________

Deaths in the Family ___Yes ___No ___unsure ____________________

Out-of-home placement / homelessness ___Yes ___No ___unsure ____________________

School History:

Ever need special education services? ___Yes ___No What for? ____________________

Ever tested for a learning disability? ___Yes ___No Results: ____________________

Ever tested for ADHD? ___Yes ___No Results: ____________________

Ever expelled from school? ___Yes ___No Why? ____________________

Out-of-school suspensions in middle and high school: ____________________

Reasons for suspensions: (check all that apply) ___fighting ___destroying property ___defiance

___alcohol/drugs ___skipping school ___disrupting class

Educational level: ___ did not finish high school ___ high school diploma ___ GED

___ some college credits ___ AA degree ___ bachelor's degree

___ other: ____________________

Legal History:

Ever arrested/cited as a juvenile? ___Yes ___No What for? ____________________

Ever adjudicated delinquent? ___Yes ___No What for? ____________________

Ever arrested/cited as an adult? ___Yes ___No What for? ____________________

Ever convicted as an adult? ___Yes ___No What for? ____________________

Consequence: ___ Jail/Prison ___Fine ___Community Service ___ Restitution ___Probation/Parole

Military Disciplinary Consequences: ***Reason:***

NJP: ___Yes ___No ____________________

Page 11 ___Yes ___No ____________________

Counseling Sheets ___Yes ___No ____________________

Captain's Masts ___Yes ___No ____________________

Court Martial ___Yes ___No ____________________

Restriction ___Yes ___No ____________________

Loss of Pay ___Yes ___No ____________________

Reduction in Rank ___Yes ___No ____________________

MPO ___Yes ___No ____________________

Confinement in Brig ___Yes ___No ____________________

HPI: (check any that apply)

Problems with:

___ Mood ___ Behavior Thinking/Attitude ___ Relationships ___ Stress

For how long? ________ days/weeks/months/years

Possibly started/triggered by: ____

____

(please circle which of the following apply):

Mood: sad angry happy numb afraid ashamed confused silly
irritated worried "on edge" moody don't care bored

Behavior: fighting breaking things irresponsible impulsive withdrawn unpredictable
odd habits/rituals work problems jumpy thrill-seeking

Thinking/Attitude: negative confused constant worrying too distracted
unmotivated guilty hopeless distrustful suspicious

Relationships: conflicts separation unfaithfulness parenting problems jealousy
domestic violence grief/loss isolation don't care arguing

Current Stressors: (check which apply)

___family	___finances	___deaths/losses
___friends	___school	___lifestyle changes
___relatives	___significant other	___health problems
___work	___separation	___other: ____________

What else should we know about you and what would be most helpful for you today?

____

____

____

____

____

____

____

____

____

____

____

____

Thank you for taking the time to complete this form. Please return this to your provider.

APPENDIX C

January 12, 2009

VETERAN: CASE #1

DIAGNOSIS:

AXIS I	309.81 Posttraumatic Stress Disorder, Chronic
AXIS II	Rule out 314.01 Attention Deficit/Hyperactivity Disorder, Predominantly Hyperactive-Impulsive Type
AXIS III	No diagnosis
AXIS IV	Combat exposure
AXIS V	GAF = 61 (Current)

RATIONALE:

Here presents a 25 y/o Caucasian male, who is a high school graduate and junior enlisted member of the XXX Army National Guard. The veteran self-reports he has served two tours in Iraq; March 2004 - March 2005 and October 2006 – January 2008.

Military Wellbeing Assessment Protocol (MWAP; Hensley, 2009a; 2009b) intake as follows:

1. Veteran is highly masculine (39) in gender role orientation (Bem Sex Role Inventory; BSRI; Bem, 1978)
2. Veteran possesses a moderately internal (MI) locus of control, indicating he believes event life outcome is generally the result of his own actions or inactions (Rotter, 1966)
3. The Revised NEO Personality Inventory (NEO-PI-R; Costa & McCrae, 1982) assesses the Five-Factor Model of Personality; consisting of neuroticism (N), extraversion (E), openness (O), agreeableness (A), and conscientiousness (C). In normalizing the MWAP in among military veterans of Operation Iraqi Freedom (OIF)/Operation Enduring Freedom (OEF), the researcher (Hensley, 2009a; 2009b) found neuroticism to be highly predictive of PTSD symptom severity, trauma-related guilt, and distress. The veteran in this case self- reports very high (5/5) predisposition to high neuroticism facets, including: anxiety (n1), angry hostility (n2), depression (n3). The veteran self-reports high (4/5) predisposition towards self-consciousness (n4) and vulnerability (n6). Assessing extraversion (E) domain, the veteran self-reports a low (2/5) overall degree of extraversion However, supporting E-domain facets are widely varied. The veteran self-reports very low warmth (e1) and gregariousness (E2), suggesting he is very much a loner who prefers to remain to himself. The veteran self-reports low excitement seeking (e5) and low positive emotions (e6), suggesting he experiences little joy or happiness in his life. Assessing the openness domain, this veteran self-reports a high acceptance of fantasy (O1). However, he scores very low in desire to venture into the unknown (Actions; o4; 1/5). He also scores low in willingness to reexamine values (o6). The veteran, overall, scores very low in agreeableness, suggesting he is often considered obstinate and unyielding by others. Specifically, he scores very low (1/5) in trust (a1), low in straightforwardness (a2), low (2/5) in altruism (a3), very

low (1/5) in compliance (a4), marginally average (3/5) in modesty (a5), and low (2/5) in tender-mindedness (a6). The veteran self-reports overall low Conscientiousness (C); specifically, he self-reports low (2/5) competence (c1), dutifulness (c3), and deliberation. Significances of these observations discussed in Impressions Section.

4. The veteran's three dominant coping strategies (Ways of Coping Questionnaire; WCQ; Folkman & Lazarus, 1988) are: confrontive coping (1.83/3.00), planful problem-solving (1.5/3.00), and escape/avoidance (1.375/3.00). Significance of observations discussed in Impressions Section.
5. In traumatic history intake (Brief Betrayal Trauma Survey; BBTS; Goldberg & Freyd, 2006) the veteran self-reports only one isolated instance of observing a person being intentionally injured by another. However, as an adult the veteran reports repeated instances of observing close and non-close others being physically attacked by others.
6. Asked to briefly describe his or her most traumatic life event—the event by which he or she defines the word, trauma (PTSD Symptom and Diagnostic Scale; PSDS; Kubany, 2004)—the veteran self-reports his primary traumatic event (PTE) as buddies being injured or killed by an improvised explosive device (IED) in Iraq. In response to questions assessing biopsychosocial response, veteran fully meets all six criteria outlined in the Diagnostic and Statistical Manual for Mental Disorders, Fourth Edition-Text Revision (DSM-IV-TR; American Psychiatric Association, 2000). The PSDS PTSD Symptom Severity Scale quantitatively assesses level of symptom severity as moderate to severe (59/80).
7. In relationship to the PTE described, the veteran self-reports mild to moderate (3/6) global guilt, moderate (4/6) distress, mild to moderate (3/6) total guilt cognitions, mild to moderate hindsight bias, mild to moderate (3/6) insufficient justifications, and mild to moderate (3/6) sense of wrongdoing.

Impressions

Hensley (2009a, 2009b) found the neuroticism (N) domain to be positively correlated with PTSD symptom severity, trauma-related guilt, and distress. One facet in particular, depression (n3) was highly correlated with PTSD symptom severity, trauma-related guilt, and distress. This veteran scored very high in, both, the neuroticism domain and depression. Gregariousness (e2), the desire for the company of others, was found to be negatively correlated to PTSD symptom severity and global guilt. This veteran scored very low (1/5) in gregariousness. Positive emotions (e6) was found to be negatively correlated to PTSD symptoms, global guilt, total guilt cognitions, and distress. This veteran scored low (2/5) in positive emotions. Actions (o4), the openness to try new ideas or experiences, was found to be negatively correlated to global guilt and distress. This veteran scored very low in actions. This veteran was extremely low in trust, indicating inherent skepticism or distrust of the intentions of others. The veteran also self-reported low straightforwardness (a2), which was found by Hensley (2009a, 2009b) to be negatively correlated with global guilt. Compliance was found to be highly negatively correlated with PTSD symptoms and distress. This veteran scored very low (1/5) in compliance. Low scorers tend to be much less aggressive and competitive than their high-scoring counterparts. Modesty (a5) was found to be positively correlated to PTSD symptoms, global guilt, and distress. This veteran scored his highest score (3/6) in the A domain in modesty. Deliberation was found to be highly negatively correlated to PTSD symptoms. This veteran scored low (2/5) in deliberation. Dutifulness (c3) was found to be negatively correlated with global guilt. The compendium of personality domains and facets suggests this veteran is highly predisposed to high PTSD symptom severity, trauma-related guilt, and distress.

Problematic are two of this veterans three most dominant coping strategies—confrontive coping and escape avoidance. Confrontive coping is reflective of his highly masculine gender role orientation. Male persons predisposed to escape avoidance are likely to engage in self-soothing remedies such as alcohol or drug use as a venue to achieve relief. Coupled with his low gregariousness, and extremely low social support-seeking score, this presents a very real probability.

Recommendations

Given that he had little exposure to/experience with highly traumatic life experiences during childhood, it is unlikely that he developed the schematic processes and short-term adaptive/long-term adaptive coping strategies from which to cope with a volatile combat environment. This assertion is supported by the relative absence of strong adaptive, or even maladaptive, coping strategies, except the ones noted. Consequently, he is suffering severe distress when the PTE is recalled.

1. This person self-reports high receptiveness to fantasy. Eye Movement Desensitization and Reorganization (EMDR), with guided journaling, would be a prudent option in this case. The veteran should be encouraged to reflect upon the most challenging event faced during the day, resources and options available, benefits and risks of each option, option selected, and outcome. This will foster greater planful problem-solving. The veteran self-reports average self-discipline; so this should be well received.
2. Evaluation for psycho-pharmaceutical intervention of very high anxiety and depression would also be prudent.
3. Enrollment in anger management individual and group therapy would be prudent.
4. By virtue of the absence of androgyny, poor social-support seeking, and other personality facets, this individual was not presented with a positive female role model, nor engaged in group activities with the opposite sex. Group activities which foster androgynous interaction and trust, such as weekend or longer wilderness programs, would be ideal.

APPENDIX D

January 12, 2009

VETERAN: CASE #2

DIAGNOSIS:

AXIS I	No diagnosis
AXIS II	No diagnosis
AXIS III	No diagnosis
AXIS IV	Combat exposure
AXIS V	GAF = 80 (Current)

RATIONALE:

Here presents a 35 y/o Caucasian male, who is/was an enlisted Army Infantryman who was deployed 12 months IVO Baghdad in 2004-2005. Military Wellbeing Assessment Protocol (MWAP; Hensley, 2009) intake as follows:

1. Veteran is decidedly masculine (37) in gender role orientation (Bem Sex Role Inventory; BSRI; Bem, 1978)
2. Veteran possesses a moderately internal (MI) locus of control, indicating he believes event life outcome is generally the result of his own actions or inactions (Rotter, 1966).
3. The Revised NEO Personality Inventory reports veteran is a highly assertive (E3), self-disciplined individual. Atypical to this veteran's profile is high propensity to reeaxamine ideas (O5) and values (O6). NEO-PI-R reveals low propensity for neuroticism (N); including, low predisposition for anxiety (N1), angry hostility (N2), and depression (N3). Veteran also presents a low degree of self-consciousness (N4). With the exception of assertiveness, which demonstrates his need to be in charge, E scale facets are largely within normal range. As stated, propensity to reexamine ideas and values are atypical in the O range. Veteran presents very low level of trust, demonstrating skepticism and distrust of intentions of others. Low modesty (A5) infers individual is self-assured and readily presents successes to others. C facets are well above median. Achievement striving (C4), in combination with high assertiveness scores argues he tends to tests his own limits and the limits of others.
4. Veteran's three most dominant coping strategies (Ways of Coping Questionnaire; WCQ; Folkman & Lazarus, 1988) are: highly developed planful problem-solving (2.6), confrontive coping (1.5), and self-control (1.43). These strategies suggest well-developed childhood and adolescent trial-and-error, with high degree of success.
5. Traumatic history intake presents no self-reported traumatic experiences in childhood and adolescence, nor adverse social interactions with close others.
6. In PTSD Symptom and Diagnostic Scale (PSDS; Kubany, 2004), veteran presents combat action in support of Operation Iraqi Freedom (OIF) as his primary traumatic event—the event by which he defines the word trauma. Response to post-event symptomology suggests the veteran meets all six criteria for a diagnosis

of PTSD in accordance with the Diagnostic and Statistical Manual of Mental Disorders, Fourth Edition-Text Revision (DSM-IV-TR; American Psychiatric Association, 2000). PTSD Symptom Severity Scale suggests symptomology is mild to moderate (37).

7. Trauma-Related Guilt Inventory (TRGI; Kubany, Haynes, Abueg, Manke, Brennan et al, 1996) demonstrates moderate-to-severe Global Guilt (5/6), mild-to-moderate Distress (4/6), mild-to-moderate Total Guilt Cognitions (4/6), mild-to-moderate hindsight bias (4/6), mild-to-moderate insufficient justification (4/6), and mild-to-moderate sense of wrongdoing (4/6).

Impressions

The amalgamation of the self-report instruments reflects a moderately internal, self-driven, highly assertive, highly masculine, male person. The veteran presents a low nsley predisposition to N-level facets, mild to moderate PTSD symptomology, and a high degree of conscientiousness (C). These predispositional factors are in stark contrast to the findings of Hensley (2009a, 2009b), which found, among 61 male and female veterans of Operation Iraqi Freedom (OIF)/Operation Enduring Freedom (OEF) that high neuroticism was positively correlated to PTSD symptom severity. Specifically, depression (n3) is positively correlated to PTSD symptomology. Additionally, the veteran self-reports average predisposition to anxiety (n1) depression (n3), and only marginally high predisposition to angry hostility. Hensley (2009a, 2009b) found gregariousness (e2) to be negatively correlated to PTSD symptom severity and global guilt. This veteran self-reported average (3/5) gregariousness. Hensley (2009a, 2009b) found positive emotions to be negatively correlated with PTSD symptom severity, global guilt, total guilt cognitions, and distress.

This veteran self-reported average (3/5) propensity for positive emotions. Hensley (2009a, 2009b) found willingness to examine/reexamine ideas (o5) was negatively correlated to global guilt and distress. This veteran self-reported high willingness to reexamine ideas. Hensley (2009a, 2009b) found straightforwardness (a2) to be very highly negatively correlated to PTSD symptoms and global guilt. This individual scored average (3/5) in straightforwardness. Hensley (2009a, 2009b) found compliance (a4) to be highly negatively correlated to PTSD symptoms severity and distress. This individual scored low (2/5) in compliance. Hensley (2009a, 2009b) found modesty to be positively correlated to PTSD symptoms, global guilt, and distress. This veteran scored marginally low (2/5) in modesty. Hensley (2009a, 2009b) found dutifulness (c3) to be negatively correlated to global guilt. This individual scored average (3/5) in dutifulness. Lastly, Hensley (2009a, 2009b) found deliberation to be highly negatively correlated to PTSD symptom severity. This veteran self-reported average deliberation.

Confounding is the self-report absence of guilt for event outcome on the PSDS, when associated with moderate to severe presentation of Global Guilt on the TRGI. This association suggests further exploration of the event outcome in relationship to his actions/inactions before, during, and after event. No psycho-pharmaceutical intervention is indicated. While this veteran self-responded adverse response to the overt questions regarding PTSD and trauma-related guilt symptomology, he does not fit the overall MWAP (Hensley, 2009) profile for a diagnosis of PTSD, trauma-related guilt, or distress. His personality profile argues for a resilient personality and his ways of coping argue he possesses highly adaptive coping strategies. Perhaps more indicative is the observation among 61 previous veterans completing the study, persons with severe trauma/distress were able to identify a singular or few PTE(s) as troubling. This veteran self-reported only "Combat action – Operation Iraqi Freedom" as his PTE. Thus, he lacks the stigmatic specificity to establish a traumatic event as his definitive baseline.

RECOMMENDED COURSE OF ACTION:

1. Brief individual assessment/counseling to assess/deconflict the confounding issue discussed above and what he could have done differently to alter outcome.
2. Group counseling (with caution). This individual will tend to lead group sessions and absorb/dominate group members, rendering the group sessions less productive for other participants. However, his presence, with the personality domains and ways of coping presented, will challenge other participants to reassess maladaptive views. Thus, counselor must moderate participation.

Respectfully submitted,
//signed//
LCDR Alan L. Hensley, USN(Ret.), PhD Candidate, BCETS, FAAETS

APPENDIX E

January 11, 2009

VETERAN: CASE #3

DIAGNOSIS:

AXIS I	309.81 Posttraumatic Stress Disorder, Chronic
AXIS II	None
AXIS III	No diagnosis
AXIS IV	Combat exposure
AXIS V	GAF = 61 (Current)

RATIONALE:

Here presents a 24 y/o Caucasian female. The veteran is a former junior enlisted active duty Soldier, who served a 12 month tour of duty IVO Karbala, Iraq as a 31B (Military Police). Military Wellbeing Assessment Protocol (MWAP; Hensley, 2009a; 2009b) intake as follows:

1. Veteran possesses an androgynous (both strong masculine and feminine) gender role orientation (Bem Sex Role Inventory; BSRI; Bem, 1978).
2. Veteran reports a moderately internal locus of control, which suggests she considers event outcome to be largely the consequence of her own action(s)/inaction (Rotter Locus of Control Scale; LOC; Rotter, 1966).
3. In the Revised NEO Personality Inventory (NEO-PI-R; Costa & McCrae, 1992), the veteran self reports an overall high (4/5) predisposition to neuroticism (N) domain facets; specifically angry hostility (n2; 4/5), depression (n3; 4/5), impulsiveness (n5; 4/5); and vulnerability (n6; 4/5). Depression (n3) was specifically positively correlated to PTSD symptom severity, trauma-related guilt, and distress. In the Extroversion (E) domain, the veteran reports high (4/5) gregariousness (e2) and very high (5/5) excitement-seeking (e5). The veteran reports high (4/5) acceptance of fantasy, very high (5/5) actions (o4), and high (4/5) willingness to reexamine values (o6). In the Agreeableness (A) domain, the veteran self-reports very low (1/5) trust (a1), very low (1/5) straightforwardness (a2), very low (1/5) compliance (a4), and low (2/5) modesty (a5). High-very high N is negatively associated with low-very low Conscientiousness (C) domain facets; specifically, very low (1/5) competence (c1), very low (1/5) order (c2), very low (1/5) dutifulness (c3), very low (1/5) achievement striving (c4), very low (1/5) self-discipline (c5), and very low (1/5) deliberation.
4. The three dominant ways of coping (Ways of Coping; Lazarus & Folkman, 1984) for this veteran are: escape/avoidance (1.87), self-control (1.71), and accepting responsibility (1.5).
5. Trauma history (Brief Betrayal Trauma Survey; BBTS; Goldberg & Freyd, 2003) reveals, as a child, this veteran was attacked by someone not close. As an adult, this veteran witnessed both, persons close and not close, physically attacked. Additionally, this veteran self-reports being repeatedly attacked as an adult by persons not close. As an adult, this veteran was sexually assaulted/forced to have sex repeatedly with persons not close.

6. In self-report (PTSD Symptom and Diagnostic Scale; PSDS; Kubany, 2004), this veteran reports her primary traumatic event (PTE), by which she defines the word, trauma, and gauges all other traumas, was being sexually assaulted/raped by a senior male enlisted person during deployment in Iraq. The PSDS reveals the veteran meets all six criteria for a diagnosis of PTSD, chronic as defined by the Diagnostic and Statistical Manual for Mental Disorders, Fourth Edition-Text Revision (DSM-IV-TR; American Psychiatric Association, 2000). The PSDS PTSD Symptom Severity Scale reveals the veteran is quantitatively assessed as suffering from moderate to severe (45/80) symptom severity. Predominantly, the symptomology affects her relationships with her family, inability to engage in intimate relationships, and ability to function in a male-dominant work environment.
7. The Trauma-Related Guilt Inventory (TRGI; Kubany & Haynes, 2004) reveals the veteran suffers from moderate to severe (5/6) global guilt, moderate (4/6) distress, moderate total guilt cognitions, moderate (4/6) hindsight bias, mild to moderate (3/6) insufficient justification, and moderate to severe sense of wrongdoing. Specifically, the veteran feels her actions: went against her beliefs and values; she contributed very little to the event; but feels partially responsible for the event; and feels biopsychosocial distress recalling the event.

Impressions

The veteran in her current state is greatly distressed in male dominated work or social environments. IVO poor self-control psycho-pharmaceutical intervention is likely to be poorly accomplished. She self-reports high predisposition for facets of neuroticism and very low conscientiousness, self-esteem, and competence. Particularly problematic is her predisposition to excitement-seeking (e5) and very low deliberation; the frequent components of frequent casual unprotected sex situations.

Normalizing the Hensley Military Wellbeing Assessment Protocol (MWAP; Hensley, 2009a; 2009b) on 61 male and female veterans of deployment in support of Operation Iraqi Freedom (OIF)/Operation Enduring Freedom (OEF), Hensley (2009a, 2009b) found high N to be positively correlated to high PTSD symptom severity, trauma-related guilt, and distress. Generally, these persons tend to experience greater negative affects such as anxiety, distress, fear, sadness, anger, and guilt than those persons scoring low in N. Because disruptive emotions interfere with adaption, persons high in N are prone to have irrational ideas, be less in control of impulses, and to cope more poorly than his or her low-N counterparts. Hensley (2009a, 2009b) found a low score on the Agreeableness domain to be predictive of high angry hostility (N2).

Agreeableness is primarily a measure of interpersonal predispositions. While agreeable persons tend to be more sympathetic and empathetic, disagreeable persons, or those scoring low in agreeableness, tend to be more egocentric and skeptical of the intentions of others. He or she also presents greater competitiveness than cooperativeness. This veteran presents both low agreeableness and high angry hostility. Hensley (2009a, 2009b) found straightforwardness to be negatively correlated to PTSD symptom severity and global guilt. This veteran self-reported very low straightforwardness. Compliance (A4) was found to be negatively correlated to PTSD symptoms and distress. This veteran scored very low (1/5) in compliance.

Deliberation (c6) was found to be significantly negatively correlated with PTSD symptom severity trauma-related guilt and distress. This veteran scored very low in deliberation (c6).

The veteran employs largely short-term adaptive/long-term maladaptive coping strategies, such as escape avoidance, which are counterproductive to long-term wellbeing. Attention needs to be focused on formulating such long-term adaptive coping strategies as planful problem-solving and social support seeking; thereby attriting the reliance on maladaptive coping strategies, such as accepting responsibility (arguably learned through co-dependency) and escape avoidance. In view of her three dominant coping strategies, the veteran is predisposed to promiscuity, risk-taking, weight disorders, and alcoholism and other self-soothing techniques. Coupled with high angry hostility, she is prone to engage in antisocial behavior and have frequent engagements with law enforcement.

Recommendations

The veteran should be enrolled in both individual and group therapy for adult victims of sexual assault/rape and anger management. Specific attention should be given to developing short-term adaptive/long-term adaptive coping strategies, such as planful problem-solving and social support. She should be encouraged to journal; focusing on the day's most challenging event, possible alternative plans of action, benefits and risks, threats and resources, action taken and outcome (positive or negative). The challenge to this plan will be a relatively low degree of self-discipline. Consequently, journaling will, necessarily, need to be counselor-monitored. The practitioner/veteran process is not expected to be short-term. Additionally, she should be enrolled in sexual assault and anger management groups to foster social-support seeking. Ideally, because this veteran is recently discharged after fulfillment of enlistment contract, a 14-21 day in-residence individual and group counseling program would be beneficial to provide structure necessary for adaptive coping strategy development and monitor maladaptive self-medication/alcohol consumption.

Respectfully Submitted,

//signed//

LCDR Alan L. Hensley, USN (Ret.), PhD Candidate, BCETS, FAAETS

APPENDIX F

January 11, 2009

PATIENT: CASE #4

DIAGNOSIS:

AXIS I	309.81 Posttraumatic Stress Disorder, Chronic
AXIS II	None
AXIS III	No diagnosis
AXIS IV	Combat exposure Problems with primary support group Other psychosocial and environmental problems (gender role incongruence/civilian versus military gender role perception)
AXIS V	GAF = 51 (Current)

RATIONALE:

Here presents a 25 y/o Caucasian female. Patient is a junior enlisted member of the XXX Army National Guard, who served a 13 month tour of duty IVO Baquba, Iraq as a 21C (Bridge Engineer). Military Wellbeing Assessment Protocol (MWAP; Hensley, 2009a; 2009b) intake as follows:

1. Bem (1978) Sex Role Inventory reflects a highly masculine gender role orientation.
2. Rotter (1966) Locus of Control Scale reflects an undifferentiated locus of control event outcome is neither largely the result of her own action/inaction, powerful/influential others, or serendipity.
3. The Revised NEO Personality Inventory (Costa & McCrae, 1992) reflects a person who is very highly (5/5) predisposed to such neuroticism (N) facets as anxiety (n1) and depression (n3). Additionally, she is highly predisposed (4/5) to angry hostility (n2), self-consciousness (n5), and impulsiveness (n5). Extroversion (E) domain facets reflect this person is low (2/5) on warmth (e1), very low (1/5) on gregariousness (e2), very high (5/5) on assertiveness, low (2/5) excitement-seeking, and very low in positive emotions. Openness (O) domain facets reflect patient is very low (1/5) in fantasy (o1), very low (1/5) in aesthetics (o2), very low (1/5) in actions (o4), and very low (1/5) in ideas (o5). The patient is low (2/5) in trust (a1), compliance (a4), and modesty (a5). However, the patient is high in the Conscientiousness (C) domain facets of competence (c1), order (c2), and achievement-striving (c4). Low self-discipline (C4) is somewhat offset by very high deliberation (c6).
4. Ways of Coping (Folkman & Lazarus, 1988) reflects an individual with, overall, poorly developed coping strategies. The three most dominant coping strategies are: social support-seeking (1.16/3.00); confrontive coping (1.00/3.00), and distancing (1.00/3.00).
5. The Brief Betrayal Trauma Scale (BBTS; Goldberg & Freyd, 2003) reflects minor psychological/emotional abuse during childhood, and forced sexual assault/rape during adulthood by a person with whom she was not close.

6. The patient self-reports the singular most traumatic event occurring during her lifetime --the event by which she defines the word, trauma—is being sexually assaulted/raped by a Soldier in her unit four years earlier (PTSD Symptom and Diagnostic Scale; PSDS; Kubany, 2004). The PSDS finds the patient meets all six criteria for Diagnostic and Statistical Manual of Mental Disorder, Fourth Edition-Text Revision (DSM-IV-TR; American Psychiatric Association, 2000) diagnosis of Post-Traumatic Stress Disorder (PTSD), Chronic. The PSDS PTSD Symptom Severity Scale quantifies the patient's symptom severity as 41/80 (moderate to severe). The PSDS has then objectified who, what, when, where; but not why or how.
7. The Trauma-Related Guilt Inventory (TRGI; Kubany & Haynes, 2004) quantifies six aspects of trauma-related guilt. The patient reflects moderate to severe (5/6) global guilt, moderate to severe (5/6) distress, moderate (4/6) total guilt cognitions, mild to moderate (3/6) hindsight bias, moderate to severe (5/6) insufficient justification, and moderate (4/6) sense of wrongdoing. Specific responses to the TRGI indicate: 1) absence of wrongdoing on her part; 2) she perceived helplessness; 3) she feels guilt for what happened; 4) what happened caused and continues to cause pain and suffering; and 5) she continues to have severe adverse biopsychosocial response upon reflecting on the event.

Impressions

This patient presents a masculine female gender role orientation. Masculine gender role in females was demonstrated to be negatively correlated with adaptive coping strategies. The Hensley Military Wellbeing Assessment Protocol (MWAP; Hensley, 2009) found positive correlations between high scores in neuroticism (N), PTSD, trauma-related guilt, and distress. This patient reported very high (5/5) N-domain scores. At the facet level, depression was highly correlated to PTSD, trauma-related guilt, and distress. This patient self-reported very high depression (n3) scores. Self-consciousness (n4) neared statistical significance with PTSD manifestation. This patient self-reported high scores (4/5) in self-consciousness. Costa and McCrae (1992) argue the emotions of shame and embarrassment is foundational to this facet. Self-conscious individuals are uncomfortable in the presence of others, are sensitive to criticism and ridicule, and are prone to feelings of inadequacy or inferiority. Gregariousness (E2), the preference for companionship/company, was found to be a negative predictor of PTSD symptoms and global guilt. This patient self-reported very low (1/5) gregariousness (e2) and is, therefore, often considered a loner by many. Very low gregariousness (1/5) is predispositional to high PTSD symptom severity and global guilt.

Positive emotions (e6), the tendency to experience joy and happiness, were found by Hensley (2009) to be negatively correlated with PTSD symptoms severity, global guilt, total guilt cognitions, and distress. This patient self-reported very low positive emotions (e6). In Hensley (2009), ideas (o5) reached negative statistical correlation with global guilt, total guilt cognitions, and distress. This patient self-reported very low ideas (o5). Feelings (o3) reached statistical significance with distress. Feelings (o3) was this patient's highest score (3/5) in the O domain. Actions (o4), being willing to experience new places and things, was negatively correlated with distress. This patient reported her lowest O-domain score (1/5) in actions (o4). Ideas (o6), the willingness to engage in philosophical or unconventional thought and discussion, were negatively correlated with distress. This patient self-reported very low (1/5) ideas. Hensley (2009) found the Agreeableness domain was positively correlated with distress. This patient reported low agreeableness. Compliance (a4) was found to be negatively correlated to distress. This patient self-reported low (2/5) compliance (a4); indicating the veterans is competitive and has no hesitancy to express anger when necessary. The noted personality facet scores project a person predisposed to, or suffering from, PTSD.

Recommendations

The relative absence of preconditional childhood experiences argues strongly that the patient's schematic perception, cognition, and response were ill-equipped to cope with this strongly sex-related offense. Current assessment of coping inventory finds a poorly developed arsenal of short-term adaptive/long-term adaptive, nor short-term adaptive, long term maladaptive coping strategies. Hence, she is predisposed to high levels of distress. This patient's personality prefers the conventional and is, therefore, adverse to fantasy. Consequently, role-playing or other types of self-awareness therapies are unlikely to be well received or effective. The fact that she self-reports little, if any, blame in the offending incident suggests cognitive behavioral therapy as a remedy is unlikely, except as a venue to reassure her that an offending sample is not necessarily representative of an entire population. Eye-Movement Desensitization and Reprocessing (EMDR) is strongly indicated to relieve extreme biopsychosocial distress. The patient's second/third most dominant coping strategy is highly problematic; if she engages in group sessions, she is likely to dissociate or resort to her alternative coping strategy—confrontation. Attention should be given to attriting her secondary coping strategies in favor of her slightly more dominant social support seeking as well as developing a planful problem-solving strategy. The therapeutic goal should, then, be on engaging the patient in therapies that encourage group interaction and trust. She should be encouraged to journal; focusing on the day's most challenging event, possible alternative plans of action, benefits and risks, threats and resources, action taken and outcome (positive or negative). The challenge to this plan will be a relatively low degree of self-discipline. Consequently, journaling will, necessarily, need to be couselor-monitored. The practitioner/patient process is not expected to be short-term. Additionally, she should be enrolled in a sexual assault group to foster social-support seeking.

Respectfully submitted,

//Signed//

LCDR Alan L. Hensley, USN (Ret.), PhD Candidate, BCETS, FAAETS

REFERENCES (for Appendices C thru F)

Bem, S. L. (1974). The measurement of psychological androgyny. *Journal of Consulting and Clinical Psychology, 42,* 155-162.

Costa, P. T., & McCrae, R. R. (1992a). *Revised NEO Personality Inventory (NEO PI-R).* Lutz, FL: Psychological Assessment Resources, Inc.

Costa, P. T., Jr., & McCrae R. R. (1992b). Normal personality in clinical practice: The NEO Personality Inventory. *Psychological Assessment: A Journal of Consulting and Clinical Psychology, 4*(1), 5-13.

Folkman, S. & Lazarus, R. S. (1988). The relationship between coping and emotion: Implications for theory and research. *Social Science Medicine, 26(3),* 309-317.

Goldberg, L.R., & Freyd, J.J. (2003). The Brief Betrayal Trauma Survey (BBTS). Retrieved January 10, 2008 from http://dynamic.uoregon.edu.

Hensley, A. L. (2009a). *Gender, personality, and coping: Unraveling gender in military post-deployment wellbeing.* In press.

Hensley, A. L. (2009b). *Gender, personality, and coping* [preliminary results]. In press.

Kubany, E. S. (1994). A cognitive model of guilt typology in combat-related PTSD. *Journal of Traumatic Stress, 7,* 3-19.

Kubany, E. S. (2004a). *Trauma Life Events Questionnaire (TLEQ) and PTSD Screening and Diagnostic Scale (PSDS).* Los Angeles: Western Psychological Services.

Kubany, E. S. (2004b). *The Trauma-Related Guilt Inventory* (TRGI). Los Angeles: Western Psychological Services.

Kubany, E. S., Haynes, S. N., Abueg, F. R, Manke, F. P., Brennan, J. M., & Starhura, C. (1996). Development and validation of the Trauma-Related Guilt Inventory (TRGI). *Psychological Assessment, 5,* 428-444.

Kubany, E. S., & Watson, S. B. (2003). Guilt: Elaboration of a multidimensional model. *The Psychological Record, 53,* 51-90.

Lazarus, R. S., & Folkman, S. (1984). *Stress, appraisal, and coping.* New York: Springer.

Rotter, J. B. (1966). Generalized expectancies for internal versus external control of reinforcement. *Psychological Monographs, 80.* (Whole No. 609).

About the Author

Lieutenant Commander Alan Hensley, USN (Retired) is a former national- and military-level Cryptologist, Intelligence Officer, and Psychological Operations (PSYOP) Officer who has served in locations around the globe both during twenty-five years in military service and subsequently as a civilian. During deployments, he has had the unique opportunity to live among, and interact with, a myriad of cultures, while studying their norms, morals, ethics, values, and spirituality in the accomplishment of their daily lives and during stressful periods.

During this time, he has also been deployed with military and civilian men and women from a wide cross-section of American and International societies. As Operation Enduring Freedom and Operation Iraqi Freedom commenced, he resumed pursuit of his PhDs in Human Services and Psychology in order to better assist the men and women of the Armed Forces identify maladaptive coping strategies and develop more adaptive resilient coping strategies during deployment, provide intradeployment crisis intervention, and provide better targeted post-deployment treatment for experiences encountered during deployment.

He is now engaged in data collection and analysis for his dissertation, Gender, Personality, and Coping: Unraveling Gender in Post-Deployment Wellbeing. Among the early findings are that deployment-related stress relies highly upon gender-associated meaning and post-deployment PTSD and trauma-related guilt is not exclusively the result of combat related events. Regardless, PTSD and trauma-related guilt resulting from non-combat-related experiences result in such behavior as suicide and domestic violence. However, the current model of assessing post-deployment PTSD has not evolved to include non-combat trauma. Consequently, he has developed the Hensley Model of Biopsychosocial Wellbeing, which is been tested during his doctoral dissertation and is being closely followed by both military and non-military medical and mental health providers. In addition to pursuing his PhD, he has become a Board Certified Expert in Traumatic Stress (BCETS) and a Fellow of the American Academy of Traumatic Stress (FAAETS). He is also a member of the American Psychological Association, the Nebraska Psychological Association, the American Counseling Association, and the National Center for Crisis Management. Additionally, he is an Oversight Committee Member and Director of Research for the Sanctuary for Veterans and their Families headquartered in Washington. Owing largely to his partial Eastern Cherokee heritage, he also specializes in assisting Native American veterans recover from combat-related stress.

Betrayal Trauma: Insidious Purveyor of PTSD

LCDR Alan L. Hensley, USN (Ret.), BCETS, FAAETS

Abstract

This paper examines the plausibility of betrayal trauma as a possible causal or mediating agent in post-deployment PTSD. The presenter explores the relationship between psychological contract and betrayal trauma through the lenses of gender, gender roles, gender associated schemas, personality domains and facets, and locus of control resulting from empirically validated gender-associated biological, psychological, and sociological predisposition; social learning; and lifetime experiences. It discusses implications of post-deployment betrayal trauma on medical and mental health providers and crisis intervention personnel using recent case examples.

Introduction

Substantial public and journalistic emphasis has been placed on apparent *Post-Traumatic Stress Disorder* (PTSD) following deployment to Iraq and Afghanistan. However, Department of Defense (DOD), Service, and Department of Veterans Affairs (VA) researchers have narrowly focused on combat proximity, intensity, and duration as the most prevalent predictor of PTSD. This assertion, however, little explains the increased prevalence of PTSD among female service members in the low combat environment observed by Mental Health Assessment Team researchers (MHAT IV; USA OSG, 2007). Hensley (2009) investigated this phenomenon, finding significant differences in traumatic or stressful events between men and women and significant differences in event meaning among the four gender role types—*masculine, feminine, undifferentiated,* and *androgynous.* Specifically, females in low combat conditions experience greater sex-oriented interpersonal trauma involving violation of trust. Many males in high, medium, and low combat conditions reporting PTSD conditions, also report death or injury of others in combat with whom a close, continuing relationship exists, trauma-related guilt, and betrayal trauma as being more fundamental to PTSD symptoms than the event itself. Interestingly, the psychological contract is not exclusive to humans, however. Rather, some males and females cited an accidental death of a pet, which depended upon the person as a protector, as his or her *primary traumatic event* (PTE). The death, they asserted, was a betrayal of trust.

PTSD Diagnostic Criteria

The *Diagnostic and Statistical Manual of Mental Disorders,* Fourth Edition-Text Revision (DSM-IV-TR; American Psychiatric Association, 2000) asserts PTSD involves the development of certain characteristic symptoms after: a) experiencing, witnessing, or envisioning the death or serious injury of self or others, or; b) learning about the unexpected or violent death, serious injury, or threat of death or serious injury of close others (Criterion A1). The person's response to the event must involve intense fear, helplessness, or horror (Criterion A2). The characteristic symptoms resulting from the exposure to the extreme trauma include persistent reexperiencing of the traumatic event (Criterion B), persistent avoidance of stimuli associated with the trauma and numbing of general responsiveness (Criterion C), and persistent symptoms of increased arousal (Criterion D). Symptoms must remain present for more than 1 month (Criterion E). The disturbance must cause clinically significant distress or impairment in social, occupational, or other important areas of functioning. (Criterion F). However, many of the veterans surveyed in Hensley (2009) report Criteria A2, B, C, D, E, and F to either result from, or are exacerbated by the perceived violation of trust to a greater extent than the mere experience of the event.

Betrayal Trauma Exemplified: My soul for a star

In the movie *The General's Daughter* (Neufeld & West, 1999), the nude body of Army Captain Elizabeth Campbell, daughter of the highly respected and politically ambitious Lieutenant General *"Fighting Joe"* Campbell, was found strangled, sexually assaulted, and spread eagle at an urban warfare training site on Army base; her arms and ankles restrained by tent stakes. Army Criminal Investigation Division (CID) Investigators, Warrant Officers Brenner and Sunhill were summoned to investigate the apparent homicide.

As the investigation unfolded, the investigators uncovered a pattern of deviant sexual behavior involving the attractive Army officer dating back to her sophomore year of her training at West Point, seven years earlier. Prior to that time, she had been a highly dedicated over-achiever, excelling at virtually every endeavor and measurably overshadowing the abilities of her male counterparts. After a particularly intense nighttime field exercise, however, her personality dramatically changed. In fact, she barely succeeded in graduating (arguably only doing so because she was General Campbell's daughter). Absent additional facts, a mental health professional might opine that her dysfunction was likely the result of stress associated with the combat-oriented event.

Seven years later, assigned to an Army Post commanded by her father, her promiscuity, involving virtually every male Soldier on his staff, became notorious. However, the General had, by all accounts, distanced himself from his daughter simultaneously with her downfall into mediocrity at the Academy. Even her sexual exploits with his staff seemed to draw little attention, until her nude, sexually assaulted body is found at the training site.

As Brenner and Sunhill continued their investigation, they unveiled a macabre, dark side of Captain Campbell's behavior, in which her one confidant, Colonel Robert Moore, was seemingly involved. Unable to make a direct connection between Moore and Captain Campbell's death, Brenner arrested Moore for *Conduct Unbecoming of a Military Officer;* a violation of the *Uniformed Code of Military Justice* (UCMJ). In the brig, Brenner questioned Moore regarding his involvement in Campbell's' death and her downward spiral into social deviance. As Brenner prepared to leave, Moore uttered, *"It was awful." "It was awful?"* Brenner responded, *"What, she violated the Code?" "It was worse,"* responded Moore. *"What, rape?"* Brenner retorted. Moore countered with, *"Worse." "What is worse than rape?"* questioned Brenner. Moore concluded the discussion with, *"When you find that out, then you'll know everything won't you."*

Questioning the Psychiatrist at West Point, Brenner and Sunhill discovered that seven years earlier Campbell had endured heinous, nearly continuous rape until nearly sunrise by several fellow Soldiers during the nighttime maneuvers in question. Left beaten, sexually assaulted, and staked in a spread-eagle position, the perpetrators told Campbell she would die if she ever revealed their identity. Upon hearing of the event, Brigadier General (one star) Campbell, stationed in Berlin, flew to his daughter's bedside. However, before meeting his daughter, General Campbell met with the post Commanding Lieutenant General (three stars). The Commanding General suggested Campbell convince his daughter to drop the charges. In return, he would be given a second star. The Commanding General argued, if disclosed, the news would harm the integration of females into the military and appointment to the academy. Meeting with his daughter afterwards, Brigadier General Campbell, the person Elizabeth trusted and respected most, advised his daughter to remain silent. *"No good can come from you pursuing the events,"* he argued. Elizabeth, feeling betrayed and alone, began to distance herself from everyone and bore little resemblance to the intelligent, strong person. Instead, she seemed to merely continue to exist.

Confronted by Brenner, General Campbell confirmed he had given his daughter an ultimatum—resign her commission or she would be prosecuted under the *Uniformed Code of Military Justice* (UCMJ). As a venue to demonstrate the extent of her psychological and emotional distress resulting from his earlier advice in the hospital room, Elizabeth concocted a scheme involving her only confidant, Colonel Moore, to stake her to the ground at the Urban Warfare site exactly as she would have been seven years earlier. Her father was then summoned under the premise of giving him an answer to his ultimatum. Seeing his daughter distraught, nude, vulnerable, and begging for him to consider the biopsychosocial distress he had caused her, the General turned in repugnance and drove away. However, the leering eyes of Army Colonel Kent had observed the sequence of events. Distraught and jealous, the Colonel, who had long obsessed over Campbell, strangled her and left her body as he had found it; nude and spread eagle with her arms and legs staked to the ground.

As Brenner concluded his detailed and accurate investigation, General Campbell told Brenner that he alone would write the approved version of the report. In return, a Letter of Commendation (LOC) would be entered into Brenner's official record for his exemplary performance. However, Brenner countered, *"This is my investigation and it will be factual." "You killed your daughter,"* Brenner further offered, *"Colonel Kent merely put her out of her misery."* Brenner concluded the discussion with, *"I once asked Colonel Moore, what is worse than rape?" "Now, I know,"* he continued, *"... betrayal."*

Some persons might argue the irrelevance of this fictional story line. However, events involving female Soldiers in Iraq and Afghanistan argue otherwise. Presented with non-combat, but personally meaningful stressors, many military veterans suffer from shame, vilification, disappointment, and perceived betrayal equivalent to, or worse than, combat-related PTSD amidst a culture of ego, arrogance, denial, and ambivalence. Denial that these events occurred, and continue to occur, represents a blatant disregard for the personal and professional wellbeing of many highly dedicated persons. This disregard, as will be described in the following actual sample cases, can result in a myriad of adverse consequences, ranging from debilitating or immobilizing cognitive dissonance to domestic violence, spouse and child abuse, homicide, and suicide.

Kayla Williams

Getting off duty on a hilltop in Iraq and needing time to decompress prior to turning in, *Signals Intelligence* (SIGINT) Specialist Kayla Williams decided to visit her friend, Matt at the *COLT Operations Center. National Security Intelligence Directives* (NSIDs), Department of Defense (DOD) directives and Army intelligence policies require, except for brief periods, at least two people man the center, except for brief periods to eat or relieve oneself. However, when Williams arrived, she found the Center darkened. As she made her way through the darkness, she found only one person on watch—and that person was not her friend, Matt. Within arm's reach, she asked the male Specialist as to Matt's whereabouts, to which he responded that he had not awakened him for his watch. As her eyes became accustomed to the dark, she noticed his pants were opened and she had obviously arrived at an inappropriate time. Uncomfortable, Williams turned to leave. However, she soon felt a hand grab her arm and pull her towards his lower extremities. As Williams continued to resist she realized she had three options. First, she could scream, which would awaken others. However, then she would be perceived as *a girl*—unable to handle the situation on her own. She had her M4 rifle, which would definitively, but violently, diffuse the situation. Lastly, she could try to reason with him. She opted for the later. Gathering her composure, she spoke to him about his girl friend and the possible repercussion for his actions. As she continued to resist, the Specialist finally released his grip. Williams hastily retreated.

That night, the distraught Williams anguished in her bunk as to what to do. If she ignored the incident, it would cause everyone the least effort. However, if she did not report the incident, his next victim might not be as fortunate. Collecting her composure, Williams reported the occurrence to her supervisor. The supervisor, under the premise of causing the least repercussions to all parties concerned, requested Williams allow him to handle the case at the *non-judicial punishment* (NJP) level. In essence, the perpetrator would be punished and reassigned; however, an official investigation would not take place. Williams relented. However, the consequences of her relenting would result in distress far greater than that of the event alone.

Approximately a month later, a Specialist who was also permanently assigned to the new site of the perpetrator was temporarily assigned to Williams' mountaintop SIGINT site. In fact, he stated, he and the perpetrator were friends. While he and Williams were on watch one night he asked Williams if it was true that she had actually solicited sexual advances that night. The person offered that the perpetrator had widely spread his version and many knew of, and believed, his version. Williams stated she was angry that she had agreed to NJP. More importantly, she felt hurt, disappointed, and betrayed by her team members—both male and female. During the next few weeks she felt increasingly self-conscious. She felt as though everyone looked at her as if she was a whore. She had never felt more vulnerable and alone. Her biopsychosocial wellbeing began to cycle out of control. As her male team members began to increasingly tell rape jokes when she was near, Williams increasingly distanced herself from them. She began having intrusive nightmares of earlier traumatic events experienced during her tour, such as the revulsion and helplessness of watching a fellow soldier die. Flies covered the blood-soaked body. She felt powerless to help him then and she felt equally powerless to help herself now. Instead of feeling like a competent, valued team member, she felt as though the men and women, who had been her teammates and friends earlier, were treating her like *"a girl ... tits, a piece of ass, a bitch, a slut or whatever"* (Williams, 2005, p. 214). Williams' appetite became virtually non-existent and her normally petite frame became emaciated. She found herself crying easily and often. Yet no one asked, nor seemed to care why. She offered (p. 215), *"all [she] wanted to do was sleep and make the pain go away."* She just *"wanted to disappear."* Lastly, Williams offered it was during this period she had actually considered suicide to end the distress; *"It would be quick, easy, and the pain would be over."* Fortunately, the deployment was over soon afterward. Unfortunately, the situation Williams found herself in was not unique.

Suzanne Swift

During her junior year in high school, easy-going Suzanne Swift found herself being courted by military recruiters with offers of education, travel, and adventure. However, the campaign in Iraq had recently begun and she did not want to be deployed there. The Army recruiter reportedly offered that if she enlisted for five years as a Military Policeman instead of the traditional four, she would avoid being sent to Iraq. In the end, Swift relented and joined the Army as a venue to save money for college.

Under the delayed enlistment program, Swift's entry was delayed until after her graduation. After Basic Training and Advanced Infantry Training (AIT), however, the 18 year-old Swift found herself being deployed to Iraq. She recalls, in addition to coping with an unfamiliar environment that she was never properly prepared for, she found herself dealing with continual sexual harassment from male unit members, including her chain of command. Swift argues, in fear and awe of her squad leader in an exigent, male-dominant environment that she was not prepared to deal with, she was groomed, manipulated and ultimately coerced, into submission of her platoon leader's sexual advances. Attempts to end the relationship, however, led to further harassment and punishment for non-existent infractions. Swift reflects the only way she endured her deployment was *day-to-day.*

The deployment behind her, Swift hoped the sexual harassment was over. However, it did not end. Instead, it continued relentlessly. Instead, officers and enlisted alike at her stateside assignment continually propositioned and harassed Swift. She endured inappropriate questions both while on duty and during the night, including the type and color of her underwear. NCOs and officers told her that her place of duty that day was naked in their rack. Swift argues that attempts to report the allegations were never taken seriously. She was told she needed to *"Cowboy Up"* and learn how to prevent sexual harassment herself in the future. She continued to feel helpless to prevent further harassment and felt betrayed by those persons who were supposed to help.

In January 2006, only nine months after return from her first deployment and nine months before the end of her mandatory 18-month decompression period, Swift found herself scheduled for redeployment to Iraq. In March 2006, the night before her scheduled departure, with her professional and personal gear packed and in transit to Iraq, the distraught Swift called her mother and told her that she did not believe that she would survive another deployment. Instead, Swift went *Absent without Leave* (AWOL). Five months later, on June 11, 2006, police surrounded the Eugene, Oregon home of her mother, Sara Rich, who is a mental health counselor. Suzanne Swift was taken into custody. For the next three days, she was detained at the Fort Lewis Brig, under the supervision of the same man who had sexually assaulted her in Iraq.

In January 2007, Suzanne Swift was prosecuted in Special Court-Martial. She maintains during pretrial negotiations for nearly two months prior to the Special Court-martial, she was offered reduced charges and reduced level of judicial punishment if she would recant her accusations of being sexually assaulted while in Iraq. While she presented substantial evidence, the court ruled that too much time had elapsed since the alleged offenses in Iraq occurred. Therefore, the accused offenses could not/would not be prosecuted. However, the alleged harassment at her stateside assignment was not so easily refuted. The perpetrator received a *Letter of Admonishment* (LOA) and was transferred to another unit. Suzanne Swift pled guilty to missing movement and being AWOL. She was ordered to serve 30 days in the Fort Lewis Brig, reduced in rank to E1, and ordered to complete the duration of her enlistment. On March 30, 2007, Swift was reassigned as a shipping clerk at Ft. Irwin, California. Swift's case was reported by local, international news, including al Jazeera. In January 2009, Suzanne Swift was honorably discharged after completion of her enlistment contract.

Gender, personality, and coping

From September through December 2008, doctoral student Alan Hensley conducted research of veterans of Iraq and Afghanistan for his dissertation, *Gender, Personality, and Coping: Unraveling Gender in Military Post-Deployment Wellbeing* (Hensley, 2009). Sixty-one veterans of deployment to Iraq and Afghanistan participated; 26 females and 35 males. Hensley found, of the 26 female veterans surveyed, three had been sexually assaulted or raped during deployment, in addition to one male. Another female reported being the victim of date rape shortly prior to deployment and others reported being victims of physical, psychological, and emotional abuse.

The three female victims of sexual assault/rape would have been classified by the Army's Mental *Health Assessment Team* (MHAT IV; USA OSG, 2007) as having been assigned to a low-combat condition during deployment. Thus, the etiology of PTSD would have been disputable in post-deployment assessment. The MHAT IV, in fact, alludes to the inability to understand the increased prevalence of PTSD in female Soldiers in low combat conditions.

Hensley (2009) undertook to investigate the reason for the increased incidence of PTSD in low-combat conditions. He investigated the relationship between sex, gender roles, way of coping, locus of control, traumatic history and the *Primary Traumatic Event* (PTE) with PTSD, trauma-related guilt, and distress. During the course of his investigation, Hensley found over 11 percent of the female Soldiers participating in his study, in addition to others who declined to participate, had been sexually assaulted during deployment. Assessment of PTSD found, though not combat-related, all three suffered moderate or greater PTSD. Perhaps more troubling, in each case the victims assert, though the act in itself was traumatic, failure of the command to validate ascribed meaning, continued presence of the perpetrator, perceived betrayal of both male and female coworkers in the aftermath, and provided greater stigmatization than the event itself. These stimuli greatly exacerbated the initial adverse biopsychosocial response, resulted in diminished locus of control, and contributed to less confidence in professional and coping abilities. The observations by the victims both supports, and is supported by, van der Kolk, McFarlane, and Weisaeith (1996), as well as Kimmerling, Oimette, and Wolfe (2002) and Scaer (2001, 2005).

Though MHAT IV (USA OSG, 2007) argues combat exposure is fundamental to the occurrence and intensity of PTSD in returning veterans, the presented cases elucidate individual-specific meaning is perhaps most fundamental. These cases provide partial explanation of the increased incidence of PTSD among female veterans of the low combat condition. However, sexual assault/rape is not inextricably the exclusive domain of female Soldiers. Recall one male veteran also reported sexual assault. Though sexual assault partially explains increased incidence of PTSD in the low combat environment, it is not the only stimuli for non-combat related PTSD, as presented in the following case.

Alyssa R. Peterson

At approximately 0900 on September 16, 2003 an aircraft, flying near the Third Brigade Landing Zone (LZ) in *Tal Afar*, Iraq spotted what appeared to be a body in a nearby grassy field. The sighting was immediately radioed in to the Tactical Operations Center, which resulted in a series of swift actions involving many in the Third Brigade members. Within 10 minutes of report of the sighting, a squad of military police personnel secured the site. Little more than 90 minutes later, members of the *Criminal Investigative Division* (CID) arrived to begin a prolonged investigation that would take nearly a month to complete. The conclusion—Army Specialist Alyssa R. Peterson had died of a self-inflicted gunshot wound to the head. Her assigned M4 rifle lay at her side.

Though her death occurred at approximately 2200 (10:00 p.m.) and several persons had heard the gunshot, no attempts were made to ascertain the origin of the gunshot, nor the safety of assigned personnel. The shot was immediately disregarded as errant. Only when she failed to report for duty at 0730 the next morning, was she reported as missing. It was not until 0900 that her body was located.

The results of the investigation (US Army, 2003) revealed many observations regarding the personality, locus of control, and ways of coping that should have been considered in the weeks leading up to the suicide. Foremost, Alyssa Peterson was, by all accounts, a devout member of the Church of Latter Day Saints. Shortly prior to enlisting in the Army, she had, in fact, been a Mormon missionary who had learned Dutch to more effectively minister to the Dutch people. This fact speaks volumes regarding the mental model of morals, ethics, and values, as well as the roles and responsibilities Peterson integrated into the biopsychosocial conceptualization of Self.

Peterson had only arrived at Tal Afar on August 25, 2003, less than a month before her death. The second night after her arrival, she performed her first interrogation in what is known by interrogators in the military as *the cage* – the most psychologically and emotionally challenging experience for any *Human Intelligence* (HUMINT) Collector. Peterson found the experience far different from the protocol she had learned in training. The empathetic Peterson found it abusive, repugnant, and morally objectionable. Her substandard performance that night caused her leadership to conduct an *After-Action Review* (AAR). The AAR further resulted in verbal counseling by her supervisor, during which he offered that she needed to be more aggressive. In the post-death investigation (p. 6), her supervisor noted she had taken the *constructive criticism* poorly. Throughout the remainder of her assignment in the cage, she continued to be criticized for her inability to be "aggressive."

Statements by other fellow Brigade members who knew Peterson reflected in the post-death investigation that she was a quiet, pensive individual who largely kept to herself during the periods she was not on duty. In confidence, she had expressed to them her eagerness to learn, but also discomfort with using the coercive techniques required in interrogation. Her team members remarked that she was unable to emotionally distance herself from the detainees she was interrogating. Unfortunately, review of her pre-enlistment activities, personality domains and facets, and ways of coping would have given insight into Peterson's mental model and associated schemas, which would have, arguably perhaps, predicted and prevented this negative outcome.

After several failed attempts at conditioning her to what she viewed as abusive, antisocial behavior, Peterson was reassigned to HUMINT collection duties at the compound *entry control point* (EP). Her duties consisted of observing, listening, and collecting intelligence from conversations at the control point without revealing her understanding of Arabic. However, in doing so, she observed continued arrogance and belittlement of local nationals at the ECP by fellow Soldiers. The empathetic Peterson attempted to assist Iraqi nationals navigate impediments. However, in doing so, she revealed that she not only understood Arabic, but was also marginally conversant. Consequently, she was again counseled for her substandard performance. Her psychological contract in disequilibrium (See Figure 1), her normally internal locus of control compromised, and her dominant coping strategies ineffective, Peterson opted to bring relief to her overwhelmed biopsychosocial Self in the only way she could envision.

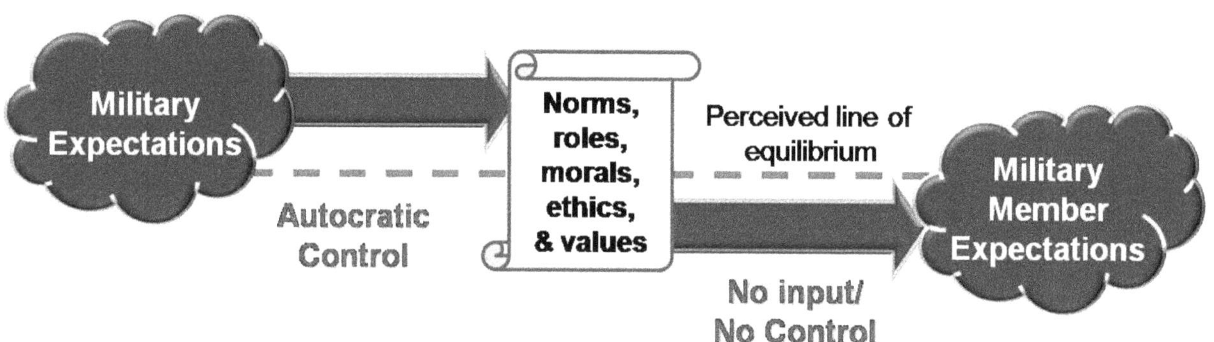

Figure 1. Psychological contract disequilibrium

On the evening of September 15, 2003, Peterson was released from duty between 2000 and 2100 hours (8:00 – 9:00 pm) to take a shower and sleep. Shortly afterward, the Company Executive Officer and Military Police personnel reported hearing the sound of two gunshots. She had walked into a nearby field and shot herself in the head, ending the month-long anguish and suffering of 27-year old Alyssa Peterson. It was not until she failed to report for duty at 0730 the following day, 12 hours after the gunshots were heard, that she was reported missing. In a farewell note, she mused how the anti-suicide training she had just received had taught her, not only why others committed suicide, but how to ensure it was done properly. This observation alludes to suicide prevention training focused more on the mechanics of suicide than on detection and prevention.

Peterson's death is only one example of the results of the multi-dimensional concept of *betrayal trauma*—perceived violation of a psychological contract with an influential or trusted other or others. The post-incident investigation largely reflects a Command mentality more intent upon making Peterson conform to the needs of the Army and more specifically, her Brigade, than concern for her physical, psychological, and emotional wellbeing.

Unfortunately, despite a wealth of empirical data, it also demonstrates the absence of understanding of mental models, schemas, psychological contracts, mutuality, reciprocity, and the consequences of actual or perceived betrayal trauma.

MHAT – The status quo

Coinciding with the commencement of Operation Iraqi Freedom, The Commanding General of the Multinational Forces in Iraq, the US Army's Office of the Surgeon General (USA OSG) requested periodic assessments by Mental Health Advisory Team (MHAT) of the wellbeing of US Army forces deployed to Iraq. The MHAT has now conducted five mental health assessments (USA OSG, 2004, 2005, 2006, 2007, 2008) of Soldiers and Marines serving in Iraq. Unfortunately, few similar efforts for Marines and Soldiers deployed to Afghanistan in support of OEF, or investigation of members of other military Services, are apparent in literature searches.

Based on anonymous self-report surveys completed by troops and on information gathered from behavioral health and primary care personnel and others, MHAT IV (USA OSG, 2007) purportedly endeavored to assess the mental health of deployed Army and Marine troops in Iraq from August 28 to October 3, 2006. While the report was completed in November 2006, it was not released to the public until May 2007.

Among the findings of the team was that combat level, family separation, and multiple deployments had the greatest effect on the respondents' mental health. However, the team failed to establish the importance of a key study finding. While, overall, no statistically significant [biological] gender differences were observed, significant differences among male and female Soldiers were observed in the low-combat condition. Specifically, whereas only one percent of the male soldiers in the LC condition screened positive for mental health problems, 17% of the females screened positive for mental health disorders (x2 (419) = 4.32, p<.03). These findings would seemingly suggest a) female Soldiers experience greater trauma/stress than males in LC conditions; b) female Soldiers assign greater meaning than males to events in the LC condition, or; c) coping strategies traditionally employed by females in the HC and MC conditions are ineffectual or not available in the LC condition. Hensley (2009) found violation of psychological contracts/betrayal trauma to be the most pervasive reason for this phenomenon.

Foundations of Betrayal Trauma

Psychological contracts are subjective, uncommunicated beliefs regarding morals, ethics, and values and rules, roles, and responsibilities between an individual, organizations and agents of those organizations (Rousseau, 1995). Fundamental to the development and maintenance of the psychological contract is the belief in mutuality and reciprocity. Also integral is a fundamental belief in honesty, integrity, and openness of the other part(ies) involved. However, this is rarely, if ever, the case. Over time, the psychological contract(s) become(s) embedded as a schema. It is through the outcome of events in relationship to the person's psychological contract(s) that the person views, understands and responds self in relationship to his or her environment.

Researchers investigating psychological contracts in the workplace (Coyle-Shapiro & Kessler, 2000; Robinson & Rousseau, 1994; Robinson & Wolfe Morrison, 1995; Rousseau & Tijoriwala, 1999; Turnley & Feldman, 2000) have found that individually, socio-culturally, and socio-environmentally influenced differences in worker psychological contracts causes them to respond differently to planned and unplanned organizational changes and perceived violation. Their research also finds that violated psychological contracts result in more intense attitudinal and emotional responses than mere unmet expectations.

Understanding the dynamics of violation of the psychological contract would be difficult without understanding the foundations of its creation.

Nature or nurture

For nearly as long as social researchers have endeavored to understand human perception, understanding, and behavior, a passionate debate has existed whether human personality is the result of nature or nurture. *Tabula Rasa* theorists, such as John Locke (1996) posit that the human mind begins life as a *blank slate* (Pinker, 2002), devoid of any predispositional abstractions or understanding. Relationships and event meaning, then, results from learning and experiences. In *The Blank Slate,* Pinker (2002, p. 44) argues, *"Differences in intelligence, scientific genius, sexual orientation, and impulsive violence are not entirely learned."* Twin studies conducted in the past few decades (Ridley, 2003; Wright, 1997) have, in fact, demonstrated that personality is the exclusive domain of neither nature nor nurture. Rather, it is a result of a complex individually defined algorithm of social learning acting upon biopsychosocial predispositional tendencies. Ridley (2003) suggests the human brain (psychological self) possesses the capacity to mediate the extent to which socio-environmental experiences reinforce or attenuate innate biological self [forming a biopsychosocial loop].

In *The Language Instinct,* Steven Pinker (1995) offers the poignant observation that if children are born with the innate desire to speak, why, then, aren't they born speaking? Why does speaking ability evolve from utterances to descriptive dialogues of complex concepts and abstractions? Who determines the relationships, relevance, and meanings of life events that are integrated into thought and those that are discarded as meaningless or irrelevant? Pinker (1995) offers that the answer has to do with brain size and other developmental factors, such as sociocultural indoctrination. In a subsequent work, *The Blank Slate,* Pinker (2002) makes an astute observation—language, like life, is not static. Rather, it evolves with the need for specificity for newly experienced phenomenon, or alternatively generalization of individual descriptors that have become individually irrelevant or linguistically laborious. Recall that the purpose of language is to convey a common meaning with others. As the world becomes increasingly mobile, some languages and dialects give way to attrition—the absence of need. Pinker (2002) argues humans innately strive to survive. As such, we are innately endowed with a genetic biopsychosocial predisposition to adapt to changing circumstances.

Mental models, schemas, promises, and mutuality

The term, *mental model,* reflects the global cognitive abstraction an individual holds about conceptually related elements, the relationship between those elements, and his or her relationship to those elements. This overarching abstraction evolves from simplistic generalization with few linkages to highly detailed conceptualizations as the individual gathers new understanding from learning and experiences. Thus, the mental model provides the referential worldview for the individual's perception, cognition, and behavior in context with his or her realm of exposure or understanding.

Similarly, the individual develops a schema, or a plan, for viewing, understanding, and responding to new or recurring experiences (Young, Klosko, & Weishaar, 2003; Stein, 1992; Horowitz, 1988; Rousseau, 2001). Initially, extremely simplistic to deal with satisfaction of such seemingly basic needs as physiological needs (e.g., food, air, and water), schemas evolve into a highly intricate hierarchy, with both vertical and horizontal aspects (See Figure 1). The vertical aspect deals with hierarchical level of abstraction, such as prioritized levels of need. Arranged in a descending hierarchy, the levels evolve from highly generalizable to levels of higher specificity. Meanwhile, the horizontal dimension deals with differentiation, such as viable options given different socio-environmental conditions. New experiences enter in a top-down approach until a viable schema is found. Unfortunately, this schema is not necessarily the most appropriate or best schema. Rather, it is merely a viable schema. Numerous studies have been conducted regarding the decision-making processes a person might use in a domestic relationship. Fig. 2 presents a possible visual abstraction of the schematic process:

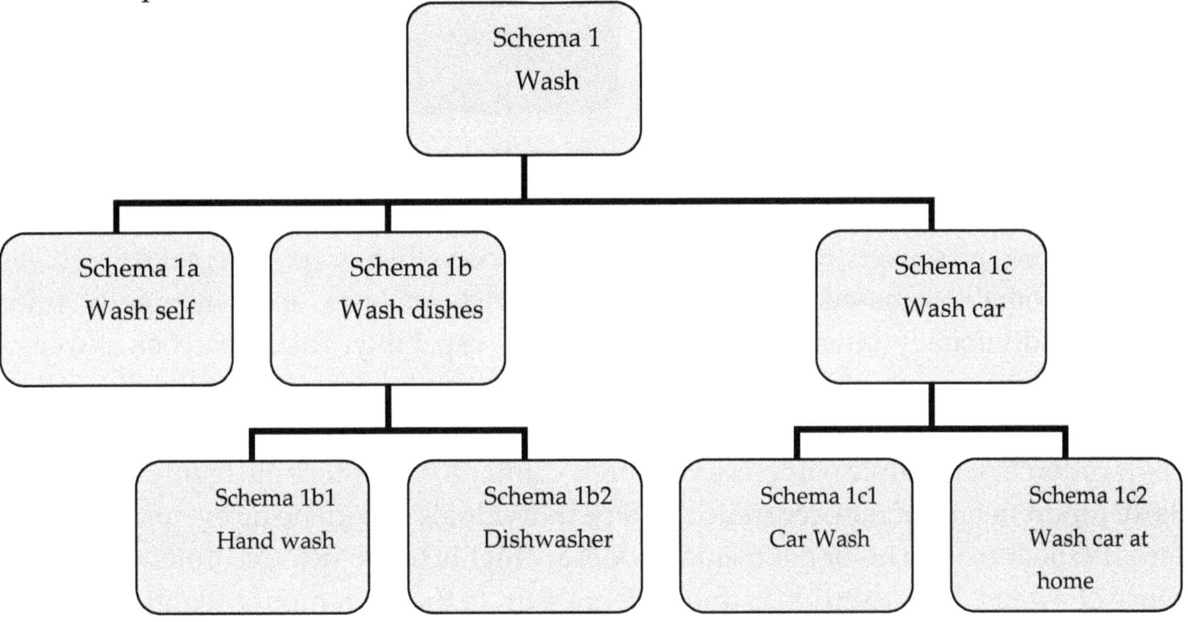

Fig. 2. Schema Hierarchy Example

Thus, though frequently used synonymously, the scope and complexity of the mental model extends well beyond that of schemas. In military vernacular, then, while a schema may be viewed as a tactical plan for dealing with a specific issue, the mental model may be thought of as a strategic plan for dealing with the myriad of issues for which the individual perceives him or herself responsible.

More salient to the present discussion, evolutionists and others studying the neuro-endocrine system (Rothschild, 2000; Wilson, 2007; van der Kolk et al, 1996) argue humans are innately endowed with the desire to prolong longevity and preserve the human species. Fundamental to this innate desire is conservation of resources and economy of effort. These researchers, and others, repeatedly report the biopsychosocial consequences of prolonged or repeated stressors. Young et al (2005) theorizes, as an adaptive psychological process to minimize biopsychosocial stress, reduce the harmful production of Cortisol and other

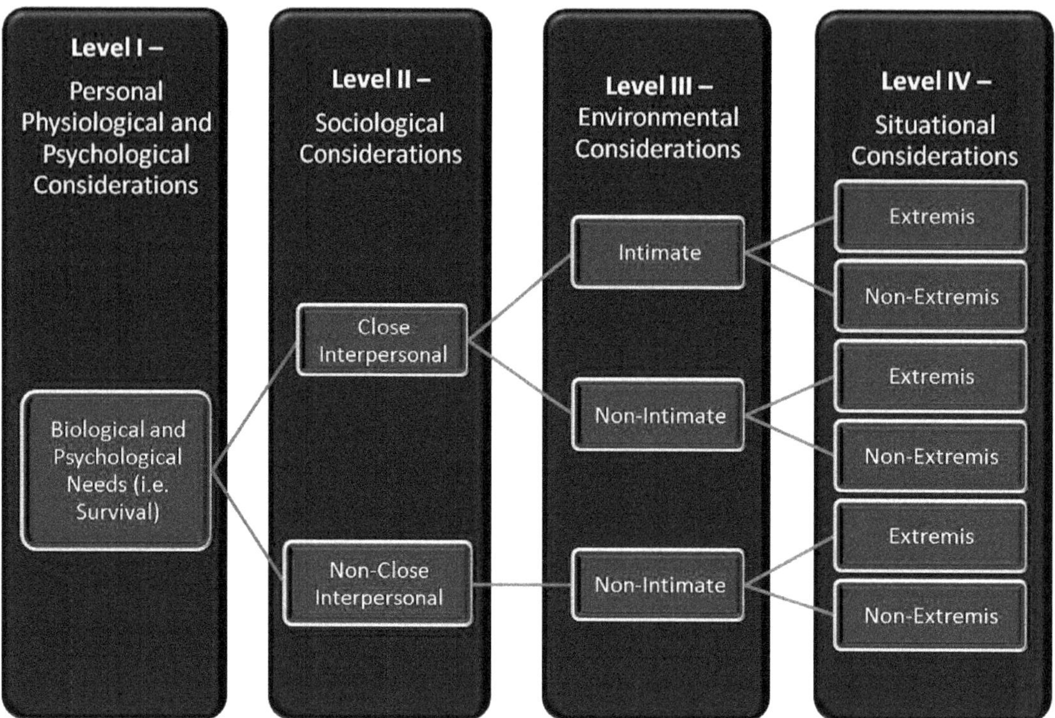

Fig. 3: Schematic Decision-making process

enzymes required for *fight, flight,* or *freeze* in exigent situations, and to minimize the over-tasking cognitive and sensory resources, humans rely upon schemas (pl. schemata) to achieve a level of automaticity based upon categorization, risk analysis, and outcome of prior experiences. Additionally, schemas provide a predictive capability. This researcher, however, also suggests schemas provide a *pre-cognitive filter* capability, which prevents illogical or irrelevant from ever reaching the level of active cognition. This hypothesis is supported by the observation that multiple witnesses viewing a common occurrence are highly unlikely to similarly report details of the occurrence. In fact, individuals experiencing events that are in extreme dissonance with his or her mental model are highly unlikely to accurately report the sequence of events. This assertion is due, in large part, to the contemporary understanding that observations are not viewed, analyzed, stored or retrieved in sequence. Rather, data is observed, analyzed, and stored as isolated sequential fragments of data.

The mental model, providing a referential capacity, provides the predictive intervening understanding from which the narrative is constructed and communicated. Thus, important details, especially preliminary details of the event contrasting greatly with established understanding are prone to be disregarded or misinterpreted in cognition. This phenomenon is well understood by anthropologists and persons engaged in *hermeneutics* – events of thousands, hundreds, and even a few years ago, cannot be understood in context of the person's current understanding of his or her world. Likewise, persons of diverse cultures are unlikely to correctly interpret intent and meaning of events occurring in another society without understanding the history, needs, morals, ethics, and values of the other culture.

One, or a few, schema[s] cannot be relied upon to accurately view, understand, or respond to all new experiences. Rather, a person actively builds and revises schemata in light of new information. As new events are experienced, schemas and even the mental model is subject to change through *accretation, tuning,* or *restructuring.* In accretion, the person assimilates the new data it into his or her existing schema without making any changes to the overall schema. In tuning, the individual realizes the existing schema is inadequate for the new knowledge. The existing schema is then modified accordingly. Restructuring is the process of creating a new schema to address the inconsistencies between the old schema and the newly acquired data.

Schemas can also serve an interpretive and inferential function, helping the person create a rational abstraction of missing or unavailable data (Crocker, Fiske, & Taylor, 1984). Unfortunately, because of the hierarchical nature of schemas, future schemas built upon erroneous schemas are likely to exacerbate misunderstanding.

Emerging Adults

Arnett (2000) suggested persons between the ages 18 to 25 are engaged in a distinctive life stage called *Emerging Adulthood*. It is during this period that persons engage in earnest relationships, establishing rules, roles, and responsibilities grounded not only in prior learning, but social experimentation. During this period, men and women develop a realistic expectation of domestic relations.

The United States is currently involved in two consecutive wars, in which many service members have now been deployed multiple times; some as many as four and five times. Nearly a quarter of the roles being filled in the military are female. Unfortunately, the roles these women are filling are, in many cases, gender role incongruent, and are in a traditionally male dominant environment or endeavor. Consequently, the rules, roles, and relationships, as well as the wartime morals, ethics, and values they learn will not necessarily reflect socioculturally acceptable expectations of gender roles for the non-military environment. Additionally, prolonged combat exposure during this period of psychosocial development is likely to produce, what will later be considered, as antisocial personalities. For example, in August 2002, four wives were the victims of homicide committed by their husbands, using techniques learned by their husbands during the course of combat deployment in Afghanistan. Not well known, is the fact that a fifth homicide by a wife occurred during that same period. This would not be the end however. In the three months leading up to December 2008, three girlfriends and wives were similarly killed. What then is the longitudinal impact on the perception of the families and children of these men and of the inability of the military to ensure learned combat skills do not become the *status quo* upon return? Recall Peterson mused that the suicide prevention training she had received two weeks earlier served as the foundation for her choice of methods for self-inflicted death—a method rarely taken by a female in a non-combat environment. The CID learned, in many of the cases described at Fort Bragg, the men perceived betrayal by their wives or girlfriends as the crime motivator. In many of the cases, the wives were estranged or seeking divorce. In 2008, Fort Bragg officials investigated over 500 incidents of domestic violence—38 percent higher than the previous year. This finding is troubling in view of the findings of MHAT V (USA OSG, 2008), which recently reported prolonged, repeated deployment is having severe consequences on the wellbeing of the Soldiers surveyed.

Gender Roles

Though the term, sex, is relatively well understood in most societies to represent male and female, the term, gender, is perhaps one of the most confused terms in the social sciences. Empirical data and research findings are fraught with conflicting data and confounded findings primarily due to the misuse of the term gender. Simone de Beauvoir (1956, 1989) eloquently stated that one is not born, but rather becomes a woman. This statement is fundamental to assertion that studies purporting to contrast the differences among males and females in any given endeavor are inherently flawed; especially in the contemporary context when men and women vie for the same occupational positions that were once the exclusive domain of one sex or the other. In great contrast to past generations, and in many cases to current non-western European cultures, American and Western European women are now being groomed as androgynous individuals, fully capable of operating in a previously male-dominated workplace. Additionally, men often now fill the ranks of teachers, nurses, and caregivers, traditionally considered the exclusive domain of women. Even within families, the traditional socially ascribed sex roles are disappearing or diminishing. Consequently, de Beauvoir's assertions become even more relevant than when asserted. While biological sex is rather indisputable based upon *x*, y-chromosomes, gender and gender roles are not nearly so clearly identified. Bem (1981) identified four gender role categories: *masculine, feminine, undifferentiated,* and *androgynous.* Undifferentiated persons present neither strong masculine, nor feminine gender characteristics. Androgynous persons, alternatively, present both strong masculine and feminine gender role characteristics.

In his dissertation research, *Gender, Personality, and Coping,* Hensley (2009) found among 61 veterans of Operation Iraqi Freedom (OIF) and Operation Enduring Freedom (OEF), military men are not inherently masculine and military females are not inherently female. In fact, while 16 of the 35 (46%) of the male veterans participating presented masculine gender role characteristics, three (8.5%) presented a feminine gender role, 13 (37%) presented an undifferentiated gender role, and three (8.5%) presented an androgynous gender role. Among females however, five (19%) of the 26 females participating presented a masculine gender role, 10 (38%) presented a feminine gender role, three (12%) presented an undifferentiated gender role, and seven (27%) presented an androgynous gender role. In analysis, Hensley found while no statistically significant differences were observed when investigating the relationship between biological sex, personality, ways of coping, locus of control, and PTSD, trauma-related guilt, and distress. When examining the relationship between biological sex and the *Primary Traumatic Event* (PTE) men more often described a combat-related event as the most traumatic event in his life, none of the women described a combat-related event as the PTE; however, three of the 26 females reported rape during deployment as the most traumatic event. In examination of the relationship of gender role to the PTE, two of these women reported masculine gender roles, one reported an androgynous gender role. Thus, while sexual assault victimization is largely the result of biological sex, response to sexual assault is biopsychosocially diverse.

One female described pre-deployment sexual assault as the most troubling event. She reported a masculine gender role. Three women described dissolution of marriages/personal relationships during deployment as the most troubling. Regarding ways of coping, distinctive differences in coping required comparison of both biological sex and gender. For example, comparison of the means between males and females (M=1.0304 and M=1.1037 respectively) in *Positive Reappraisal* yielded little significance. However, examination of the means between masculinity and femininity yielded far greater significance (M=.7319, M=1.1739 respectively). Examining *Planful Problem-Solving,* however, while the comparison between masculinity and femininity yielded little statistically significant difference (M=1.6025, M=1.7623 respectively), examination of the relationship between males and females yielded greater statistical significance (M=1.7115, M=1.4088 respectively).

Examining gender role differences, the greatest mean difference in ways of coping are observed between androgynous and masculine persons in Positive Reappraisal (M=1.350, M=.7317 respectively) and in *Social Support-Seeking* (M=1.6243, M=1.0690 respectively). Thus, while Planful Problem-Solving appears to be more significantly predicted by biological sex, indicating a greater biological or intrinsically learned sociocultural component, Social Support-Seeking and Positive Reappraisal are more significantly predicted by gender, indicating a greater extrinsically learned component. Through gender role conditioning and interaction with the same and opposite sex, persons develop highly subjective expectations of acceptable morals, ethics and values and rules, roles, and responsibilities. Additionally, psychological contracts developed from these interactions serve as the foundation of trust.

Psychological Contracts

Largely an outgrowth of the employment sector, theorists espousing the psychological contract theory (Rousseau, 1996; Conway & Briner, 2005), suggest not all facets of norms and expectancies can be included in a formal written, or even verbal, contract. In fact, while formal contracts define norms and expectancies between an employer and employee, interpretations of *who, what, when, where, why,* and *how* of roles, responsibilities, and relationships is often highly subjective and reflects the worldview of the person interpreting the roles, responsibilities, norms, and expectancies. These theorists and others (Freyd, 1995, 1999; Freyd, Klest, & Allard, 2005; Erikson, 1959, 1982) suggest violations of psychological contracts are, in fact, the basis of feelings of betrayal and distrust. Holistic conceptualization of Maslow's (1970) *Hierarchy of Needs,* Erikson's (1959, 1982) *Stages of Psychosocial Development,* Rousseau's (1996) *Psychological Contract Theory,* Young's *Schema Theory* (Bartlett, 1932, 1958; Mandler, 1981; Young, Klosko, & Weishaar, 2003), and Freyd's *Betrayal Trauma* Theory suggests violation of the psychological contract at an early age, which is subsequently reinforced, is likely to result in feelings of betrayal and maladaptive schemas by which the person subsequently views, understands, and responds to his or her environment.

Betrayal trauma

In 1991, Jennifer Freyd (1994) introduced the term, betrayal trauma in a presentation at the Langley Porter Institute. Though the term is, fact, a very real concern, researchers (Goldberg; Freyd, Allard) erroneously use it. In that Freyd and others refer to a dysfunction resulting from the offense, the contextual meaning of the term would be more aptly phrased *betrayal trauma dissociation.* Specifically Freyd referred to traumatic amnesia, a consequence of the insult, resulting from childhood abuse. *Betrayal trauma,* then, would refer to the offense itself, which might result in a continuum of consequences ranging from minor distress to PTSD or trauma-related dissociation.

Discussion

A careful review of the post-incident investigation into Specialist Peterson's death speaks volumes regarding the perception of both Alyssa Peterson on one end of the psychological contract and those individuals comprising the amalgamated category, Army, on the other. Not only does it exemplify, in explicit detail, the relationships between schemas, promises, and trust, it demonstrates the extreme consequences of failure to consider personality in occupational assignment, dual role expectancy, diminished locus of control, and betrayal of trust.

The Company Commander recounted that four days prior to her death, he had spoken at breakfast with Peterson. He reflected that she was angry at observation that detainees were considered guilty and treated aggressively until proven innocent. This procedure, she said, was unwarranted, in that only three of 43 detained interrogated during her first interrogation, were found to be worth further interrogation. She argued the abusiveness with which they were handled was sending the wrong message to the Iraqi people. In closing, Peterson stated she intended to reclassify into another specialty. Problematic, his concluding remark in his written statement (USA, 2003) states, "Her behavior did not concern me. She seemed as any other soldier."

Virtually all persons providing statements described Peterson as quiet, reflective, and eager to learn. Some of the respondents indicated a sympathetic, big-hearted, caring and friendly individual. Others suggested she was sullen and antisocial. Peterson's Platoon Sergeant observed that (p.12) *"she never participated in any off-duty activities with the Section and never accepted anything from any Section members."* He continued, *"She always stated she did not want to owe favors or anything to anybody."*

Initially assigned in "the cage" to interrogate detainees, she demonstrated extreme distress being aggressive. When advised by her fellow interrogators that she, in fact, needed to be two persons, Peterson responded (p.14), *"I don't know how to be two people; I can't be one person in the cage and another outside of the wire."* She was reassigned to the entry point as a human intelligence (HUMINT) collector. However, on more than one occasion, she had to be counseled not to reveal the fact that she understood Arabic on watch. Peterson spent off-duty time reading or working on her language skills with native interpreters. However, when accompanying other team members to meet with trusted sources, she was counseled not to speak Arabic because it disrupted the flow of communication between the more experienced linguists and the sources.

A team member (p.14) observed, *"She took criticism very personal."* She had, following one verbal counseling session (p.14), stated, *"every time [she] took initiative to do something, [she] was wrong."* Her typically high internal locus of control was being challenged by a persistent view of failure by powerful and influential others. Attribution for this failure by Peterson and others were at bipolar extremes. Despite her intense desire to learn the language properly and assist the locals, the highly empathetic Peterson was not being provided with the opportunity to do so. Instead, she was being coerced to use her skills in a manner she considered morally repugnant. She had been in country 25 days; leaving over 11 months remaining. Thus, relief from her cognitive dissonance was unlikely and trusted persons were non-existent.

Interestingly, one of the respondents providing a statement also provided a glimpse into Peterson's childhood. He reflected (p.18) that she had told him that she came from a financially austere family. Though her parents tried, they were not able to provide much assistance and her father had been unable to obtain/maintain employment. As such, she was required to largely use her own planful problem-solving to provide for her own needs. This speaks greatly to her *modus operandi* of not wanting to owe anything to anyone.

Seventeen days prior to Peterson's death, the entire Company received mandatory suicide training. However, none of the persons issuing statements reflected observing signs of suicidal behavior. Thinly veiled in her book, *Love my Rifle More Than You,* Kayla Williams

(2005) reflects on meeting Peterson four days before her death. A civilian linguist came to Williams asking if she knew Peterson. She had been having some family problems and, because Williams was a female, he thought perhaps she could help.

Williams reflected Peterson did not appear irrational. Rather, she was (p. 222) *"fidgety,"* twirling her hair with her fingers. Williams described her as shy and reserved. As Williams listens, she relates that she had not told her family that she was being deployed to Iraq. Regarding the relationship, Peterson only stated (p. 222), *"It's not a good situation, you know."* Disrupted by others, the two conclude with the promise to talk when Williams comes back from her mission the next day. Four days later, Peterson was dead.

Williams reflects, not on the anguish Peterson must have felt, but rather her own anger for the Command organizing a memorial service and requiring all command members to attend, whether they knew her or not. Sitting on folding chairs under the blazing sun, she recalls (p. 255) thinking, *"Don't we have anything better to do than memorialize a girl who couldn't take it?"* However, distress soon began to set in. *"I should have done more,"* she thought, *"I should have noticed something."* Williams' cycle of anger and guilt at Peterson is disrupted by intense anger and repulsion of her Brigade Commander as she reflects on the memorial service (p. 227):

> "When I first heard about [Peterson's] death, I was shocked and saddened ... but, as time passed, I experienced another emotion ...I'm angry, because [Peterson] caused this because she never reached out for help .... [She] never went to the chain of command, never went to the Chaplain. This is her fault ... It should never have come to this."

Removing guilt by denial and external attribution to others has long been identified as a coping strategy to resolve extreme cognitive dissonance. Was this a Brigade Commander actually condemning the actions of a person who committed an irrational act because of interminable suffering? Or, alternatively, was this a person who, like Williams, reflected in retrospect so many signs of perceived betrayal and resulting biopsychosocial distress were presented, yet unrecognized or not acted upon? What can be learned from this event?

Though many have subconsciously entertained similar thoughts, the brigade members were angry and repulsed by her remarks. What effect, then, would this attribution have on the perception of trust and compassion afforded them by the Army as a whole through the acts of one senior leader? Would a victim of sexual assault be afforded understanding and compassion or, alternatively, would they be condemned for placing themselves in a position where they could be raped.

Substantial research (van der Kolk et al., 1996; Scaer, 2001, 2005) finds that women in the general US population are nearly twice as likely to experience PTSD as their male counterparts. In the general population, statistical analysis of crime statistics also finds that, while men are exposed to more potentially traumatic experiences, women, proportionately, experience greater personal trauma (e.g., rape and assault). Would this assertion, likewise hold true in a military deployed environment? Researchers, such as van der Kolk et al (1996) find that, generally men experience more potentially traumatic experiences. The MHAT IV (USA OSG, 2007) asserts that combat-related proximity, intensity, and duration are the greatest predictors to post-deployment PTSD. Why then, do females in the low combat environment experience greater PTSD than their male counterparts? Hensley found by virtue of biological sex, three females and one male reported sexual assault. The three females would have been categorized as being members of the low combat condition. Arguably, perhaps, they experienced sexual assault as one cause of their biological sex. However, none of the three demonstrated feminine gender roles; two presented masculine gender roles and one presented an androgynous gender role. Thus, all three females presented greater masculine gender role characteristics than feminine. All three women demonstrated satisfaction of the DSM-IV-TR criteria for PTSD of the moderate to severe range.

The masculine females presented greater PTSD symptoms than the androgynous female. In statistical analysis, Hensley found masculine gender role females reported less use of short-term adaptive/long-term adaptive and short-term adaptive/long term maladaptive coping strategies. Both masculine and androgynous women, reported greater use of distancing as a viable coping strategy. Peterson, Swift, and Williams all reported use of distancing, not necessarily as a conscious coping strategy, but as a statement of fact. Feminine and androgynous females reported the least reliance on social support seeking. Masculine and undifferentiated females, however, report the least reliance on social support-seeking. Peterson, Swift, and Williams clearly reflect low reliance on social support-seeking. Interestingly, Williams clearly identifies her desire to just disappear and to sleep as a venue to relieve stress. Escape avoidance is most typical among feminine and androgynous females.

Peterson, Swift, and Williams all identified highly androgynous gender roles, which are supported by their ways of coping. However, androgynous persons, arguably, have higher understanding and expectations of mutuality and reciprocity with persons of the opposite sex as well as persons of their own sex. In essence, they have a more firmly established psychological contract, reinforced by past favorable experience. Betrayal of these psychological contracts would be more traumatic or distressing than persons with weak psychological contracts. This might partially explain Williams' extreme expressed disappointment, not only in the males in her unit, but in the females with which she physically and biopsychosocially identified. However, Williams' most dominant coping strategies were arguably unavailable because of the previously unexperienced nature of her traumatic experiences. Likewise, Peterson's lifetime experiences and achievements argue that she, too, found herself in a repressive environment in which her primary coping strategies were ill suited to handle her biopsychosocial distress.

Members of Swift's court-martial questioned, and adversely viewed, the fact she had waited until after deployment to report the sexual assault she experienced during deployment. In fact, commanding officers, the chain of command, and criminal justice practitioners frequently question why female soldiers often wait until after deployment to report acts of sexual assault. Freyd's betrayal trauma theory provides a plausible explanation for this phenomenon, in which delayed reporting might be the result of conscious deliberation or even a subconscious coping strategy of denial and dissociation to overcome betrayal trauma and to preserve the trusted relationship while needed and viable. Unfortunately, these possibilities also incur adverse post-deployment consequences, such as shame, guilt, helplessness, and other manifestations of PTSD and comorbid disorders and dysfunction as the person endeavors to reconcile lifetime events in context of reestablished sociocultural normalcy.

RECOMMENDATIONS

Researchers (Schnurr, Friedman, Engel, Foa, Shea, et al., 2007) argue many male and female service members join the active duty and reserve military or National Guard to escape an undesirable environment. Closely associated, post-deployment assessment at the VA facilities indicates that female military personnel are far more likely than male counterparts to have been exposed to some type of trauma(s) prior to joining the military or being deployed. A wide body of empirical data argues that, not only does prior trauma leave the person vulnerable to subsequent retraumatization; it also potentially prompts development of maladaptive schemas by which the person views, understands, copes, and responds to future experiences (Young, 2003, 2007). The implications of prior traumatization are significant in that prior victimization is influential in development of complex PTSD, in which prior meaningful trauma and stress becomes interlinked with seemingly disassociated deployment related stressors. Thus, prior trauma should be examined prior to deployment to a further trauma/stress inducing environment. Personality and ways of coping should be assessed both prior to, and after deployment as a venue to develop better preventative, interventional, and treatment programs for male and female veterans.

REFERENCES

American Psychiatric Association. (2000). Diagnostic and statistical manual of mental disorders: DSM-IV-TR. Washington, DC: Author.

Beck, A. T. (1967). *Depression: clinical, experimental, and theoretical aspects.* New York: Harper & Row.

Bem S. L. (1974). The measure of psychological androgyny. *Journal of Consulting and Clinical Psychology, 42 -2,* 155-162.

Bem, S. L. (1981). Gender schema theory: A cognitive account of sex typing source. *Psychological Review, 88,* 354.

Bem, S. L., & Bern, D. (1973). Does sex-biased job advertising aid and abet sex discrimination? *Journal of Applied Social Psychology, 3,* 6-18.

Betz, B., & Fry, W. R. (1995). The role of group schema in the selection of influence attempts. *Basic and Applied Social Psychology, 16,* 351-365.

Beauvoir, de, S. (1949). *The second sex.* Retrieved January 12, 2008 from http://www.marxists.org/reference/subject/ethics/de-beauvoir/2nd-sex/introduction.htm.

Beauvoir, de, S. (1956, 1989). *The second sex.* NY: Vintage.

Cox, T. (1993). *Cultural diversity in organizations: theory, research, and practice.* San Francisco, CA: Berrett-Koehler.

Coyle-Shaprio, J. A.-M., & Kessler, I. (2000). *Mutuality, stability, and psychological contract breach: a longitudinal study.* Paper presented at Academy of Management, Toronto, August.

Crocker, J., Fiske, S. T., & Taylor, S. E. (1984). *Schematic bases of belief change.* In J. R. Eiser (Ed.), Attitudinal judgment (pp. 192-226). New York: Springer.

Erikson, E.H. (1975). *Life history and the historical moment.* NY: Norton.

Folkman. S., & Lazarus, R.S. (1988). *Manual for the Ways of Coping Questionnaire.* Palo Alto, CA: Consulting Psychologists Press.

Hensley, A.L. (2009). *Gender, personality, and coping: Unraveling gender in military post-deployment wellbeing* (in press).

Horowitz, M. J. (1988). *Introduction to psychodynamics: a new synthesis.* New York: Basic Books.

Insko, C. A., Scholper, J., Hoyle, R. H., Dardis, G. J., & Graetz, J. A. (1990). Individual-group discontinuity as a function of fear and greed. *Journal of Personality and Social Psychology, 58,* 68-79.

Locke, J. (1996). *An Essay Concerning Human Understanding,* Kenneth P. Winkler (ed.), pp. 33–36, Indianapolis: Hackett Publishing Company.

Neufeld, M., & West, S. (1999). *The General's Daughter* [Motion picture]. United States: Paramount.

Nicholson, N., & Johns, G. (1985). The absence culture and the psychological contract: Who's in control of absence? *Academy of Management Review, 10,* 397-407.

Pervin, L. A., Cervone, D., & John, O. P. (2005). *Personality: Theory and research* (9th ed.). New York: Wiley.

Pinker, S. (2002). *The blank slate: The modern denial of human nature.* New York: Penguin.

Ridley, M. (2003). *Nature via nurture: Genes, experience, and what makes us human.* New York: Harper Collins.

Rousseau, D. M. (1989). New hire perceptions of their own and their employer's obligations: study of psychological contracts. *Journal of Organizational Behavior, 11,* 389-400.

Rousseau, D. M. (1995). *Psychological contracts in organizations: understanding written and unwritten agreements.* Newbury Park, CA: Sage.

Rousseau, D.M. (1996a). *Psychological Contracts in Organizations: Understanding Written and Unwritten Agreements.* Newbury Park, CA: Sage.

Rousseau, D. M. (1996b). *Managing diversity for high performance.* New York: Business Week Executive Briefings.

Rousseau, D. M. (1996c). Changing the deal while keeping the people. *Academy of Management Executive, 10,* 50-58.

Rousseau, D. M. (2001). Idiosyncratic deals: flexibility versus fairness. *Organizational Dynamics, 29,* 260-273.

Rousseau, D. M., & Ho, V. T. (2000). Psychological contract issues in compensation. In S. L. Rynes & B. Gerhart (Eds.), *Compensation in organizations.' current research and practice* (pp. 273-310). San Francisco, CA: Jossey-Bass.

Rousseau, D. M., Robinson, S. L., & Kraatz, M. S. (1992). *Renegotiating the psychological contract.* Paper presented at the Society for Industrial Psychology meetings, Montreal.

Rousseau, D. M., & Schalk, R. (2000). *Psychological contracts in employment: cross-national perspectives.* Newbury Park, CA: Sage.

Rousseau, D. M., & Tijoriwala, S. A. (1999). What makes a good reason to change? Motivated reasoning and social accounts in organizational change. *Journal of Applied Psychology, 84,* 514-528.

Rumelhart, D. E., & Norman, D. A. (1978). Accretion, tuning, and restructuring: three modes of learning. In R. Klatsky & J. W. Cotton (Eds.), *Semantic factors in cognition* (pp. 37-53). Hillsdale, NJ: Lawrence Erlbaum.

Scaer, R. C. (2001). *The body bears the burden: Trauma, dissociation, and disease.* Binghamton, New York: The Hayworth Medical Press.

Scaer, R. C. (2005). *The trauma spectrum: Hidden wounds and human resiliency.* New York: W.W. Norton.

Schnurr, P. P. (2007). Cognitive behavioral therapy for posttraumatic stress disorder in women: A randomized controlled trial. *JAMA, 297,* 820-830.

Schnurr, P. P., Friedman, M. J., & Rosenberg, S. D. (1993), Pre-military MMPI scores as predictors of combat-related PTSD symptoms. *American Journal of Psychiatry, 150,* 479-483.

Schnurr, P. P., & Green, B. (2004). Understanding relationships among trauma, posttraumatic stress disorder, and health outcomes. *Advances in Mind-Body Medicine, 20,* 18-29.

Stein, D. J. (1992). Schemas in the cognitive and clinical sciences. *Journal of Psychotherapy Integration, 2,* 45-63.

Steinberg, L. (1987). Single parents, stepparents, and the susceptibility of adolescents to antisocial peer pressure. *Child Development, 58,* 269-275.

Tekleab, A. G., & Taylor, M. S. (2000). *Easing the pain: determinants and effects of psychological contract violations.* Paper presented at Academy of Management meetings, Toronto, August.

Thomas, H. D., & Anderson, N. (1998). Changes in newcomers' psychological contracts during organizational socialization: a study of recruits entering the British Army. *Journal of Organizational Behavior, 19,* 745-767.

Turnley, W. H., & Feldman, D. C. (2000). Re-examining the effects of psychological contract violations: unmet expectations and job dissatisfaction as mediators. *Journal of Organizational Behavior, 21,* 25-42.

United States Army (2003). *Report of proceedings by Investigating Officer/Board of Officers.* Fort Campbell, KY: Author.

United States Army Office of the Surgeon General (USA OSG, 2004). *Operation Iraqi Freedom (OIF-II) Mental Health Assessment Team (MHAT) report.* Washington D.C.: Author.

United States Army Office of the Surgeon General (USA OSG, 2005). *Operation Iraqi Freedom (OIF-II) Mental Health Assessment Team (MHAT) II report.* Washington D.C.: Author.

United States Army Office of the Surgeon General (USA OSG, 2006). *Mental Health Assessment Team (MHAT) III report: Operation Iraqi Freedom 04-06.* Washington D.C.: Author.

United States Army Office of the Surgeon General (USA OSG, 2007). *Mental Health Assessment Team (MHAT) IV report: Operation Iraqi Freedom 05-07.* Washington D.C.: Author.

United States Army Office of the Surgeon General (USA OSG, 2008). *Mental Health Assessment Team (MHAT) V report: Operation Iraqi Freedom 06-08.* Washington D.C.: Author.

Van der Kolk, B.A., McFarlane, A.C., & Weisaeth, L. (Ed.) (1996). *Traumatic stress.* New York: Guilford.

Wright, L. (1997). *Twins: And what they tell us about who we are.* New York: John Wiley & Sons, Inc.

Young, J.E., Klosko, J.S., & Weishaar, M. (2003). *Schema Therapy: A Practitioner's Guide.* New York: Guilford Publications.

Native American Culture and Spirituality in Counseling Native American Veterans, Families and Communities

LCDR Alan L. Hensley, USN (Ret.), BCETS, FAAETS

ABSTRACT

Since World War I, Native Americans have represented the highest *per capita* rate of any ethnic population in the military. Unfortunately, culturally and spiritually sensitive awareness to provide preventative and therapeutic care is woefully lacking. This absence of understanding has been unfortunate, not only in past wars, but continues to be so today. While some reservations and non-reservation communities suffer the maladaptive consequences, such as alcoholism, domestic violence, and other incursions with law enforcement, other reservations remorse that their veteran population dwindles rapidly from suicide and alcohol-related incidents. This discussion examines possible healing strategies through the lenses of culture and spirituality.

Introduction

On March 23, 2003, three days into the US invasion, it was slightly before dawn in the Iraqi desert. A slow moving convoy reached a bridge over the Euphrates River. On the other side—the Iraqi-held town of *al Nasiriyah,* far away from where they were supposed to be. The 507th Army Maintenance Company—a support group of clerks, cooks, and others—had definitely taken a wrong turn in the desert. As the convoy lumbered through the Iraqi checkpoint on the other side, the guards waved and motioned the convoy further. Their weapons—M-16's and .50 Cal's—all largely disabled from days of blowing sand, the tired, poorly equipped band of support personnel soon found themselves the target of elite Iraqi soldiers and *fedayeen,* armed with rocket-propelled grenades (RPGs) and AK-47 assault rifles. What would transpire is considered one of the bloodiest days of the invasion phase. Eleven soldiers of the 507th died in that one attack. Nine others were wounded.

In one of the Humvees were two distinctively different women. One would die. One would live on, despite extensive life-threatening injuries, to tell the true story of that fateful day that would have otherwise been part of a carefully orchestrated misinformation program to garner support for, what many believed to be, an otherwise questionable effort. On the days following the attack, one woman would become unwilling fodder for international media—a rallying figure to garner American support from both deployed military and civilians back home. A petite blond-haired, blue-eyed epitome of femininity who had joined

Army to travel and go to college, she would soon be projected as the all-American girl who continued to fire her guns against the heavily armed Iraqi forces. The other woman, a Hopi Indian from Arizona. She was a single mother of two children who had joined the military as one of the few options she had available to provide for her children. The name, Jessica Lynch, would become, and still is, a household name. Despite becoming the first woman killed in Operation Iraqi Freedom and the first Native American woman ever to die in combat, few would recognize the name Lori Piestewa were it not for the persistent efforts of Jessica Lynch. Rallying around Lynch, Native Americans and non-natives alike would then hail Lori Piestewa a hero—a warrior who had given her all. She would become a source of pride for a long-disrespected segment of American society.

Largely through the efforts of Lynch, Squaw Peak near Phoenix, the second highest point in the Phoenix Mountains, was renamed Piestewa Peak. Unfortunately, in their haste to find something to honor her service, the state and federal governments brought an inextricable derogation to their efforts. For example, if one performs a search on the term, Piestewa Peak, prominently displayed (Arizona Leisure, 2007) is Piestew*a Peak (Squaw Peak).* Thus, naming of the mountain, though perhaps not intended, is in itself, a harsh reminder that Lori Piestewa was, in fact, an Indian.

Since World War I, though they represent less than one percent of the total US population, Native Americans have joined the military at the largest *per capita* rate of any ethnic group (US Senate, 2003). However, few have been officially recognized. Unfortunately, when recognized, federal and state governments often demonstrate myopic understanding of the cultural implications of their actions. For example, in their rush to right centuries of wrongs, and to rally around Lynch, what has America learned? Who are the Hopi? Even more important, what are the cultural and spiritual foundations for which Native Americans have evolved? We now know what Native Americans have done for America in combat. What is it we need to know about Native American culture and spirituality to help them when they need America?

ENVIRONMENT

The late 1800's, with the Western European migration pressing westward; thousands of Native Americans were slaughtered or dislocated onto barren sections of the United States without regard to cultural identity. It would be as much a terrible injustice, today, to attempt to reflect upon the culture and spirituality of each tribe and clan, as it was to relocate and attempt to remove any vestige of cultural heritage from Native Americans for the past 140-plus years. This discussion will then focus on two different Native American cultures—the warrior culture *Oglala Lakota* and the peaceful people, the *Hopi.* From opposite extremes of the geographical, cultural, and philosophical US, the Oglala Lakota and Hopi will be examined in an effort to identify similarities and differences in Native American culture and spirituality that should be considered by medical and mental health professionals, whether dealing with veterans, families, or communities, or attempting to help in the aftermath of a disaster.

Oglala Sioux – the warrior society.

The two-million acre Pine Ridge Indian Reservation is located in the southwest corner of South Dakota near the border with Nebraska. It is the eighth largest Indian Reservation in America—larger than Delaware and Rhode Island combined. This immense, desolate reservation is home to nearly 38,000 members of the Oglala Sioux Tribe. Largely within Shannon and Jackson Counties, in an area known as *the Badlands,* this area has the distinction of being the poorest area in the US. Unemployment hovers between 85 and 97 percent. However, the reservation also has a more pronounced distinction; it has the lowest life expectancy of any population in the Western Hemisphere. The average life expectancy is just 47 years for males and 52 for females—far less than the average of 77.5 for the remainder of the US. The infant mortality rate is 300 percent higher than the national average. Despite extensive farming on the reservation, only 1/3 of the profit is returned to members of the reservation. Relatively few other employment opportunities exist on the Reservation. In the past, members of the tribe have attempted other ventures, such as a meat-processing facility and a moccasin factory; however, both ventures failed. The Prairie Wind Casino, which provides jobs for 250 persons, is the sole exception.

A majority of the scarce, poorly constructed homes on Pine River were built in the 1970's. Unfortunately, these homes, resembling dilapidated gardening sheds for many Americans, which were built for families of 4, now house 10-12 people. Houses constructed for families of 6-8, now house upwards of 17, and sometimes as many as 30 persons. Nearly 40 percent of these homes lack running water, sewage, heat, and electricity. Small propane heaters heat most. Many of these homes are infested with black mold, *Stachybotrys.*

Of the approximately 28,000 tribal members, nearly 14,000 are under the age of 18. More than half of these adolescents are battling life-threatening illnesses, such as tuberculosis, diabetes, alcoholism, and malnutrition. Alcoholism affects 80% of the families on the reservation. The death rate for alcohol-related deaths is 300 percent higher than the national average. Owing largely to the loss of cultural identity and spirituality, many of the youth engage in drug abuse and domestic violence. Few children born today are raised in a dual parent environment. In fact, grandparents are raising 58 percent of the children being raised today. The teen suicide rate is four times the national average.

The rate of tuberculosis on the reservation is nearly 800 times that of the remainder of the US. More than 50 percent of persons over 40 suffer from some form of diabetes. In fact, diabetes on the Reservation is nearly 800 times the national average. Consequently, diabetes-related blindness, organ failure, and amputations are not uncommon. Cervical cancer on the reservation is nearly 500 times the national average.

Many of the wells on the Reservation are contaminated, pesticides, mining operations, and other poisons. Buried military ordinance and hazardous materials from a military bombing range on the Reservation provide further contamination.

A Federal Commodity Food Program is active; however, the food supplied is largely high carbohydrate or high sugar content foods, which are wholly unsuitable for a population with the high incidence of diabetes. Because of physical, cultural, and other reasons, however, it would be virtually impossible for persons or groups outside of the reservation to provide for the needs of even a portion of this population. For this reason, integration with the Oglala Sioux Tribal Council, tribal elders and the tribal infrastructure is a necessary imperative.

The Indian Health Services (IHS) was established to provide health care for Native Americans in exchange for large grants of land. Unfortunately, the IHS is sorely underfunded. Consequently, it is understaffed and ill equipped to address the needs of even a portion of the needs of Native Americans. Nowhere, is this more apparent than on Pine Ridge Reservation. The *Porcupine Clinic,* built in 1992, is the independently owned Native American-operated health clinic in the US. Among its many patients, are non-English-speaking tribal elders. Despite meager resources, the clinic does not refuse service to any tribal member.

Despite these adversities, the Oglala Lakota are a proud, determined people, working hard to overcome Reservation problems. Against many odds and with minimal resources, the Oglala Lakota continue trying to provide a better environment for their children than they inherited. This, then, provides a glimpse into the environment from which many Native American veterans come and to which they are destined to return.

The Hopi – the peaceful people

Compare the Pine Ridge Reservation with the Navaho Reservation from which Lori Piestewa came. Many Native- and Non-Native Americans create a vision of a female warrior who left the reservation to continue a noble warrior heritage. The sad truth is, many Native American women, like Lori Piestewa, join the military to escape a curse that would limit their life expectancy or to provide for the hope that their children will not have to experience the life that they experienced. In fact, Lori Piestewa grew up in an arid, desolate, and poor Navaho Nation community near Tuba City, Arizona, north of Phoenix.

The Navaho Nation is a semi-autonomous reservation covering approximately 26,000 square miles. It occupies virtually all of northeastern Arizona, the southeastern portion of Utah, and northwestern New Mexico. In fact, the Navaho are the single largest tribe in the US, and the reservation is the largest in the US. Of the 298,215 Navajo people living throughout the United States, 173,987 were within the Navajo Nation boundaries in 2000. The Navajo Nation economy exists on traditional endeavors, such as sheep and cattle herding, wool production, weaving, jewelry making, and art trading. Unemployment, unlike the 85-90 percent on Pine Ridge, hovers near 40-45 percent. Reservation employment opportunities extend to, not only Native Americans, but also Non-Natives as well as the Navaho Nation endeavors to encourage tourism. Similar to Pine Ridge, many homes on the reservation do not have natural gas or electricity. Therefore, heat is limited to wood burning stoves.

Like Pine Ridge, the Navaho Nation has serious health concerns. One in 2,500 babies born have *Severe Combined Immunodeficiency* (SCID), a condition in which children are born with virtually no immune system. Cancer rates are substantially higher than the national average. Of particular concern is that young Navaho females experience nearly 17 times higher incidence of cervical cancer than the remainder of the US. Scientific environmental studies find mining has caused a high incidence of uranium poisoning from abandoned mines in the water system. Studies on mice have revealed high Uranium exposure resulted in higher estrogen levels, which might partially explain the increased cervical cancer. As with the Oglala Lakota, diabetes, four times the national average, is a serious concern among Reservation inhabitants. High carbohydrate, high sugar consumption on a physiology typically used to protein is seen as a potential cause. Alcohol consumption by a body not innately designed to cope with it results in an untold number of deaths each year.

Like many Native American women on the reservations, Piestewa grew up fast, married young, became a mother of two children young, and divorced young. The one thing she was not able to escape was the curse of dying young. Unlike many Hopi, however, she integrated Christianity into her Hopi spirituality. Note, that she did not integrate her Hopi spirituality into her Christianity. That is because her Hopi culture and spirituality defined who she was as a person. In fact, she regularly attended spiritual ceremonies at nearby Moenkopi Village.

Poverty, lack of opportunity and hope for a better future forced Piestewa to make a difficult, life-changing decision. This decision meant she would have to leave her children for long periods. However, this decision was not unusual in that, like the families of Pine Ridge, grandparents and extended family now raise many children on the Navaho Reservation.

Two distinctively different Native American cultures, similar problems—isolation, indifference, and the desire to retain traditional culture and spirituality in a country that would have them leave their heritage behind and enter into mainstream America.

CULTURE

Though raised on the Navaho Nation Reservation, Lori Piestewa was, in fact, not Navaho. She was, instead a member of the rival Hopi tribe, geographically surrounded by the Navaho tribe. As of 2000, the Hopi tribe was comprised of 6,946 people. In conjunction with the Arizona Tewa People, a system of villages, built in the traditional pueblo style surrounds three mesas. In fact, the Hopi village, Old Oraibi (founded circa 1150), has the distinction of being the oldest continuously inhabited village in the world.

The Hopi are believed to have migrated from the area now known as Mexico around 500 BC in a journey not unlike the journey of Moses and the Israelites. As the Hopi separated into groups during the migration, the Hopi divided into clans, such as the *Bear, Spider, Badger, Antelope,* and *Snake* Clans—groups of individuals who can matrilineally trace their ancestors back to common ancestors. As agricultural conservation became more important for survival and, arguably to prevent inter-clan rivalry, tillable land was divided among the clans. Land would pass matrilineally. While women in the family owned the land, male members of the clan farmed it. Steeped in mysticism, cultural and spiritual beliefs, and tradition, there are now 34 clans. Each of the clans possesses their own beliefs about how all Hopis came into existence. Hopi history, mythology, and parables that are not always told consistently. Each Hopi mesa, village, or clan may have its own version, which is imperative to understanding the philosophical, cultural and spiritual foundations of the person. Unfortunately, secrecy of Pueblo ways to outsiders, while preserving the cultural identity, is potentially problematic to outsiders attempting to assist in the aftermath of a disaster.

Clan membership also dictates which ceremonial positions a person may hold, as well as certain rules, roles, and responsibilities. Special duties, responsibilities and honors are attributed into members of each clan. Some are responsible for hosting ceremonies. The *Badger* clan, for example, conducts the *kachina* ceremony. Elaborately masked men from the Badger Clan, portraying the kachina, visit Pueblo villages during the first half of the year to bring harmony and balance to the world, as well as bring rain to the crops. The kachinas also dance, bring gifts for the children, and even administer disciplinary scolding. The *Antelope* and *Snake* clans are responsible for performing the sacred Snake *Dance*—a prayer for rain. Others are responsible for keeping and honoring certain sacred objects. As a matrilineal society, in which the mother determines inheritance and social status, the objects and, in fact, all property is passed down through the mother's family. Somewhat antithetical to Amish and other conservative Western societies, Hopis are forbidden from marrying another person from their own clan, in that a clan is considered a family.

The Hopi lived a peaceful existence until 1540, when the Navaho, pressured by Coronado and the Spanish, began attacking, not only the Spanish, but the Hopi as well. Over the next 300 years, the Navaho and Hopi would continue to be adversaries. In 1870, the United States laid claim to the Hopi lands, forcing the Hopi to fight them as well, until they were forced onto the Reservation at Black Mesa.

Despite hundreds of years of battle with the Navaho, and attempts by the Spanish and United States to force Catholicism upon the Hopi people as early as 1629, they continue to retain traditional cultural and spiritual values.

SPIRITUALITY

The stories (Kaiser, 1991) reflect the Hopi belief they were the first inhabitants in North America and entered the *Fourth World* (Courlander, 1987) from a corrupt *Third World*, existing in the netherworld through Sipapu—a crack in the Earth's crust. They were, they argue, the chosen people to survive a great flood. Only a few survived, and then only because they were the pure of heart. The Third World, they offer, was destroyed by the great flood. In analysis, reference to Sipapu should not be taken literally perhaps; but, rather as a metaphor representing a journey from another land.

Though varied in the many interpretations by the clans, many believe in the *First World*, Tawa—the Sun Spirit—out of Tokpella—endless space, created earth. Tawa then created *Sotuknang*—the nephew—who was sent to create the nine universes according to his plan. Sotuknang then created the *Spider Grandmother*, who served as an intercessorary for *the Creator*. She creates all life.

Masauwu—Spirit of Death—is the master of the Upper, or Fourth, World. He was here when the *good people* escaped the wicked *Third World* in promises of a better world. Though some describe him as a hideous being, others describe him as handsome and benevolent. In fact, some clans of the Hopi believe it is Masawu that sited them at Oraibi and charged them with being the protectors of the earth. Among the stories of the Hopi, it was Masauwu that warned them to be watchful of the return of Pahana—the *lost white brother*. Others of the clans argue the Spider Grandmother was grandmother to the Sun and it was she who beckoned them from the Third World. Another version was that Tawa destroyed the world in a great flood. Before the flood, the good people were guided into hollow reeds, which were used as flotation devices. According to the stories, sacred stones or tablets, depicting the images of the Pahana, were given to the Hopi by various deities. Pahana left for the East at the same time as the Hopi entered into the Fourth World. Upon his return, the wicked will be judged and the world will enter into peace once again. He will be wearing red. Based upon this belief Hopis are buried facing east. Based on the testimony of John Young and Andrew Gibbons (Waters, 1963), this assertion is well grounded in red marble tablets unlike any material indigenous to the region. Pahana will bring the missing fourth of the sacred stone. The Hopi believe, if they succumb to the White forces, no one will remain to care for the Fourth World (Kaiser, 1991). The world will then end in catastrophe. The Hopi offer (Kaiser, 1991) that there are two ways of life—the Hopi (Good) way and the way of the White man. If the Hopi stray from the good way, they, like others, will perish. The Fourth World will end, they argue. Preceding the end will be a period of disorder, confusion, pain, and suffering—not unlike the prophecy offered in the Bible. A powerful, central figure, who was present at the beginning, will return, beginning a period of judgment. Three previous worlds existed. The first was destroyed by fire, the second by ice, and the third by flood. Only a few pure Hopi will survive to begin the Fifth World. However, the Hopi offer, the time is not too late—destruction can be averted if the people voluntarily return to the way ordered by the Great Spirit.

Regardless of the correctness of any of the versions, correlation to the events of the Bible can be readily envisioned. Secondly, the importance of the femininity in Hopi culture and spirituality, in direct contrast to many other cultures such as the Western European culture, can be seen. Women were/are valued not only as the keepers of property, but also as the keepers of knowledge and history.

Central to Native American spirituality is the medicine wheel or *sacred hoop*—the unending circle of life, representing the importance of the four directions—North, South, East, and West, the seasons of the year, and the seasons of life. In the Hopi sacred circle, north is the cardinal direction. With the color white, North represents the human body, animals, and plants. It also represents the white-skinned people and infancy. The East represents the mind and air. Colored yellow, east represents the yellow-skinned people and adolescence. The South, colored red, represents the red-skinned people, adulthood, heart, and fire. Finally, the West, colored black, represents the black-skinned people, water and eldership.

In contrast to the Hopi—the peaceful people, in the Sacred Circle of the Lakota warrior society, life begins and ends in the east. South represents childhood, west represents adolescence, and north, home of the white buffalo, represents adulthood. The Lakota Sacred Hoop reflects the importance of women in the Lakota culture. As elucidated by the medicine man Crow Dog (Lame Deer & Erdoes, 1972), *"This holy woman brought the sacred buffalo calf pipe to the Sioux. There could be no Indians without it. Before she came, people did not know how to live. They knew nothing. The Buffalo Woman put her sacred mind into their minds."* According to Lakota legend, one summer, the *Council of Seven Fires,* representing the entire Lakota Nation, came together. There was no meat and the people were starving. Among the camps, were the *Itazipcho*—the *Without-Bows.* One morning, Chef Standing Hollow Horn sent two of his men to look for game. In front of them, the men were confronted with a hill from which they could see the whole countryside. Halfway up the hill, however, they spotted a form coming down towards them. At first, the form was merely a vision. However, as the form came closer, the two men could tell is was a beautiful woman, well ordained with a white buckskin dress and ornaments. However, the form appeared to be floating instead of walking. The *wakan* (holy) stranger was *Ptesan-Wi* --the White Buffalo Woman. One man was awe-stricken. The other desired the maiden's body. As he reached for her, lightning struck him and he turned into a pillar of bones. To the man who had behaved appropriately, the White Buffalo Woman said (Neihardt, 1972): *"Good things I am bringing, something holy to your nation. A message I carry for your people from the buffalo nation. Go back to the camp and tell the people to prepare for my arrival. Tell your chief to put up a medicine lodge with twenty-four poles. Let it be made holy for my coming."*

The hunter returned to the camp to tell the chief and others what he had seen and been told. The chief ordered the camp to make ready for the holy woman. After four days, the woman approached carrying a bundle with her. The chief beckoned her to enter the medicine lodge. She entered circling clockwise. The chief began the conversation by telling Ptesan-Wi the Lakota were happy she had come, after which she began to instruct them on the holiest of rituals. An altar of red dirt was to be constructed in the center of the tipi with a buffalo skull and a three stick rack for what she had brought them. A design was traced on the smooth surface of the altar. After instructing all present how to recreate the design, she arose and circled the tipi sun-wise. Stopping in front of the chief, she opened her bundle and presented him with a chanupa—a sacred pipe.

Ashamedly, the chief offered that because there had been no meat for so long and the people were starving all he had to offer her was water with *wacanga* (sweet grass). This was the beginning of an enduring tradition. Holy people dip sweet grass or an eagle's wing into water and sprinkle it on members of the tribe to be purified.

Ptesan-Wi showed the people how to use the pipe. After filling it with *chan-shasha*, red willow-bark tobacco, she circled the tipi four times, representing the circle without end, the sacred hoop, and life's journey. The *chan-shasha* was lit, and passed from person to person, representing *peta-owihankeshini*, the flame without end, to be passed from generation to generation. The smoke arising from the bowl, she told them, was *Tunkashila's* breath, the living breath of great Grandfather Mystery.

After all had smoked of the pipe, *Ptesan-Wi* showed all present how to pray with the proper words and proper gestures. She showed them how the pipe was to be lifted to grandfather sky and grandmother earth, and then to the four directions. With the pipe directed toward the heavens, the people were told, they would form a living bridge between the sacred beneath to the sacred above. All people would become one with all living things, humans, animals, trees, plants and grasses. The pipe, she advised, binds all to one another.

The bowl of the pipe, she offered, represents the buffalo. The buffalo, with four legs, represents the universe, the four directions, and the four seasons of man's life. The buffalo is placed in the west and holds back the water. Each year it loses its hair and each year it loses a leg. The *Sacred Hoop of Life,* she offered, will end when all the hair and legs of all of the great buffalo are gone, and the water comes back to cover the Earth (Note the reference in both the Hopi and Lakota teachings that speak of the great flood). The wooden stem of the pipe represents all that grows on the earth, she told all present. Twelve feathers from the spotted eagle, the Great Spirit's messenger, hung from the stem. Engraved in the bowl were seven circles of various sizes, each representing a ritual or practice to be performed with the pipe as well as the *Ocheti Shakowin*—the seven sacred campfires of the Lakota nation.

As *Ptesan-Wi* continued, she spoke to the women present. They were from *Mother Earth,* she told them. Their contributions were equally as valuable as those of a warrior. The pipe, then, holds men and women together in a circle of love, she offered. Both men and women have a part in making their own pipe. The man carves the bowl and makes the stem. The woman, then, adorns it with bands of porcupine quills. When a man takes a wife, both hold the pipe at the same time. A red cloth is wound around their hands, thus binding them together for life. She then showed the women how to properly cook the other items she had brought in her bundle, such as corn and wild turnip.

Ptesan-Wi then spoke to the children, telling them they have wisdom beyond their years. They would be the upcoming generation, she told them; for this reason, they were the most precious. One day, they too would hold and smoke the pipe and have families of their own. One day, they too would pray with it. Thus, it was the unending symbol of passing down life

Lastly, speaking to all, she offered that the Lakota were the purest among tribes. For that reason, the chanupa had been bestowed on them. In exchange, they were responsible for taking care of all Indian people on the Turtle Continent. To Chief Standing Hollow Horn, said (Lame Deer & Erdoes, 1972) *"Remember: this pipe is very sacred. Respect it and it will take you to the end of the road. The four ages of creation are in me; I am the four ages. I will come to see you in every generation cycle. I shall come back to you."* She then left saying, "*Toksha ake wacinyanktin ktelo*—I shall see you again."

As she walked off silhouetted in the sun, she dropped and rolled over four times. The first time, she became a black buffalo. The second time, she became a brown buffalo. The third time, she became a red buffalo. The fourth and final time, she became a white buffalo calf. Among the Lakota, then, the white buffalo is the most sacred living object—a prize beyond price. The White Buffalo Woman, *Ptesan-Wi,* then disappeared over the horizon. Remarkably similar renditions of the story of the White Buffalo Calf Woman are found in Lame Deer and Erdoes (1992), Neihardt (1972), and Marshall (2005). Prior to his death in 1976, Lakota Medicine Man John (Fire) Lame Deer reflected (Lame Deer & Erdoes, 1992) he had seen the White Buffalo four times in his visions four times in his life.

Notice the spiritual similarities in the two versions. Regardless of the correctness of either version, both versions reflect upon the inviolability of cultural and spiritual rituals in being. Each reflects upon the importance of retaining cultural heritage. Finally, each, though preceding modern theorists and researchers such as Erikson (1959, 1968, 1982), are inextricably bound to seemingly timeless wisdom.

STATUS QUO

Despite valiant attempts by tribal organizations and members, Native American reservations in the US are analogous to or, sometimes, in more dire need of assistance than the Third World countries who are seen to advertize daily on television stations around the US. Americans, however, are poorly informed regarding the conditions on the reservations and when disasters such as the 1998 Pine Ridge tornado destroyed 150 homes, America is ill prepared to render assistance. Remember, Native American culture is a sharing, communal culture. The destruction of one home is equivalent to displacing upwards of 30 people. Potentially then, 4500 people might have found themselves without shelter or the basic needs for survival. Having personally viewed the conditions on Pine Ridge Indian Reservation, I was abhorred at the indifference that would allow such conditions to continue. The conditions described in this discussion do not even begin to describe the conditions we allow Native Americans to live in. Even more salient to the present discussion, is the absence of cross-cultural understanding that would potentially preclude us, as medical and mental healthcare providers, from rendering needed assistance when needed most. Native Americans, per-capita have contributed the most of any ethnic population to our military since World War I. Yet we, as medical and mental healthcare providers, do not have the basic skills necessary to help veterans help themselves or others. Instead, we relegate them to return to a life they left on the reservation, only to become one of the many unknown statistics inherent to a life of poverty, indifference, and isolation.

CONCLUSIONS

To the world outside of the Reservation, life continues on the reservation with Native Americans thriving in their own sections of America. Relegated to obscure areas of the US and both geographically and socially, nothing could be further from the truth. However, few persons outside of the reservation will ever know the truth without a concerted effort by a prominent person of media interest, such as Jessica Lynch.

Existing resources for Native American veterans, families, and communities are, at best, disorganized and poorly funded. Fraught with structural, cultural, and spiritual barriers, scant resources are not desirable or viable for many Native Americans. Consequently, many suffer in silence; resorting to such maladaptive coping strategies as depression, alcohol abuse, drugs, resulting in domestic violence, frequent interaction with the law and even suicide. While tribal groups such as the Hopi and Zuni arduously protect secrecy of knowledge and beliefs, history has demonstrated many will, of their own volition, integrate external beliefs and ideas if they are proven to be of value to the maintenance of their own cultural and spiritual beliefs, in a manner similar to what the New Order Mennonites have done.

What messages is America sending to the Native American people when, though hundreds have died in combat, it is only through the efforts of an adopted white sister that the contributions of one Native American is honored? What message are we, as Americans, sending, when a mountain with a defamatory name is renamed in honor of the sacrifices of one Native American, in addition to a nearby freeway? Eight mothers of Navaho and Hopi veterans are now part of the Gold Star Mothers, reflecting the death of their child in Iraq and Afghanistan. What subliminal message does naming of Piestewa Peak send to the other Gold Star Mothers regarding the worth of their sons and daughters? Why did Jessica Lynch need to solicit Ty Pennington and the *Home Makeover: Extreme Edition* crew to build a veteran center on the Navaho Nation Reservation in 2005, when so many from that reservation, and other reservations, suffer in silence; oblivious to all outside of the reservation? What would Lori Piestewa have wanted her death to mean, and more importantly, what have we learned from her death? Are we any closer to healing the ills of generations, of understanding and helping the people who come to America's rescue when needed? The Native American culture is a communal culture. Would the fact she was honored, while so many other Native Americans continue to suffer have brought her pride and joy, or sadness and shame?

Few, perhaps today, recall the name Ira Hayes, a Pima Indian, from Gila River Indian Reservation in Sacaton, Arizona. Hayes and five other Marines are indelibly engraved in the Pulitzer prize-winning photograph taken by photographer Joe Rosenthal while raising the flag at Mount Surabachi, Okinawa on February 23, 1945. Of the six Marines, only Hayes, Rene Gagnon, and John Bradley lived to return home. Hayes' notoriety drew particular attention. Hayes returned to the reservation and found it much as he had left it. Though crops surrounding the reservation were lush and green, water was diverted from the reservation, with the exception of one small ditch. Haunted by the loss of others who had not returned, and plagued by the unwanted attention, Hayes turned to alcohol as a coping mechanism. He became a drifter and a loner, often performing odd jobs. He was often intoxicated and had frequent involvement with law enforcement. The jail was often home for Hayes after many days of drinking. Alone, on the morning of January 24, 1955, Hayes, 33, was found dead, lying face down in his own vomit and blood near an abandoned hut close to his home. Ten weeks earlier, Hayes had been invited to Washington DC to commemorate the Iwo Jima monument. Lauded as a hero by President Eisenhower, a reporter asked Hayes after the ceremony how he liked the fanfare, his response was reportedly (BBC, 2003), *"I don't."* Questioned afterwards (BBC, 2003) regarding his statement, Hayes responded, *"How could I feel like a hero when only five men in my platoon of 45 survived, when only 27 men in my company of 250 managed to escape death or injury?"* Four movies have been made depicting the raising of the flag on Iwo Jima. Only one (Grainger & Dawn, 1949) portrayed Hayes as a Native American. Oddly enough, Hayes and two fellow survivors, Rene Gagnon and John Bradley, briefly portrayed themselves. In all other movies, White men, such Lee Marvin (Aurthur & Frankenheimer, 1960), Tony Curtis (Bartlett & Mann, 1961), and Adam Beach (Spielberg & Eastwood, 2006), played him.

Disaster response organizations donate millions of dollars and send untold numbers of medical and mental health professionals to faraway lands in the aftermath of disasters. Unfortunately, many Native Americans are now living in similar conditions. How well will we, as medical and mental health professionals, be physically and culturally ready to help them in the aftermath of inevitable disasters? On the other hand, will we even care?

RECOMMENDATIONS

Cultural and spiritual misunderstanding and differences have been foundational to virtually all wars throughout the history of humanity. However, a concerted effort among Hopi clans for well over 2,500 years, demonstrates agreement to coexist through mutual understanding and acceptance is possible. Unfortunately, in the current half-full mentality, people of the US unfortunately disregard the view that the glass is also half-full; giving hope for more instead of less. Only through mutual understanding that cultural and spiritual differences do exist and agreement to assimilate those differences into a holistic sacred circle that includes all American people, will hope for wellbeing of all people be possible.

Steeped in centuries of learning and experience, Native American cultures thrived in relative harmony since the gleanings of life in North America. Though often considered rudimentary, Native American cultural and spiritual beliefs, in many ways, reflect a more experience-grounded understanding of the human being. For example, upon reflection, the Sacred Hoop embraces relevance to virtually every aspect of human life, from geographic directions, to seasons of time and seasons of life. The Sacred Hoop ardently reflects understanding of the human psychosocial development, predating Erikson (1959, 1968, 1982), by centuries. Thus, Native American culture and spirituality should not be automatically disregarded as an elementary and flawed process.

The focus of the present discussion deals with understanding and integrating Native American culture and spirituality into assisting veterans, families, and communities to overcome the effects of combat. While many psychotherapeutic interventions are understood and available to counselors based upon biological, psychological and sociological theory and research we, as medical and mental health providers have only begun to understand and integrate holistic understanding of faith into our repertoire. By convention, Native Americans integrated both pharmaceutical and psychotherapy into psychological intervention for centuries. For example, extensive public and media interest has been devoted to quantifying and qualifying *post-traumatic stress disorder* (PTSD) among veterans returning from Iraq and Afghanistan. Untold resources have been devoted to understanding the genesis and progression of this disorder. Though progress has been made, researchers (e.g., Van der Kolk, Mc Farlane, and Weisaeth, 1996) argue understanding remains embryonic. In contrast, though varied versions exist regarding the conceptualization, virtually all Native American cultures reflect that a shadow being (bear) exists in all human beings.

In periods of exigency, the shadow being emerges with a high degree of automaticity and even to a higher degree through conscious evocation. The shadow being then controls our very biopsychosocial being, from physical to psychological consideration of morals, ethics, and values. The shadow being stays at the forefront until its presence is no longer required. Unfortunately, awareness of the absence of need does not operate with the same degree of automaticity as the shadow being is summoned. The Plains warrior societies often banned returning warriors from reentering the tribe until cleansed, which often consisted of days and weeks. In fact, virtually all of the Native American cultures integrated a cleansing ceremony into the reintegration process. Formal rituals were held, prayers for forgiveness and healing were offered, and songs sung to the Great Spirit for forgiveness. The ceremonies fulfilled several purposes. Foremost, was to allow the warrior to reflect upon all he had seen and experienced in battle. Secondly, it offered the awareness to the warrior that the people realized he had seen and possibly done terrible things. However, they were necessary, and often were the consequence of the dominant shadow being. Lastly, it provided a near-term venue for the warrior to reflect and forgive himself.

Unfortunately, as the White man ventured westward, Native American societies were conquered and forced upon reservations that did not reflect their mental model constructed over centuries. Far in excess of mere cognitive dissonance—in this case, the confusion occurring when confronted with situations not within the mental model—*biopsychosocial dissonance* occurred. Proven practices were found to be no longer effective and, in the process, cultural and spiritual rules, roles, rituals, processes and procedures have become diluted. As children were forced into Christian schools and, consequently, often endured treatment far different from the psychological contract they were led to believe. Realizing that neither their traditional culture could protect them from trials and tribulations and the White population could not be trusted to honor either written, spoken, or psychological contracts, coping strategies became dysfunctional.

As a venue to better themselves from the meager, at best, existence on the reservation, many Native Americans joined, and continue to join the military. Unfortunately, cultural sensitivity in understanding, acclimating, and healing Native American veterans leaves much to be desired.

Though approached from generations of differences in understanding, both, Western societal understanding of PTSD and the Native American conceptualization of the shadow being, serve a functional purpose in healing, especially among Native Americans. Perhaps, however, this combined understanding might be functional to Non-Native Americans as well.

Rather than focusing on differences in religious and spiritual beliefs, focus should be placed on commonality. Healing programs should reflect a mutual understanding and acceptance.

Programs to counsel Native American veterans, families, and communities must not be the traditional White, Anglo-Saxon, Western European model *whitewashed* with enough Native American rituals to be *Indian-like.* Rather, each clan or tribe is unique. While some practices and rituals are nearly universal, others are not. Therefore, counseling Native American clans and tribes requires cultural and spiritual awareness. Despite over a century of repression, aggression, and segregation on the reservations, many elders continue to retain the wisdom of the healing ceremony. Proven counseling practices should be integrated into programs built upon the clan or tribe cultural and spiritual framework, not *vice-versa.*

REFERENCES

Allen, P. G. (1992). *The Sacred Hoop*. Boston: Beacon Press.

Aurthur, R. A. (Producer) & Frankenheimer, J. (Director) (1960). *Sunday showcase: The American* [Television Broadcast]. United States: NBC.

Bartlett, S. (Producer) & Mann, D. (Director). (1961). *The outsider* [Motion Picture]. United States: Universal Studios.

BBC (2003). *Ira Hayes – An unwilling hero.* Retrieved February 1, 2009 from http://www.bbc.co.uk/dna/h2g2/A1118396.

Centers for Disease Control (2006). *Tobacco use among adults-U.S.* 55(42):1145-148. Retrieved January 20, 2009 from http://www.cdc.gov/mmwr/preview/mmwrhtml/mm5444a2.htm.

Centers for Disease Control and Prevention (2005). *Corrected data tables: Tobacco use, access and exposure to tobacco in media among middle and high school students in the United States. MMWR 54(12).* Retrieved January 20, 2009 from http://www.cdc.gov/mmwr/indrr_2005.html.

Cobb N., Paisano R. E. (1997). *Cancer Mortality among American Indians and Alaska Natives in the United States: regional differences in Indian health 1989-1993.* Rockville, MD: Indian Health Service. HIS Pub. No. 97-615-23.

Courlander, H. (1987), *The fourth world of the Hopis: The epic story of the Hopi Indians as preserved in their legends and traditions.* New Mexico: University of New Mexico Press.

Erikson, E. H. (1959). *Identity and the life cycle.* New York: International Universities Press.

Erikson, E. H. (1968). *Identity: Youth and crisis.* New York: Norton.

Erikson, E. H. (1982). *The life cycle completed.* New York: W. W. Norton.

Gaw, A. C. (Ed., 1993). *Culture, ethnicity, and mental illness.* American Psychiatric Publishing.

Grainger, E. (Producer) & Dawn, A. (Director) (1949). *Sands of Iwo Jima* [Motion Picture]. United States: Republic Pictures

Lame Deer, J., & Erdoes, R. (1972). *Lame Deer: Seeker of visions.* New York: Simon & Schuster.

Lame Deer, J., & Erdoes, R. (1992). *Gift of power: The life and teachings of a Lakota medicine man.* Rochester, VT: Bear & Company.

Marshall, J.M. (2005). *Walking with grandfather: The wisdom of the Lakota elders.* Boulder, Colorado: Sounds True.

Neihardt, J.G. (1979). Black Elk speaks. Lincoln, NE: University of Nebraska Press.

Spielberg, S. (Producer) & Eastwood, C. (Director) (2006). *Sands of Iwo Jima* [Motion Picture]. United States: Dreamworks Pictures & Warner Brothers.

U.S. Department of Health and Human Services. (1998). *Tobacco use among U.S. racial/ethnic minority groups – African Americans, American Indians and Alaska Natives, Asian Americans and Pacific Islanders, and Hispanics: a report of the Surgeon General.* Atlanta: U.S. Department of Health and Human Services, Centers for Disease Control and Prevention.

U.S. Senate (2003). *Murray stands up for Native American veterans in health care battle.* Retrieved February 2, 2009 from http://murray.senate.gov/news.cfm?id=220410.

van der Kolk, B. A., McFarlane, A. C., & Weisaeth, L. (1996). *Traumatic stress: The effects of overwhelming experience on mind, body, and society.* New York: Guilford Press.

Waters, F. (1977). *Book of the Hopi.* New York: Penguin Press

National Guard Family Services: Wyoming Family Assistance Centers Program

Debbie Russell and Daniella Hamilton

The Family Assistance Centers (FACs) are a Department of Defense (DoD) directive. We have six strategically placed FACs in the state of Wyoming. This helps to ensure that we have contact with even the most secluded areas of the state. We are not a unit specific entity; we are in contact with all DoD Deployed Service Members and their families throughout the five deployment phases:

1. **Pre-deployment**: This begins with the warning order for deployment. This stage ends when the Guard member departs from home. The time frame may be a couple days to more than a year.
2. **Deployment**: This begins with the Service Member's departure from home through the first month of the deployment. A roller coaster of mixed emotions is common during the deployment stage.
3. **Sustainment**: From the first month through a month before the Service Member is scheduled to return home. This is a time of establishing new sources of support and routines. Many rely on FACs who serve as a close network to handle problems and disseminate the latest information. FACs provide a variety of training modules for the families to provide them with as many tools as possible to help them be successful during the deployment as well as assisting them with self sufficiency. Many rely on FSGs to serve as a close network that meets on a regular basis to offer support. Some are more comfortable with family, friends, and church as their main means of emotional support. We want the family member to use all forms of support available to them!!
4. **Re-deployment**: One month before the Service member is scheduled to return home is generally one of intense anticipation. There can be a surge of conflicting emotions, such as some apprehension and then on the other hand, there is excitement that the Service Member is returning home.
5. **Post-deployment** (Reunion)**:** This phase begins with the arrival home. Like the pre-deployment state, the time frame for this stage is also variable depending on the particular family. Typically, this stage lasts from three to six months.

The Family Assistance Center has adapted to the many changes of deployment and reunion. We try to educate and assist with those changes. In the Pre-Deployment stages we contact family and military members to help insure that all questions regarding the deployment are answered. We have briefings for both the family member and the service member. Those are the Family Academies. There are also age specific briefings for the children and siblings of the Service Members. During the Deployment stage we have contact with the family members and help answer any questions that may come up and have a monthly function to help family morale and assist in building relationships between the families that have a Service Member deployed.

During the Re-deployment stage, we hold reunion briefings to help the family member understand some of the emotions that come after a service member returns home. During these briefings, we like to have a parent and also a spouse that has been through the deployment previously to help answer questions regarding the reunion. We continue to contact family members up to one year after the service members have come home. This is to make sure that everyone is adjusting well and are back to a new normal routine.

Some of the other programs that we offer for all military members are our PREP, Marriage Enrichment Seminars. At this retreat they are given the tools to effectively communicate with each other. We highly recommend the families attend this retreat both before the deployment and after the deployment.

Our goal is to make sure that the soldier and their family is well-educated and understands the benefits that they have after their return.

About the Authors

Debbie Russell is a Specialist with the Wyoming Family Assistance Program (FAC). She supervises and trains the Family Assistance Center Representatives and assists in training the Lead Volunteers. Debbie Russell began working with the Family Program in 1987 as a volunteer and then accepted the position as the FAC Supervisor in 2003. Being a parent and spouse of a service member for 26 years, she recognizes the need for providing assistance to families before, during and after deployment. Contact: Debbie.russell@us.army.mil

Daniella Hamilton is a representative with the Wyoming Family Assistance Program. She accepted a position with the Family Assistance Center in 2003 when her husband was deployed. Daniella currently is in charge of the Central Region and the Northeastern Region of the state. Being a spouse of a Military member for 16 years has helped her in understanding and assisting others with the challenges they face in military life.

Department of Veterans Affairs: Services to Returning Combat Veterans

Shellie Franklin, MA, LPC and Marti Salas, LCSW

ABSTRACT

Veterans returning from service in Operation Enduring Freedom and Operation Iraqi Freedom (OEF/OIF) have their own unique set of needs and challenges. Every VA across the nation has a specialized program in place, designed to assist these veterans with a smooth transition from deployment to civilian life. Whatever it takes, it is the mission of the OEF/OIF program to make sure all returning combat veterans are provided with the healthcare, benefits, and community resources they deserve. VA resources, as well as the process for obtaining these resources were explained. Shellie Franklin spoke from her perspective as both an Iraqi veteran, as well as a current readjustment counselor for combat veterans.

Operation Enduring Freedom and Operation Iraqi Freedom (OEF/OIF) veterans are facing a variety of challenges once they return home from the combat zone. Post Traumatic Stress Disorder (PTSD) and Traumatic Brain Injury (TBI) are considered signature wounds of these wars. Additionally, each and every service member returning from deployment goes through a readjustment period, which can often times be very difficult to navigate. They return home to find that they have changed, and others around them say they have changed—they will never be the same person they were before they deployed. The challenge then becomes one for the service member, their family members, friends, and employers to navigate together.

There are many common psychosocial issues related to this readjustment period: anxiety, sleeplessness, feeling constantly on guard and watchful, relationships become stressed and often dissolve, employment is lost, substance use begins and/or increases, driving related accidents have increased, suicide and homicidal behaviors are on the rise. It is important for these veterans to feel supported and to have a sense of belonging. Many find it helpful to be able to spend time with others who have served in the war, as they feel that their families and friends won't be able to understand. They are a very stoic, heroic generation that often does not seek the help of others. It is critical for the service members and care givers to know that services and support are available to them, to understand that what they are going through is normal, and be willing to be patient because readjustment is a process that does not happen quickly.

The VA has established a program for this group of veterans who are returning from combat zones. Each VA facility across the nation has an OEF/OIF team, which is responsible for providing outreach to returning veterans and case management services to those veterans who need such services. The ultimate goal is to ensure they receive assistance as they transition home, and to help make this transition as smooth as possible. For the first five years after they come off of active duty orders, these veterans are eligible for free healthcare services for anything related to their combat service; they may also be seen for conditions not related to their combat service, but will be charged co-pay for these services: $15 for office visits, $8 for 30-day supply of prescriptions, and $50 for specialty clinics. Once their five-year period has expired, they remain enrolled for VA services, but are moved to co-pay status for all services. The co-pay is based on income and other factors, so in some cases the veteran may have no co pay at all. A separate service available is through Veteran's Benefits. For any injury, illness, or condition the service member sustained during their time in service, the veteran may file a claim to receive a service-connected disability. If they receive a service-connected rating, this will open up another set of resources to the veteran, based on their individual rating.

The OEF/OIF team is available to assist these veterans with enrolling for healthcare, scheduling appointments, and arranging assistance for filing their claims when applicable. If the VA cannot provide a needed service, the OEF/OIF team members are very familiar with numerous community resources that may be available to the veterans and their families. Services available within the VA include but are not limited to: Primary Care, Audiology, Physical Therapy, Occupational Therapy, Optometry, and Orthopedics, 24 hr Emergent care, Chaplain Services, Social Work Services, and Mental Health Services. Mental Health services include medication assessment and management along with counseling for PTSD, depression, anxiety, military sexual trauma, and general readjustment issues. Mental Health clinics are established at VA hospitals and clinics. Vet Centers are also part the VA system, but are located at a site separate from the VA hospitals and clinics. They do not diagnose, and they do not prescribe medications, but do provide PTSD and readjustment counseling for combat veterans. All returning combat veterans who present for an appointment at the VA are automatically screened for PTSD, depression, alcohol use, TBI, Military Sexual Trauma (MST), and infectious diseases. Any positive screen generates a referral for further assessment of that condition. Assessment and rehabilitation for TBI is an important part of the services available at the VA. A team of professionals from Occupational Therapy, Physical Therapy, Speech Therapy, Recreational Therapy, Social Work and Mental Health all work together to provide treatment for veterans with mild, moderate, or severe TBI. Each VA has a Suicide Prevention Program with its own coordinator, as well as an MST coordinator.

About the Authors

Shellie Franklin, MS is a Licensed Practicing Counselor in Cheyenne, and received her Master of Science degree in Counseling from University of Wyoming. She has served in the Colorado, California and Wyoming Army National Guard for 30 years. During that time, Shellie worked full time as the State Family Coordinator for 10 years, and the Education Officer for 7 years while working on her Master's degree in counseling. Shellie is currently in the Army Reserves and was deployed for 15 months to Kuwait for Operation Iraqi Freedom in May 2006. Shortly after coming home, Shellie began working for Fort Collins and Cheyenne Vet Centers under the Cheyenne VA. She is now working for the Vet Center in Cheyenne, which includes travel to Laramie WY, Kimball, Sidney, and Gering/Scottsbluff,

NE. Shellie has specialized training in Eye Movement Desensitization Reprocessing (EMDR), Hakomi body centered therapy, and critical incident stress management (CISM).

Marti Salas, LCSW, is a Licensed Clinical Social Worker in the State of WY. Marti received her MSW from the University of WY in 1999, and began her career working within the child welfare system with children and families and is a child and family therapist. In 2007 Marti started at the Cheyenne VA as a case manager for returning combat veterans. She quickly developed a passion for ensuring that the heroes who are defending our freedom receive every service and resource that they have so valiantly earned. She now works full time as the Program Manager for returning combat veterans at the Cheyenne VA.

Summary of Additional Presentations

The 7th Rocky Mountain Region Disaster Mental Health Conference in Laramie, Wyoming in November 2008 included a large number of presentations. Papers or articles were submitted for publication by most. However, in an attempt to make these proceedings more complete, summaries are presented below for those few without papers.

Linking Disaster Victims to Resources: A Case Study of Equity in Post-Katrina Crisis Counseling Referrals

Kelli R. Pribanic, MA candidate

Previous disaster research reveals that socially marginalized groups and communities are more vulnerable in disaster recovery and often do not receive the same quantity or quality of post-disaster assistance. Data collected from a crisis counseling organization named Mississippi Project Recovery is used as a case study for examining how equitably Katrina affected residents were linked to recovery resources. Using referrals distributed in crisis encounters as a proxy for measuring access granted to resources, race, class, and gender are assessed for their effects in the distribution of referrals. Preliminary findings were discussed for how pre-existing social and mental health vulnerabilities were potentially magnified.

Kelli Pribanic provided an engaging presentation and discussion on her research findings and work in her home state of Mississippi. Kelli is a native of Pascagoula, MS and is working and collecting information on recovery efforts along the Mississippi Gulf Coast. Her presentation provided a specific example of one post-Katrina mental health care program delivered in an impact area that has gained little publicity. She is an M.A. candidate in the Department of Sociology at the University of Wyoming. She currently works for the Gulf Coast Fair Housing Center in Gulfport, MS. Areas of research include race, class, gender, social vulnerability and natural disasters, disaster mental health, and cross-cultural trauma. Kelli has been invited back to present the final results of her research and work at the 9th Rocky Mountain Disaster Mental Health Conference to be held in Cheyenne, Wyoming in November 2009.

Trauma and Forgiveness

Dennis B. Klein, PhD

The Keynote presentation for the third day of the conference was presented by Dennis B. Klein, PhD. He is the Director of the Jewish Studies Program and is Professor of History at Kean University in Union, New Jersey. His address was on Trauma and Forgiveness.

Dr. Klein's travel and other expenses and presentation were co-sponsored by the Departments of Social Work, Sociology, Psychology, Religious Studies, and History at the University of Wyoming and also by St. Matthew's Cathedral in Laramie. Dr. Klein also gave a Public Address at the University of Wyoming on Friday. His presentation provided additional, relevant and important insights into the conference topics and emphases.

First responders and follow-up caretakers can speed a trauma victim's recovery by considering forgiveness in a new light. Forgiveness conventionally understood is conditioned on the prior expression of contrition, but recent philosophical and psychological theories are exploring the possibilities of granting forgiveness before or without an offender's apology. This perspective confers strength and independence, a victim of assault is no longer a victim. By examining Holocaust survivors' memoirs, a classic example of post-traumatic testimony, we will also observe that victims can forgive their offenders even as they remember and condemn the offense. This realistic position makes forgiveness tenable and a promising method of negotiating trauma.

Dr. Dennis B. Klein is director of the Jewish Studies program and professor of history at Kean University in New Jersey. He is author of four books, including *Jewish Origins of the Psychoanalytic Movement* (University of Chicago Press, 1985) and *Hidden History of the Kovno Ghetto* (Little, Brown in cooperation with the U.S. Holocaust Memorial Museum, 1997).

He is founding editor in chief of *Dimensions: A Journal of Holocaust Studies* and founding director of the Anti-Defamation League's Braun Center for Holocaust Studies. He is a Fulbright-Hays Fellow, Phi Beta Kappa, and recipient of numerous research awards. Dr. Klein is listed in *Who's Who in the World, Who's Who in American Colleges and Universities, Dictionary of International Biography, and the Directory of American* Scholars. In 2006 he was a Research Fellow at the University College London and Resident Fellow at Oxford University.

About the Editor

George Doherty resides in Laramie, WY where he founded the Rocky Mountain Region Disaster Mental Health Institute, Inc. He is currently employed as the President/CEO of this organization and also serves as Clinical Coordinator of the Snowy Range Critical Incident Stress Management Team. He has been involved with disaster relief since 1995, serving as a Disaster Mental Health Specialist with such incidents as the UP train wreck in Laramie, Hurricane Fran in North Carolina, the Cincinnati floods in Falmouth, KY and Tropical Storm Allison in Southeast Texas. He served as Supervisor for Disaster Mental Health for flash floods in Ft. Collins, and spent a month as the Red Cross Disaster Mental Health Coordinator for western Puerto Rico in the aftermath of Hurricane George. He has also published numerous articles in disaster mental health and traumatic stress publications and served as Guest Editor for 2 Special Editions of the journal *Traumatology* (1999 & 2004). He served as an officer in the US Air Force and was an OTS instructor, squadron commander and other positions. Additionally, he served 11 years involved in Air Search & Rescue with Civil Air Patrol in WY as Squadron Commander, Deputy Wing Commander, Air Operations Officer, and Master Observer. Certified Instructor with the Wyoming Peace Officers Standards and Training (POST). He has extensive experience conducting CISM debriefings with first responders and others and is a member of a national crisis care network, providing assistance to companies and other organizations following critical incidents involving sudden deaths and similar traumatic events.

He is a Licensed Professional Counselor in private practice and has been an adjunct instructor for a number of colleges, including Northern Nevada Community College, Warren National University and the University of Wyoming. Organizational memberships include the American Counseling Association, Voting Associate Member of the American Psychological Association, American Academy of Experts in Traumatic Stress (AETS), Association of Traumatic Stress Specialists (ATSS), Traumatic Incident Reduction Association (TIRA), Certificate of Specialized Training in the field of Mass Disaster and Terrorism, Wyoming Department of Health Emergency Preparedness Advisory Committee; Research Advisor and Research Fellow: American Biographical Institute (ABI), Editorial Advisory Board Member and Book Reviewer: PsyCritiques (APA Journal), Life Member of the Air Force Association, and Life Member of the Military Officers Association of America, Life Member: Pennsylvania State University Alumni Association, Alumni Admissions Volunteer - Pennsylvania State University.

Publications include: *Crisis Intervention Training for Disaster Workers: An Introduction.*; Editor and contributor for the *Proceedings of Rocky Mountain Region Disaster Mental Health Conferences* (2005, 2006, 2007, 2008). Served as Guest Editor for Special issues of the journal *Traumatology* on Disaster Mental Health (1999) and Crises in Rural America (2004); .Cross-cultural Counseling in Disaster Settings. - *Austral-Asian Journal of Disaster and Trauma Studies* (1999). Published reviews include: Understanding Oslo in Troubled Times; Responders to September 11, 2001: Counseling: Innovative Responses to 9/11 Firefighters, Families, and

Communities; Genocide: A Human Condition? Stress Management, Wellness and Organizational Health., .Leadership Competency and Conflict.; Leadership: Lessons from the Ancient World - all in PsyCritiques. Conference Director for annual Rocky Mountain Disaster Mental Health Conferences 1999 -present.

Additional past positions include: Masters Level Psychologist – Rural Clinics (State of Nevada), 1980 – 1986; Veterans Counselor (VA Contract) – 1980-1986, NV; Counselor – pre-delinquent children and families – CORA Services (Philadelphia, PA).1972-1975; Program Coordinator - Community Action Programs (EOAC, Office of Economic Opportunity – Waco/McLennan County, TX) 1968-1971.

About The Rocky Mountain Region Disaster Mental Health Institute

Mission:

The Rocky Mountain Region Disaster Mental Health Institute is an independent, nonprofit, 501(c) (3) corporation whose mission is to promote the development and application of practice, research, and training in disaster mental health, Critical Incident Stress Management, traumatology and other emergency response interventions and the promotion of community awareness, resilience and recovery. This includes hazards vulnerability and mitigation research, planning and training for first responders, mental health professionals, chaplains and related personnel.

Purpose:

The purpose of the Institute is to provide a forum for presentation of research results, education, training and consultation in Disaster Mental Health Services (DMHS) and Critical Incident Stress Management (CISD/CISM), advances in delivery of DMHS and CISD/CISM, discussion and sharing of information, ideas and plans, development of a DMHS and CISD/CISM research and service delivery network, presentation of Continuing Education training for mental health professionals, first responders and chaplains, training for newly recruited DMHS and CISD/CISM volunteers and first responders, and publication of program proceedings and papers as appropriate for dissemination to DMHS and CISD/CISM professionals and first responders locally, regionally and nationally.

Significance:

Mental Health Services before, during and following disasters, critical incidents, crises, and terrorist activities are becoming an integral part of disaster and critical incident preparedness, mitigation, response, and follow-up. Disaster Mental Health Services is a relatively new field which has expanded significantly within the past ten years. Critical Incident Stress Debriefing and Critical Incident Stress Management have been around since the early 1980s. In order to continue to grow and meet identified needs, both will require continued development as well as focused research and training. Research will help identify how Mental Health Services can best be utilized as well as how relevant changes need to be made in practice. Networking and sharing experiences can also help develop resources.

The long-term goal includes training emergency Disaster Mental Health teams and CISM teams to conduct interventions for corporations, states, municipalities and rural communities in the Rocky Mountain region and to evaluate their effectiveness in reducing the effects of trauma on first responders and others as well as affected communities and organizations.

Who Should Attend

The conference is a must experience for anyone working in the fields of: emergency medical services and trauma units, crisis intervention, mental health, traumatic stress, emergency services, disaster mental health, military, National Guard & Reserve, schools, law enforcement, firefighters, chaplains and other first responders.

Certificates of Attendance

All conference delegates will be provided with Certificates of Attendance. Each presentation will be listed on the reverse with the number of contact hours. It is the responsibility of the delegate to have each presenter sign off on their certificate. Your Certificate of Attendance will be printed with your name exactly as it appears on your Registration form. Please make sure that you print it clearly. A small fee of $5.00 will be assessed to make and mail a duplicate certificate. If you register late or onsite, your certificate will be printed and mailed approximately 3 weeks post-conference.

ROCKY MOUNTAIN REGION DISASTER MENTAL HEALTH INSTITUTE
PO BOX 786
LARAMIE, WY 82073-0786

http://www.rmrinstitute.org/rocky.html
email: rockymountain@mail2emergency.com
Phone: 307-399-4818

The Rocky Mountain Region Disaster Mental Health Institute is a 501(c)3 Non-profit Organization.

Index

T

V

W

SOCIAL SCIENCE / Disasters & Disaster Relief US$24.95/£12.95

Proceedings of the 5th Rocky Mountain Region Disaster Mental Health Conference

Recent years have seen an extraordinary number of major disasters, critical incidents and other events that have had major impacts on our world. The 2004 tsunami, hurricanes Rita and Katrina, and the wars in Iraq and Afghanistan affect millions of lives daily. Potential events such as Avian Flu pandemic, global warming and the increasing threats of spreading unrest in the Middle East are concerns that weigh heavily on us all.

November 8-11, 2006, the Rocky Mountain Region Disaster Mental Health Institute held their Annual four-day Disaster Mental Health Conference. The theme of the conference was **TAKING CHARGE IN TROUBLED TIMES: Response, Resilience, Recovery and Follow-up**. This edition contains the major papers presented at the conference and summaries of additional presentations. They address some of the major crisis events confronting our societies in recent years, namely, large disasters such as hurricanes Katrina and Rita; case studies such as Abu Ghraib, and traumatic events such as a night club suicide bombing, the role of cultural sensitivity and ethics in disaster settings, resilience, and the importance of planning, education and taking care of our first responders and mental health professionals. An additional concern with information includes information about preparation of communities and families for deployment and return of military personnel. The importance of planning for how mental health personnel can respond in the event of an Avian Flu Pandemic is also discussed. Presenters are drawn from researchers and responders from Wyoming, the United States, and the United Kingdom.

"This compilation of 10 papers deals with people's reactions to a wide variety of disasters, including not only terror and Hurricane Katrina, but child abuse and the trauma suffered by families of service members. Taken together, the papers are fascinating. The "Proceedings of the 5th Rocky Mountain Region Disaster Mental Health Conference" provides insight into the nature of the individual's response to terror and disaster. They should be interesting reading for everyone who either indirectly or directly has been affected."

—Linda Benninghoff, Reader Views

SOCIAL SCIENCE / Disasters & Disaster Relief **US$24.95/£12.95**

Proceedings of the 6th Rocky Mountain Region Disaster Mental Health Conference

Events around the world continue to present challenges for first responders and mental health professionals. Natural and man-made disasters continue. Evidence mounts concerning potential events such as global warming and the effects this may have worldwide. Avian Flu remains a concern as do forms of biological terrorism and natural hazards such as tsunamis, floods, hurricanes and earthquakes. The 2004 tsunami in Sri Lanka and Thailand continues to have a significant impact on that area of the world. Wars in Afghanistan and Iraq continue to impact those countries, the Middle East and the United States. Preparing our communities and families not only for deployments and support of those deployed and their families, but also for the aftermath and return of our military and National Guard personnel into our communities is important for all.

What can we expect from all of these? How do communities and first responders handle these? What role does mental health play? How do first responders and mental health professionals plan together for responding to future events and learning from past ones. Using a strategic planning approach, how do we identity potential threats and identify target populations and groups? What resources are available for which identified threats? How do we do such planning, how often, and how do we exercise such plans prior to events? What can we learn from such events and how do we incorporate what we learn into future planning?

It is crucial that response, resilience, recovery and follow-up be included in our planning. Additional variables important in responding include cultural knowledge and sensitivity. We need to prepare to respond appropriately within a culture not our own, whether locally, nationally, or internationally.

November 8-10, 2007, the Rocky Mountain Region Disaster Mental Health Institute held their Annual Disaster Mental Health Conference in Cheyenne, Wyoming. The theme of this conference was: **From Crisis To Recovery: Resilience and Strategic Planning for the Future**.

"*Proceedings of the 6th Rocky Mountain Region Disaster Mental Health Conference* is a must have for first responders and mental health professionals. Addressing the needs of people who work in these fields is critical. The better trained they are to be emotionally equipped for disasters, the better they can help others. I think that the 120 pages of information covered in this book will be some of the most important information needed by people in this field today."

—Page Lovitt, *Reader Views*

Social Science: Disasters & Disaster Relief US $29.95 / £ 14.95

Crisis Intervention Training for Disaster Workers

George W. Doherty, MS, LPC

This book provides information about training for mental health professionals and first responders who work with victims of disaster related stress and trauma. It helps prepare them to relate with disaster victims and co-workers. Warning signs and symptoms are explored together with stages, strategies and interventions for recovery.

The book will introduce you to disasters, the community response, the roles of first responders, Disaster Mental Health Services and Critical Incident Stress Management (CISM) responders and teams. It provides a brief overview of these and their roles in responding to the needs of both victims and disaster workers. The role of CISM is presented and discussed both for disasters and other critical incidents. This includes discussion about war, terrorism and follow-up responses by mental health professionals. The book is designed to help readers identify appropriate methods for activating Disaster Mental Health Crisis Intervention Teams for disaster mental health services for victims, co-workers, and self.

The content includes general theory and models of Disaster Mental Health, CISM, crisis intervention techniques commonly used in these situations, supportive research, and practice of approaches used in responding to the victims, workers and communities affected by disasters, critical incidents and terrorism threats and events.

"Provides a breadth and depth of knowledge as well as practical tools for beginner to expert. Should be required reading for all disaster responders, and, especially, mental health professionals considering disaster work."
—Bruce L. Andrews, MS, LPC (ARC Disaster Mental Provider/Instructor)

"This text serves as a wonderful adjunct and lead into the discipline of CISM. It provides a brief survey of disaster mental health and disaster mental health services."
—Thomas Mitchell, LPC

Rocky Mountain
Disaster Mental Health Institute
Press

"Learning from the past and planning for the future"

RMRInstitute.org

www.ingramcontent.com/pod-product-compliance
Ingram Content Group UK Ltd.
Pitfield, Milton Keynes, MK11 3LW, UK
UKHW050615260726
13967UKWH00008B/2873

9 781932 690866